𝒟

Black Ribbon

Ruffly Speaking
Bloodlines
Gone to the Dogs
Paws Before Dying
A Bite of Death
Dead and Doggone
A New Leash on Death

Susan
Conant

Black
Ribbon

DOUBLEDAY

New York

London

Toronto

Sydney

Auckland

A Dog Lover's
Mystery

PUBLISHED BY DOUBLEDAY
a division of Bantam Doubleday Dell Publishing Group, Inc.
1540 Broadway, New York, New York 10036

DOUBLEDAY and the portrayal of an anchor with a dolphin are
trademarks of Doubleday, a division of Bantam Doubleday Dell
Publishing Group, Inc.

Excerpts from American Kennel Club rules, regulations, guidelines, and official
breed standards reprinted by permission of the American Kennel Club.

Excerpt from *Surviving Your Dog's Adolescence* (New York: Howell Book House),
Copyright © 1993 by Carol Lea Benjamin, reprinted by permission of the
author.

Book design by Paul Randall Mize

Library of Congress Cataloging-in-Publication Data
Conant, Susan J., 1946–
Black Ribbon: a dog lover's mystery/Susan Conant.—1st ed.
p. cm.
1. Winter, Holly (Fictitious character)—Fiction. 2. Women
journalists—Maine—Fiction. 3. Women dog owners—Maine—Fiction.
4. Resorts—Maine—Fiction. 5. Dogs—Maine—Fiction. I. Title.
PS3553.O4857B53 1994
813'.54—dc20 94-19547
CIP

ISBN 0-385-47415-6

1 3 5 7 9 10 8 6 4 2

BLACK RIBBON
Frostfield Arctic Natasha, CD, TT, CGC, VCC
February 9, 1986–March 31, 1993
Radiant spirit, joyful noise

Stay with me, my good girl. I loved you every minute
of your life.

Acknowledgments

MANY THANKS to Sally Jean Alexander; Susan Bulanda, Coventry Canine Search and Rescue; Debra Goodie; Officer Warren F. Harnden, Rangeley Police Department, Rangeley, Maine; Ted Sprague; and Jan Thomas, Chesrite Kennel, all of whom expertly answered my questions. Thanks also to Roseann Mandell, Geoff Stern, and Margherita Walker, who read my manuscript when they could have been training Duchess, Kody, Audrey Rose, Basil, and Blossom, to whom I apologize for time stolen and points lost. I am also grateful to Jean Berman, Judy Bocock, Dorothy Donohue, and Tracy Katz. Wayne Morie's wonderful Chesapeake Bay retrievers, CH Brackenwood Spartan, UD and Chesrite's Tyme To Heel, CGC (Sparty and Elsa) taught me to love the breed. Special thanks to Elsa for the use of her name; my fictional Chessie would answer to no other. Vanderval's Tundra Eagle, CDX, one of the great obedience malamutes of all times, appears with the blessing of her breeder, owner, and handler, Anna Morelli. For the title of Holly's canine romance, I am indebted to P.J. (Pam) Richardson. Best of Breed among editors once again goes to perfection itself, my beloved Kate Miciak. Many thanks also to William Walker, D.V.M.; to his skilled and compassionate staff at the Rotherwood Animal Clinic, Newton, Massachusetts; to a great and caring veterinary surgeon, Joel Woolfson, D.V.M.; to Theresa Hawley and Corinne Zipps; and to everyone else who helped to save the rescue malamute now called Kashina. For kindness to Kashina, special thanks to my husband, Carter Umbarger, who finds himself at ever-increasing risk of becoming a dog person.

Without an Alaskan malamute to guide me through the bleak landscapes of the soul, I would wander forever without finding Holly's voice. I am deeply grateful to my new lead dog, Frostfield Firestar's Kobuk, CGC, in whose unerring path I humbly follow, and to his baby half-sister, Frostfield Perfect Crime, called Rowdy.

Black Ribbon

One

CONSIDER THE ETERNAL QUEST for Order.

Loyal Order of Moose, Fraternal Order of Eagles, Patriotic and Protective Order of Stags, Order of the Blue Goose, Ancient Order of Foresters, Modern Woodmen of America, Knights of Pythias, Tall Cedars of Lebanon, Order of DeMolay, Independent Order of Odd Fellows, Knights of Malta, Ancient Arabic Order Nobles of the Mystic Shrine, Constellation of Junior Stars, Red Cross of Constantine, Supreme Conclave True Kindred, Grand Order of Galilian Fishermen, Mystic Order of Veiled Prophets of the Enchanted Realm . . .

Or so it once was. No longer the Loyal and multitudinous Order of yesteryear, Moose International, Inc., recently substituted bright-colored blazers for the traditional black satin cape. No more *tah*, either; no more backward spelling at all. Modernization is paying off: 168,000 new Moose last year. Progress. Or so the poor Moose suppose. Total membership: 1.27 million. Pitiful. Masons: 4.1 million in 1959. Today? 2.5 million. Elks, too. Eagles. Decline, decline. Thus falters the quest for Order: The Lodge dislodges; the fez falls apart; the conclave cannot hold. Snippets of rite drift from the aeries where Eagles soared. Bits of regalia lie scattered where once roamed droves of Patriotic and Protective Stags. Tall Cedars of Lebanon petrify to dead wood.

But hark! Is that a yelp I hear? A yip, a ruff, a bold, resounding *woo-woo-woo?* It is all these things and more. Read the numbers: in the United States of America, 54 million dogs, 2.1 million Masons, thus 25.7 dogs for every Mason; and 4.1 million Masons in 1959, peak membership, but only 2.5 million Masons today, 1.6 million fewer members. And remember that number, because American Kennel Club individual dog registrations last year alone equaled exactly 1,528,392, a figure that rounds off to . . . Well, work it out for yourselves! Indeed! For every member lost to Freemasonry since 1959, the American Kennel Club has registered a new canine in the past year alone. Out of order, chaos; and out of chaos, the Ancient, Benevolent, and Protective Order of Mystic Stalwarts of the Highborn Pooch.

"Boy, oh, boy," said my editor, "do you ever need a vacation."

Any editor who phones at seven A.M. deserves a brush-off. But a *dog writer's* editor? Sorry, but if you can't endure the ordeal-by-pun, you don't belong in dogs, the land of Lixit waterers, Rebark booties, Pupsicle frozen beef treats, and antiparasitics with brand names so gut-wrenching that you don't even need to shove the products down Fido's throat, but can just catch his eye and holler: *Erliworm! Panacur! Evict!* or *Good Riddance!*

"And the other organizations are even worse off!" I exclaimed into the phone. "Thirty-six dogs per Elk, and the Moose are really trying hard, but you've got to feel sorry for them, because for them, it's—"

Bonnie groaned. "The camp is called Waggin' Tail," she said. "It's in Maine." She paused. "Vacationland," she added significantly.

"I grew up there," I reminded her.

"On the coast. This is in Rangeley. Doesn't your grandmother . . . ?"

"She's in Bethel. It's nearby."

"There. You see? The cool north woods of home. And, Holly? Maxine McGuire has mortgaged her soul to get this thing going. You will *love* it." Bonnie was instructing, not predicting. "And your dogs will love it even more than you will. That's very, very important. They'll adore every second. Focus on the dogs. Their reactions, their quirks, their experience. You're in the picture, but you're in the background."

Teaching your grandam to suck rawhide.

Bonnie persisted. "Max is sending you the preregistration packet. Camp's the last week in August. I want the article as soon as possible after camp ends. *Compris?*"

" 'How We Spent Our Summer Vacation in Dog Heaven.' "

"Wonderful! There you go. And I also need something very, very positive about . . ." Bonnie's voice faded.

"I can't hear you."

"AKC!" she shouted. For those of you new to the fancy, I should explain. AKC: Antiquated Kennel Club. "Write me something about AKC. About shows?"

Bonnie is a good editor. If there's one thing that AKC does splendidly, it's a dog show. The American Kennel Club itself does not hold shows; it approves them. Clubs run shows— kennel clubs, national breed clubs, obedience clubs—1,169 all-breed shows, 1,729 specialty shows, and 405 obedience trials last year alone, and if I were a few hundred people instead of just one, I'd have attended every all-breed show, every specialty, and every trial in the country, and I'd have had fun at every one. Have I lost you? *Specialty:* a single-breed dog show, limited to Siberian huskies, Pulik, German shepherd dogs, whatever. Preferably, from my point of view, Alaskan malamutes.

"Sure," I told Bonnie. "Anything you want except one more article on the search for a new president. That one's been done to death."

"Do me a nice hands-on, how-to piece," Bonnie said.

"How to Amateur-Handle Your Dog to Best of Breed at Westminster." Short article. Entire text: *Don't. Hire a professional.*

Bonnie added a thought. "Something about judges. Etiquette for exhibitors. Making the judge's job easy. *Do's* and *Don't's.* You have the guidelines?"

In what may at first seem like a digression, let me point out that in conventional Masonry, *G* stands for God and Geometry. In the fancy, it means Guidelines: "Guidelines for Dog Show Judges" and "Guidelines for Obedience Judges." *R* is also sacred to us: "Rules Applying to Dog Shows," "Rules Applying to Registration and Discipline," "Obedience Regulations," single copies of which used to be free, sort of like Gideon Bibles, but now cost a dollar apiece. Before long, the Gideons'll start tacking a nominal rental fee onto motel rates. Anyway, in Masonry, *G* refers to God's compass, and in our order, it refers to Guidelines, which is to say that in both orders, *G*, the last letter in you-know-what, defines the limits of good and evil. Have I lost you? Well, the Moose may have discarded the *tah*, but in the fancy, we're as backward as ever.

The promised preregistration packet arrived a week after Bonnie's call, on a July day when the sun burning over Cambridge, Massachusetts, was as red as the letters that spelled out the camp name and motto on the big white envelope:

WAGGIN' TAIL
Where All the Dogs Are Happy Campers
And All the Owners "Ruff It In Luxury"!

Torn open and upended on my kitchen table, the thick envelope yielded one color-glossy promotional brochure for Waggin' Tail Camp and dozens of photocopied pages that I

spread out and sorted through. The brochure, a slick professional product, displayed several appealing photographs: one of a sunset reflected in a sapphire blue lake; one of a gigantic log cabin with miniature clone-cabins arrayed on either side; one of a mastiff bitch, Maxine McGuire's, no doubt, with a large litter of pups similarly clustered about her. Maxine and my editor, I might mention, belonged to the same lodge—Bonnie's mastiffs went back to Maxine's lines—thus Bonnie's loyalty to Maxine and the eagerness of *Dog's Life* magazine to support Maxine's new enterprise.

The text of the camp's brochure contained a great many exclamation points. It was principally devoted to persuading the reader that, in contrast to competing institutions, Waggin' Tail offered a high degree of—and here I don't just talk the talk, but quote the quotes—"civilization." For the last week of August, Waggin' Tail, it proclaimed, had exclusive possession of the newly refurbished Mooselookmeguntic Four Seasons Resort Lodge and Cabins, located in Maine's beautiful and unspoiled Rangeley Lakes region, where campers would enjoy home-cooked gourmet meals featuring sumptuous regional delicacies ("including lobster!!!"), a daily cocktail hour, wine with dinner, and various other alcoholic and nonalcoholic extravagances unavailable at competing camps!!! "Ruff It in Luxury!"

Despite the promises of lavish accommodations, epicurean delights, and copious tippling, what obviously set Waggin' Tail apart from numerous similar camps was that it cost a ridiculous amount of money. The fees appeared not in the brochure, but on one of the photocopied enclosures. Of necessity, the figures were in fine print; otherwise, they wouldn't have fit on the page. I had no idea why I'd even been sent the fee schedule. In return for the laudatory piece I'd been assigned to produce, my dogs and I were on full scholarship.

The remaining material consisted of a five-page welcome-to-camp form letter from Maxine McGuire; a tentative schedule of camp activities that included every dog sport and activity I'd ever heard of and a bewildering number of workshops, seminars, and courses on topics such as leash-braiding and canine first aid; detailed directions to the resort; a long list of items to pack; two copies of a lengthy contract entitled "Waiver of All Liability and Release and Indemnification Agreement," one of which had to be signed and returned; and two health certificates to be filled in by my veterinarian. The absence of a corresponding form to be completed by my M.D. was, I thought, a sure sign that Maxine McGuire was a real dog person, which is to say, someone who demands written proof that a dog is fecal negative and up-to-date on his shots, but assumes that a mere human being doesn't have anything worth catching, anyway.

Ah, but speaking of real dog people, let me explain why my bitch, Kimi, didn't go to camp by remarking on how ill-deserved is the Old Testament's reputation for antidog bias! It's there, of course, and it's perfectly understandable. Even by my standards, the ancient Egyptians really were dog nuts, and I can imagine that if I were held in bondage by a bunch of reptile-worshippers, I probably wouldn't run out and get a pet chameleon the second I finally got free, so if establishing the Mount Sinai Kennel Club and chairing its first all-breed show wasn't exactly Moses's top priority, you can't blame him, or God, either. I mean, by comparison with Job, Biblical dog lovers got off easy, and in return for their trials, received more than fair compensation in the consoling verse that I recited to myself on the morning of Sunday, August 22, when I left Kimi, as well as my Cambridge three-decker, in the care of my cousin Leah, and headed for Rangeley, Maine, accompanied only by my male malamute, Rowdy, a creature of many purposes and times, but one blessedly free of the cycles to which Kimi is subject. Indeed, in the words of Ecclesiastes, to every thing there *is* a season.

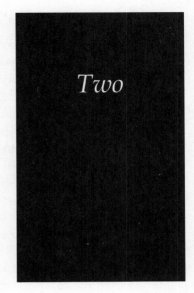

Two

EXPERIENCED WORLD TRAVELERS, I'm told, pack lightly. Experienced dog people do, too, at least for ourselves: By the time we've jammed in everything the dogs will need and found room for such absolute dog-show necessities as folding chairs and ice chests, it's a miracle if there's room left for a change of human underwear. But Waggin' Tail Camp wasn't a show: So by leaving the grooming table at home, I squeezed in an entire suitcase for myself. When I backed out of my driveway, the remainder of the Bronco held Rowdy's crate and the bare minimum of paraphernalia he'd need for the week: an orthopedic dog mattress with a fake fleece zip-off cover, a small bag of premium dog food, a canister of liver treats, a supply of cheese cubes in a Styrofoam cooler with two freezer-packs to keep the cheese fresh, a container of large and small dog biscuits, Rowdy's five favorite chew toys, an X-back racing harness, a longe line, a tracking harness, a thirty-foot tracking lead, two obedience dumbbells—one wooden, one nylon—three white work gloves for the Directed Retrieve, a set of scent discrimination articles in a plastic mesh carrier, a twenty-six foot retractable lead, assorted metal and nylon training collars, a Wenaha doggy backpack, three leather leads, a wire slicker brush, an undercoat rake, a finishing brush, grooming spray, dog shampoo, a food dish, a water bowl, and a king-size sheet to protect the bedspread of my own bed in case Rowdy decided to sleep there instead of in his crate and in case I decided to let him, as he certainly would decide and as I certainly would, too.

Within the folding crate was Rowdy, who'd realized for a week that we were going somewhere and, now that we were finally heading out of Cambridge on Route 2, rested his big head smugly on his big white snowshoe paws and eyed the front passenger seat.

"Forget it," I told him. "You hated that seat belt harness."

Having used the rearview mirror for the incidental purpose of checking to see whether a Boston driver was about to smash into me, I again caught Rowdy's eye and, just as Ford intended, admired my big, beautiful dog. AKC judges have done so too, not in mirrors, of course, but they have, conformation judges somewhat more ardently than obedience judges, I might add. Rowdy finished his breed championship easily. Putting the X for Excellent on his Companion Dog title, however, had taken us more attempts than I care to report, thank you. Need I explain? The Alaskan malamute is the heavy-freighting dog of the Inuit speakers of *Mahlemut*, a dialect of Inupiat in which the sounds rendered in English as the command *Come!* actually mean: "Hightail it in the opposite direction, dash in giant figure eights, drop to the ground, roll onto your back, and wave your paws in the air until the judge cracks up and the spectators are in stitches." That's Mahlemut for you: succinct. I've studied up. My research has given me a great respect for the people who developed this breed. Extraordinary language. Ungodly beautiful dogs. Big-boned. Low-slung. Like small-eared wolves with dark, gentle eyes and an expression warm enough to melt the Arctic night and sweet enough to turn blubber into honey, and . . .

And what does all this have to do with dog camp? Let's just say that five hours after we left Cambridge, when I parked the Bronco in the Waggin' Tail lot, leashed Rowdy, and led him across a field of rough, weedy rural Maine grass toward what a cardboard arrow informed me was the camp registration table, I had a dog I was proud to be seen with. And he had heavy competition, too: a handsome young mastiff; three sleek basenjis; numerous Labs in yellow, black, and chocolate; a darling papillon; a perfectly matched brace of Pomeranians groomed for the show ring; three English springer spaniels; a pretty briard with a barrette in her hair; one bichon; two Boston terriers; a very old Pembroke Welsh corgi; a young whippet; a beautifully proportioned, well-balanced Chesapeake bitch with that dark brown coat favored in this part of the country; an Australian cattle dog; a Bernese hitched to a festively decorated cart; two drenched goldens and a flatcoat fresh from the lake, all three cooling off everyone in shaking distance; dozens of multiethnic, culturally pluralistic mixes and crosses, and . . . Well, I could go on and on, and, if I'm not stopped, will probably do so at extreme length and in minute detail. But, as I've indicated, even judged against heavy competition, mine was certainly the most outstanding dog of all. This happy realization, of course, filled me with the comforting sense of being exactly where I belonged, right in the midst of my own Blue Lodge, secure in the knowledge that everyone around me shared the Unifying True Secret known in our fellowship as the Transcendent Paradox: Everyone else present at Waggin' Tail at that moment was thinking exactly the same thought I was. And every single one of us was absolutely right.

Never been to Maine? If so, I'll do my best to take you along, but I have to admit that I notice pines, firs, spruce, hemlock, maples, and birches principally in their absence. If

the Mooselookmeguntic Four Seasons Resort Lodge and
Cabins had been denuded of vegetation, I'd probably have
winced at the cruel, raw look of recent clear-cutting. If the
mountains had flattened out since my last visit, or if a big dry
hollow had stretched itself in the background where the lake
belonged, or if the big log-cabin lodge and matching little
cabins hadn't been there at all, I might have wondered
whether I'd taken a wrong turn and landed us in the Desert of
Maine. As it was, tall trees and thick undergrowth surrounded
the big grassy field on one side of the newly blacktopped parking lot, and mature trees rose here and there around the numerous buildings, which, as the brochure had promised,
looked newly refurbished. What had obviously been an old
fishing and hunting camp had, indeed, become a resort. The
logs and the cedar siding had fresh coats of stain, every roof
was brand-new, and every paintable piece of trim—doors,
window frames, window boxes, shutters—was a bright, high-
gloss crimson. If I'd randomly turned in at the long drive to
the resort in search of a place to spend the night, I wouldn't
even have bothered to ask whether there was a vacancy; I'd
have taken one look, turned around, and driven off to find a
room I could afford. I wouldn't really have cared. Whenever I
feel poor, I remember that I'd rather have my dogs than other
people's money.

So, scholarship camper that I was, I proudly led Rowdy
across the grass to the crowded registration area that had been
set up in the field.

"Holly Winter," I told the woman who stood behind the
table running her eyes and hands through the manila folders
crammed into a portable plastic file box. At first glance, I
assumed that she must be an agility instructor. Quick introduction to agility: timed obstacle course for dogs. Canine
playground. Anyway, the filing woman had straight, bristly
hair cut so short that its color vanished into her scalp, a style I
associate with agility people, who are so single-mindedly de-

voted to their sport that they pare down all other aspects of their lives to become the ascetics of dog athletics, lean fanatics with sinewy muscles and burning eyes. Their hair and everything else, too: If it gets in the way of agility, bind it back, or cut it right off. No breasts showed through the woman's plain white T-shirt. I wondered whether she'd carried her commitment to excess. Like almost everyone else, however, she wore a name-tag pin, a white square with an outline of red curlicues, the words *Waggin' Tail* across the top, and the motto *Ruff It In Luxury* across the bottom. In between, hand-printed in red Magic Marker, was her name, Heather, with something illegible beneath.

"Chief Fecal Inspector," said Heather, her voice and expression as flat as her chest.

Holding out Rowdy's health certificate, I stammered, "He's, uh, he's negative. We just had a stool sample checked."

Heather tapped a blunt-nailed finger against her name tag. "I saw you looking. It's my job. Chief Fecal Inspector." The corners of her thin lips inched upward. "Camp rule," she explained. "Clean up after your dog, or I'm the one who yells at you." She glanced at Rowdy, who was eyeing the Chesapeake bitch. "And don't let him leave his mark on the agility equipment, either! Winter? And Rowdy."

I nodded compliantly. My customary friendliness and volubility were hard to suppress. For example, I had to fight the urge to ask Heather whether she was, in fact, a double Amazon. She removed a fat brown envelope from one of the manila folders, thrust it into my hand, and directed me to the next stop on my registration pilgrimage. "Get a pin," she ordered me. As an apparent afterthought, she said, "Welcome to Waggin' Tail." The camp's name seemed to embarrass her. I began to like Heather.

"Welcome to Waggin' Tail!" The cry, unabashed this time, emanated from a fortyish woman with a soft, round face, faded blue eyes, a mop of springy yellow-gray curls, and pale skin brightened by networks of prominent veins, red on her face, blue on her legs. Despite the SPF-30 pallor, she had an outdoorsy look. She was plump in the middle and nowhere else, and wore khaki shorts and a Waggin' Tail T-shirt, gray with red letters.

"Maxine," I said. When I'd asked Bonnie what Maxine McGuire was like, she'd provided the only introductory information of any concern to anyone in the fancy: *"Very* nice dogs," Bonnie had pronounced. As I've said, Bonnie and Maxine both had mastiffs. The only representative of the breed in sight, the adolescent male who'd already caught my eye, was dozing under a nearby tree. So how did I recognize Max McGuire? Let me explain that after extended periods of time spent in the company of dogs, even an unlikely ESP prospect like me acquires the ability effortlessly to discern the names of total strangers. Get a dog! It'll change your life. Actually, I read her name tag. "I'm Holly Winter," I told her.

In contrast to Heather, Maxine greeted this unremarkable piece of information with an effusive and nervous-sounding display of surprise and delight. The surprise couldn't have been genuine—I'd sent in all my forms—but the delight was certainly heartfelt. Its object, of course, was the article ˙I'd write for *Dog's Life.* If Rowdy and I had looked like the wolfman accompanied by the bride of Dracula, Maxine would still have gushed over us. "What a *beautiful* dog! You *do* show him, don't you?"

I nodded. Rowdy preened. Maxine fired off an anxious volley of questions, instructions, comments, and bits of information. I had my registration packet, didn't I? But I needed a name tag. Had I seen my cabin yet? It was right on the lake. Phyllis and Don Abbott had the other half of the cabin, but I wasn't to worry: The entrances were separate, so I'd have plenty of privacy to write. I used to have goldens, didn't I? I showed them in obedience? Well, maybe I'd shown under Phyllis Abbott, and I knew who Don Abbott was, didn't I?

Yes, AKC, very big in dogs. Right. *Lovely* people. Wasn't the heat terrible? Max wasn't used to it, but we had the lake, didn't we? And it always cooled off at night. I had brought a bathing suit, hadn't I? Rowdy was the camp's only malamute. Did he like to swim? He didn't? Well, maybe he'd at least like to wade. I could drive right up to my cabin to unload, but afterward, would I please leave my car in the lot. There was an orientation meeting in front of the main house at four o'clock. A lot of people were taking dips in the lake to cool off. What an eager group! Cars had begun arriving at eleven o'clock, two hours before camp was supposed to start, and nothing was scheduled until four, when we had our orientation meeting. Had she mentioned that already? I'd find the schedule in my registration packet. I had picked it up, hadn't I? Of course I had.

Maxine's nervous verbal barrage held Rowdy's attention slightly longer than it did mine. When she paused for a breath, I moved fast. "It *is* terribly hot, and I'd love a swim, and Bonnie sends her best, and she says your dogs are gorgeous, and Rowdy is desperate for some water. Which cabin are we in?"

Ah, the Maine log cabin. The oh-so-charming outdoor plumbing that smells worse than a dog-show Porta Potti on an August afternoon, the ropes of oakum that slip loose to admit snow in the winter and bugs in the summer, the carcinogenic reek of creosote, the nauseating redolence of damp wood stove, the ephemeral stench of moldy mattress in which small rodents have nested, produced their young, perished, and half-decomposed, usually right under the spot on which you lay your weary head. That's how it used to be. Then tourism triumphed. The indoor flush had no sooner vanquished the outhouse than oakum lost to synthetic caulk, and creosote to odor-free preservative stains. Even as I speak, the mattress-nesting field mouse, Maine's official state rodent, is probably becoming an endangered species.

In the combination bedroom and living room that occupied the front of my own cabin, the creature was already extinct, its ecological niche destroyed by Blueboard, plaster, and paint, its familiar breeding place replaced by a king-size bed that Rowdy sniffed with mild interest. The beige carpeting had been installed by someone other than a local jack-of-all-trades, as had the pleated blinds, one of which I immediately raised to get a look at the lake and thus the reassurance that I was, after all, in northern Maine. The principal source of my disorientation was, I suppose, the powerful-looking air conditioner built into one wall. Rangeley, Maine, is, after all, the precise spot toward which God Herself directs each immaculate exhalation; the air in Rangeley needed artificial conditioning about the way that water in the Vatican baptismal fonts needs chemical filtration. With water on my mind, I checked out the bathroom. Only a year or two ago, I suspected, when the enterprise had still been a serious fishing and hunting lodge, the shower must have been one of those rusted metal stalls with a dirty plastic curtain magnetically attracted to the human body and a slimy floor with a drain that reliably failed to deserve the name and periodically backed up to spew the contents of the septic tank around the end-of-a-long-day feet of the angled-out fishermen and shot-out hunters who'd come North to escape the city and had only to open their noses and wiggle their toes to understand just how completely they'd succeeded. Pale blue tile with white grout now covered the walls and floor of the room. The toilet was a low-slung, water-conserving model, the dead-white fiberglass tub and shower unit didn't show a trace of stain, and when I experimented by turning on the faucet at the foreign-looking wash basin, the water didn't smell like fish or beavers. I hoped that the proprietors of the refurbished lodge weren't counting on the return of the old customers, who'd take one whiff, turn around, and head back to Boston and New York. The real sportsmen—the *sports*, as they're called in Maine—would hate the place now.

Me? *I* grew up in Maine. I thought the bathroom was wonderful.

Having overcome the impulse to fill the tub and have a civilized soak instead of a swim in the lake, I returned to the big front room, where Rowdy had taken advantage of my absence. Dogs aren't allowed on my bed unless they are explicitly invited. Rowdy understood the rule perfectly: Unless invited, he was to stay off the bed, that is, my bed at home. We weren't at home. Therefore, this one was up for grabs. And he'd got it first. So his face proclaimed. Have I mentioned Rowdy's face? White, an "open face," without the dark markings that make up Kimi's full mask, but a handsome, commanding face, richly expressive. What it expressed at the moment was intense curiosity about exactly how I intended to lay claim to that bed.

I respect Rowdy too much to lie to him. "Very clever," I remarked. He flattened his ears against his head. His wagging tail thumped the expensive-looking and probably hand-woven beige bedspread that I was supposed to protect from dog hair. His dark eyes smiled.

Two seconds later, he was off that bed. The secret? Obedience training. How do dogs and people ever survive without it? It's the essence of human-canine teamwork, perfect interspecies cooperation in which two radically different minds think as one. For instance, the thought on Rowdy's and my joined mind happened to be food. When I reached into my pocket, extracted a small dog biscuit, and called, "Rowdy, come!" he instantly leaped off the bed. Rowdy is a brilliant trainer. He has shaped my behavior so that I exemplify what the AKC regulations call "the utmost in willingness, precision, and enjoyment." I now have my CPX—Companion Person Excellent title—and you may look forward to seeing me in the Utility ring soon.

There is, however, one training technique that Rowdy has yet to master. It's frequently neglected by many human trainers as well. No one uses it anymore. No one but me. I'm the last true believer in the good old-fashioned talking-to. "That is *my* bed!" I announced. "Mine! And no one invited you on it, and furthermore, dogs are not allowed to deposit hair on the nice bedspreads here, and even if the other dogs were permitted to do it, *you*, buddy, would be forbidden! And the next time I leave you alone in this lovely room that's a lot fancier than we are, I expect to return and find you on the floor or in your crate or somewhere else where you belong! I do not *ever* want to see you on that bed again unless I have specifically given you permission. Is that understood, buster? That is *my* bed!" I whirled around, raised my arm, and pointed dramatically at the bed.

As it turned out, my fingers led my eye to a buff-colored envelope that rested on the pillow like a sort of stationery version of mints. I wondered whether it contained some tactful reminder to protect the good linens from my dog or whether it might simply be a note of welcome. I opened the envelope. The greeting card inside showed a small watercolor picture of pink-flowering trees, green hills, and a soon-to-set sun. Blue letters across the top of the card read: *With Sympathy on the Loss of Your Pet.* A sentence beneath the watercolor went on: *Our pets are our better selves, honest, trusting, pure.* Bewildered, I opened the card. The preprinted message inside was this: *I know how much you loved your pet and how deeply you are grieving now.*

The card was unsigned.

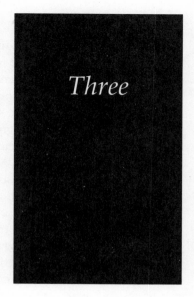

Three

KIMI? IMPOSSIBLE. Her face appeared in my mind's eye. As intensely as ever, she fixed her gaze on me. My heart pounded. I live with many ghosts. The dogs who wait for me keep permanent watch. Don't they trust me? Of course they do. So why the scrutiny? It's a reminder, that's all, a necessary and even comforting reminder that I have no real cause for grief. The worst has not happened and never will. My dogs have merely died. They have not stopped loving me.

This is a grotesque mistake, I thought. The sentiment felt hideously familiar. My last golden, Vinnie, died of cancer, or would have if I hadn't stopped her pain first. Even so, her death felt like some vicious practical joke. *Okay, enough!* I kept wanting to shout. *Hah-hah! Very funny! See what a good sport I am? Very clever! Sure had me fooled, you did. And now? Game's up! Did you hear me? Enough, I said! Give her back, do you hear me!* Then my pitiful whisper: *Please, please give her back. Give me back my dog. Give me back my wonderful dog.*

I groped for reality. Kimi was young and healthy. Vinnie's death had felt like a horrible mistake; this sympathy card must actually be one. Maxine McGuire had wanted to offer condolences to some other camper who'd just lost a dog, but in her nervous frenzy about the opening of camp, she'd forgotten to sign the card and left it in the wrong cabin. Besides, if, God forbid, I really had lost Kimi, someone would have told me in person; leaving me an unsigned sympathy card would have been no one's ludicrous idea of a gentle way to break the news.

I shoved the card in a bureau drawer, slipped Rowdy's training collar over his head, attached a six-foot leather lead, and set out for the main house in search of a telephone so that I could call Leah, make sure that Kimi was all right, and issue dozens of warnings about hazards to dogs that I'd failed to mention in the countless diatribes on the subject that I'd been delivering almost nonstop since my decision to entrust Kimi to my cousin's care.

The door of my cabin opened onto a deck that faced the lake. Originally, I thought, the cabin must have been a single unit with an old-fashioned screened porch. When decks came in vogue, did bugs go out? But the deck was bigger than the porch must have been; it extended about ten feet toward the lake and wrapped itself across the front of the cabin and around the sides, where it ended in stairs. The effect was chalet-like and spacious; the wooden railing that divided the deck in half left plenty of room on both sides for twin sets of red-painted Adirondack chairs and big pots of scarlet geraniums in garish bloom. On the side of the deck that wasn't mine, a vaguely familiar-looking, round-headed man was sitting in one of the chairs doodling on legal pad and talking intently into a portable phone. I couldn't help overhearing.

He spoke impatiently. "No," he said. "That was in the Board's modified recommendation. This was in the Ad Hoc Committee on Committees recommendations. Their own Delegate Committee presented the whole thing in full." English? A dialect thereof. AKC, actually, which is a kind of

reverse *Mahlemut.* Remember *Mahlemut?* Succinct. Not so
AKC. I understood every word he said, and if you did, too,
well, God help us both. If you didn't, don't let it bother you.
Except to the extent that the man was discussing the politics
of the nation's largest dog registry, he wasn't talking about
dogs at all. He wasn't looking at dogs, either. From the long,
narrow dock that stretched out into the lake directly in front
of my cabin, the Chesapeake bitch I'd noticed earlier took an
energetic dive into the water. Rowdy's feet sounded on the
deck. His tags jingled. The bitch was as good a Chesapeake as
Rowdy was a malamute. Even when Rowdy wagged his tail
and rested his big, handsome head on the railing that divided
the deck, the man's eyes never left his legal pad.

"Rowdy, this way." I patted my thigh and shortened the
leash. "Let's go call Leah."

The Mooselookmeguntic Four Seasons Resort Lodge and
Cabins occupied the shores of a deep cove. Viewed from the
lake, the buildings consisted of the main lodge, a vast two-
story log cabin with low, motellike wings; and double rows of
small cabins along the lake shore on both sides. From that
watery perspective, the long dock by my cabin was to the left
of the lodge, directly in front of which was a long, narrow
stretch of rocky beach. On the pebbles to the far right of the
beach rested ten or twelve upturned canoes painted the same
fiery red that brightened the doors and window trim of the
buildings. Gaudy geraniums bloomed in pots on the decks and
in baskets that hung from the eaves of the unscreened porch
of the main house. Each double row of little cabins consisted
of six set directly on the water with another six staggered in
back to assure a view of the lake. In the state of Maine, and
perhaps elsewhere, the distinction carries considerable economic and social weight. *Right on the water* is definitely the
place to be; a mere *view* is worse than second best because
glimpsing the lake or the ocean from an aqueously disadvan-
taged spot requires the viewer to take in the superior places of

those who can afford to be *right on the water*, and the result is, of course, envy, jealousy, and spite far worse than any land-locked, no-view vacation spot could possibly engender.

"Right on the water," a woman spat. "I don't call this *right on the water*." In her left hand was a doughnut. She gave it a vicious bite. Her right fist gripped the boxy black-plastic handle of a retractable lead. With no regard for the hefty yellow male Lab at the other end of the lead, she shook her fist at the cabin from which Rowdy and I had emerged. Her gesture thus encompassed us as well. *"That's* right on the water." The woman bore so remarkable a physical resemblance to an obese bulldog that I must have stared at her. From the official bull-dog standard: "heavy, thick-set, low-slung body, massive short-faced head, wide shoulders, and sturdy limbs." With regard to temperament, however, the standard goes on to specify an "equable and kind" disposition and a demeanor both "pacific and dignified." Also, according to her red-and-white pin, she was called Eva, which seemed like a funny name for a bulldog, and her accent was definitely Long Island with a rock-hard *g*, whereas a self-respecting bulldog would have ut-tered nothing less than pure Oxbridge and would have done so in low, self-effacing tones. Bullbaiting was no upper-crust sport, but the breed long ago overcame its rough origins. Eva had obviously not done likewise.

The embarrassed-looking recipient of Eva's outburst was a very young woman with short blond curls and careful make-up. She wore a neatly ironed outfit, shorts and a sleeveless top in a shade of bright pink that matched her fingernails. Accord-ing to the words emblazoned on her pink tote bag, she loved Cairn terriers. Cradled to her breast was what I gathered was supposed to be one, a little gray dog with an almost incredible number of glaring deviations from the standard of the Cairn terrier: a very narrow skull, a long, heavy muzzle, an under-shot bite, big yellow eyes, gigantic ears, a silky coat, and a flesh-colored nose. Other faults were presumably covered by the loving hands and forearms of his owner. According to the woman's name tag, she was Joy, or so I assumed; the pin on her bright pink blouse read "Joy and Lucky."

"Craig and I are just *so* happy to be in a cabin," Joy told Eva. "He was afraid we'd get stuck in the bunkhouse." She nodded toward a large structure visible through a stand of pines and white birches. Despite cedar siding, red trim, and yet more geraniums, the building retained the look of a small sawmill, and the only shore on which it sat belonged to the parking lot. "And then we would've had to decide whether to come at all," said Joy. As Rowdy and I approached, she added in quiet tones of deep shock, "It's coed, you know! *Men* and women! And with shared bathrooms."

Horrors. I was beginning to suspect that Joy did not belong to the fancy. Our members aren't necessarily crazy about sharing bathrooms, but we aren't bothered by human nakedness and other such secular trivia. An Order is, after all, for Higher Things. What worries us is that someone won't clean the tub after bathing the dog. We ourselves don't mind showering with fur underfoot, of course; in fact, we've learned that a nice, thick abrasive layer of guard coat acts as a natural sole-smoothing callus remover, a sort of woofy loofah; but hotel managers, innkeepers, and the like always object, and we live in perpetual fear that our careless brethren will drive the proprietors thenceforth to ban the Sacred Animal from comfortable lodging establishments near popular show sites.

As if to confirm my suspicion about her noninitiate status, Joy took a look at Rowdy and cried, "What a beautiful husky!"

When I first got Rowdy, I welcomed these displays of ignorance as happy opportunities to spread the Good Word. "Thank you," I'd say, "but he is an Alaskan malamute." Then I'd pin the ignoramus in a corner and deliver a two-hour lecture on Otto von Kotzebue, Scotty Allen, Arthur Walden, Short Seeley, the Byrd expeditions, Paul Voelker, the reopening of the stud book, the key differences between the Kotzebue and M'Loot lines, the Husky Pak formula, Sergeant Preston and Yukon King, the breed standard, and the particulars in which Rowdy epitomized the ideal and thus looked nothing whatsoever like a Siberian husky. At that point, my exhausted victim would gasp something like, "Well, like I said, lady, nice dog," and vanish, never again to admire any dog at all. Bit by bit, however, I began to delete key points of the original malamute vs. Siberian discourse; these days, unless the call of the wild rings in the admirer's eyes, I sometimes limit myself to an inadequate word of thanks.

And was about to do just that when Rowdy caught sight of the doughnut in Eva's left hand, perked up his ears, and wagged his tail. There was nothing aggressive about the posture; Rowdy intended to beg for the doughnut, not to steal it; he falls back on theft only when charm fails. Maybe Eva's big-boned yellow Lab misread Rowdy, or maybe he was looking for an excuse for a fight. In either case, he growled viciously, and lunged toward Rowdy and me so fast and so unexpectedly that I barely had time to haul Rowdy back and spoil the fun. As apparently unprepared for the Lab's attack as I'd been, Eva flung the doughnut aside, and, instead of using the flex lead to reel in her dog, adopted a stiff pose, put on a deadly serious expression, and commanded in the stern tones of old-fashioned formal obedience, "Bingo, *come!*" Bingo was no dope; he completely ignored her. Impressed? Take heart. Your dog, too, can easily learn not to come when he's called. Just look and sound as if you'll kill him when he gets in striking distance. Works every time. But don't count on teaching a Labrador retriever to lunge at other dogs. The typical Lab needs to be prevented from kissing everything on four paws.

By then, I'd retreated out of the radius of Bingo's retractable lead and had Rowdy sitting politely at my left side with his attention fixed on my face and his mind intent on the intriguing question of whether my mouth did or didn't con-

tain a lump of cheese or a bit of hot dog that would sail his
way if he kept watching. If I haven't mentioned it already, let
me say that Rowdy honestly is a good dog.

As I was telling him so, Eva finally had the sense to start
reeling Bingo in. As the Lab turned his attention from Rowdy,
however, he spotted the remains of Eva's discarded doughnut,
which rested on the ground about midway between Eva and
Joy, who had dashed away and clutched the frightened-look-
ing Cairn, Lucky, in her arms. Or I think that's what happened; I'm giving Bingo the benefit of the doubt. When he
headed full tilt toward Joy, I think that he just wanted the
doughnut; I don't think that he meant to attack Lucky. Even
so, Joy can't be blamed for screaming and turning tail. And
Bingo can't really be blamed for going after her, either; in the
eyes of a dog, a person who shrieks and runs becomes interesting prey. What we advise kids in dogwise courses is to "be
a tree." Then some bright kid always pipes up and says, "But
I'll get peed on!" and we say, "Sure, maybe you will, but
what's worse, getting peed on or getting bitten?" Gets 'em
every time.

Fortunately, though, despite Joy's distinctly nonarboreal
dash for safety and despite Eva's ludicrous repetition of the
reliably useless "Bingo, *come!*" the Lab eventually found the
doughnut, and while he was gulping it down, Eva finally managed to reel him.

"Good boy, Rowdy," I said. "Okay!" That's his release
word. The one that triggers the rapt attention is "Ready!"
Why *ready?* The sacred rites of the obedience ring require the
judge to ask each exhibitor two ritual questions, the second of
which is, "Are you ready?" One acceptable answer is, of
course, *yes*, but as an attention-triggering word, it has obvious
disadvantages. A second acceptable answer does dual service
as a reply to the judge and a cue to the dog: "Ready."

Awakened from his trance, Rowdy became a normal malamute again; he eyed Bingo, and his hackles rose.

Eva addressed Joy, not me. "That's a malamute, not a husky. Malamutes are part wolf."

My own hackles rose higher than Rowdy's. *Be a tree*, I thought. "All dogs are descended from wolves," I said quietly. I'd barely arrived at camp. We'd be here for a week. I didn't want a fight. My smile encompassed Eva and Joy. "I'm Holly Winter. And this is Rowdy. I'm sure the dogs will do fine once they get used to each other. They're bound to be a little nervous. The new setting and everything?" I hate to have Rowdy watch me roll belly-up, but I continue to retain a remote sense of human diplomacy—as opposed to malamute diplomacy, a form of negotiation with a single rule: *Never back down.*

"Lucky is just beside himself," Joy said with relief. "We drove all the way from Oregon, and he's been cooped up in the car, and now all these dogs! He's totally overwhelmed." It seemed to me that if I were clutched in someone's arms as nervously as the Cairn was in Joy's, I'd lose a little self-confidence, too, but I didn't say so.

Eva did. "Put him down. You're making him nervous. The way you grab him like that, he thinks he can't stand up for himself."

Joy's eyes darted to Bingo. She tightened her grip on Lucky. "Well, how could he? I mean, poor Lucky only weighs fifteen pounds, and he really isn't used to big dogs. He's scared of them."

"Should've taken him to puppy kindergarten," Eva snapped.

Shameful apology pinched Joy's face. "I didn't know about it then. When I got Lucky, I didn't know anything." She paused. "He came from a pet shop. I just didn't know." She massaged the little dog's big, hairy ears. "He isn't show quality. We had him neutered." She took a breath. "But Lucky is a very good dog. He's great with kids, he loves everyone, and he's *so* smart. I didn't want a show dog, anyway. I just wanted a pet."

I could almost read the words about to spring from the pendulous lips of Eva's pushed-in bulldog face: *You sure got one*, she was about to say. Person-to-person and in my *Dog's Life* column and articles, I am an ardent bad-mouther of pet shops, the puppy mills that supply them, and the entire wholesale commercial dog industry. But Joy had already gotten the message.

I spoke up. "Lucky has a very sweet face."

Joy's whole body radiated pleasure. "Thank you. But *your* dog is really beautiful."

"Thanks." I felt awkward, as if I'd made a polite remark about some ghastly art-object of Joy's, a Day-Glo matador on black velvet, a lamp in the shape of Michelangelo's David, and in return, she'd praised my Rembrandt.

"Good-looking dog," conceded Eva, eyes on Rowdy. "Maybe a little small for the breed," she told Joy, "but he's still a good-looking dog."

I am the first person to admit to the faults in my dogs. Kimi lacks Rowdy's perfect ear set. One of my goldens, Danny, had a gay tail; he carried it a little too far above the horizontal. *Gay* has nothing to do with sexual preference, by the way; in fact, whenever Danny was anywhere near a bitch in season, I always wished it did.

"Which breed did you have in mind?" I asked Eva.

She looked baffled.

"Never mind," I said. *Be a tree.* But on another occasion, I realized, maybe I actually would rather get bitten.

Four

"EVA SPITTELER is a prize *b-i-t-c-h*."

Cam White lowered her voice to spell out the word. Even without the special treatment, the *bitch*-as-in-s.o.b. meaning would have been unambiguous, and as for *prize*, well, if Eva had been the only dog entered in a kiddie pet parade, she still wouldn't have made it into the ribbons.

To get away from Eva and Bingo, I'd pretended to have forgotten something in my cabin. After I returned there and waited a few minutes, I reemerged and immediately spotted two Lodge sisters, Cam White and Ginny Garabedian. I'd seen Cam in the ring, and we'd hung around together at shows, but I also knew her from photos in *Front and Finish*, which perhaps I should explain is the official publication of the Exhausted Order of Obedience Fanatics, a monthly tabloid for dog trainers that's crammed with pictures of OTCH dogs (Obedience Trial Champions); ads for equipment, videos, trials, and, yes, indeed, dog camps; and chatty, informative columns about everything from the evils of animal-rights extremism to the methods of the top handlers to what are euphemistically referred to as the "challenges" of working with northern breeds. *(Front and Finish*, P.O. Box 333, Galesburg, IL 61402–0333. See? We aren't a *secret* society at all.)

As I was explaining, Cam White had an OTCH sheltie named Nicky who appeared in *Front and Finish* in his own right, sometimes with a grinning Cam at his side, and who also inspected the reader from the photo at the top of Cam's column, which was about the fine points of the obedience regulations. In the typical column, Cam presented a scoring dilemma that she then resolved. *At a recent outdoor trial*, a reader would write, *mine was the first dog in Open A. On the Retrieve on Flat, he was casting back and forth in long grass looking for his dumbbell when he came across what the spectators later described as the remains of a peanut butter sandwich. After wolfing it down, he gave a loud burp and then promptly located and retrieved the dumbbell. The judge took a substantial deduction. Shouldn't we have been allowed to repeat the exercise?* And Cam would discuss the judge's obligation to inspect the ring, distinguish between the excess length of the grass and the presence of the sandwich, explain that the judge could have permitted the dog to repeat the exercise, opine that the deduction was for slowness in retrieving rather than for eating or burping, lament the failure of clubs to follow the regulations stating that grass is supposed to be "cut short," and argue that the regulations should be revised to specify precisely how short, preferably in millimeters. Then she'd launch into the fascinating theoretical question of whether burping alone merited a deduction and, if it did, how many points it should cost.

The obsessive streak evident in Cam's dog writing harmonized with her almost compulsive neatness. Her clothes retained visible creases—deliberate ones, that is—and her short, dark hair waved in evenly spaced rows of controlled curls. Her lipstick never smudged. Her mascara never ran. She arrived at shows with her gear meticulously packed in clever canvas cases she'd designed and sewn herself. Nicky was always under perfect control. Although the Shetland sheepdog is to the rough-coated collie what the Shetland pony is to the full-size horse, sheltie people resent having their dogs demeaned as miniature collies. Thus I hesitate to report that the sable-and-white Nicky really looked a lot like a rerun of Lassie on a very small screen.

Cam was in her early or midthirties, about my age. Ginny Garabedian, her companion and cabinmate at Waggin' Tail, looked about sixty, as she'd done for the ten years I'd known her and would probably continue to do for another two or three decades. An AKC tracking judge and breeder of Labrador retrievers, Ginny was a compact, sturdy person who braided her gray hair into an extremely long plait that she wrapped around and around her head and fastened tightly in place. Bareheaded, she looked as if she wore an elaborately woven basket upturned on her head. Like a lot of tracking people, however, she frequently wore a real hat, and when I first met her, the double *chapeau* effect always made me wonder whether Ginny had some haberdashery-specific neurological disorder that caused her to perceive two hats as one.

After a while, though, I learned to ignore the oddity of Ginny's head. For one thing, I ran into her a lot and got used to it. She showed in breed, casually and routinely put Novice obedience titles on her dogs, taught tracking clinics, attended seminars on canine nutrition and diseases, wrote a few articles for the dog magazines, belonged to D.W.A.A.—the Dog Writers' Association of America—and otherwise gaited my own rings of the *haut monde du chien*. For another thing, I learned something about Ginny that diverted me from her trivial quirk of appearance, namely, that she had outlived five husbands. I was astounded. Topped by the plait alone, Ginny had a vigorous, outdoorsy, and distinctly unisex attractiveness. If she'd been a bird, I thought, she'd have belonged to some appealing species shown in the field guides with a single illustration and the notation "sexes alike." After I heard about the five dead husbands, I wondered about them whenever I saw Ginny. So complete was her dedication to dogs that I found it difficult to imagine her being interested in one man, never mind five, unless they'd all looked like Labrador retrievers. Or maybe, with canine opportunism, she'd married the men to support her dogs. If the full truth be known, I also wondered what had killed the five husbands and how much life insurance each had carried. As it turned out, everyone else in dogs harbored the same suspicions about Ginny that I did. Never having been married, however, I kept mine to myself until the day a dog acquaintance of Ginny's and mine confronted me on the subject. "Look," she said, "here are the rest of us, fighting and scheming and begging whenever it's time to get a new show puppy, and then there's Ginny, and, I mean, you have to ask yourself: What did *she* do to deserve that kind of luck?"

"Prize *b-i-t-c-h*," Cam repeated. "And in my area, everywhere you go, there's Eva." Cam's area, if I remembered correctly, was New York or New Jersey. By *everywhere*, she did not mean supermarkets, movie theaters, and dinner parties; she meant only the places that counted. "You can't go to a show without seeing her! And she is *so* obnoxious. She'll stand outside the breed rings and say awful things about everyone's dogs—"

"At the top of her lungs, too," added Ginny, who was not, by the way, wearing a hat. We were standing in the shade of a big old white birch midway between my cabin and the main lodge.

"Yes," Cam agreed, "and she doesn't know what she's talking about, either, and Ginny, I am really sorry to say this, but that dog does not belong on the grounds of an AKC show." Cam and her husband, I remembered, had connections at AKC. Among other things, he was a delegate. For AKC types like Cam—and like me, as well—the fancy spins on the axis of the American Kennel Club. A dog with Bingo's temperament,

I should point out, didn't belong on the grounds of any show, AKC, UKC, or any other KC, either.

"*I* don't mind," Ginny said. "I know when I've made a mistake. I should never, ever have sold to Eva. She ruined that lovely puppy. I have never had temperament problems in my lines. My dogs live right in the house with me, and they all get along, and I can take them anywhere, and they never so much as look cross-eyed at another dog." As if to verify Ginny's claim, the chocolate Lab bitch she had with her strolled over to Rowdy, lowered her head, tilted it, stuck out a long pink tongue, and licked Rowdy's muzzle. He regarded her with the air of an emperor accepting obeisance from a serf. "This one's the worst of all," Ginny commented. "Her name's Wiz, but everyone always ends up calling her Kissy Face."

"I knew that dog of Eva's looked familiar," I said happily, "but I couldn't place him. Bingo. Bingo looks like that big male of yours. I knew he reminded me . . ."

Ginny's face contorted in pain. Her body seemed to shrink.

Cam caught my eye, frowned, and briefly raised a finger to her lips. "Merlin died," she informed me quietly.

"I am *so* sorry," I said. "I had no idea. He was a wonderful dog. So beautiful."

And he was, too. Without spilling the sordid contents of "the Labrador mess"—a prolonged controversy about revising the AKC standard of the Labrador retriever—let me explain that the breed has become separated into two distinct lines, bench and field, show dogs and hunting dogs, and that Ginny's were show dogs. So dirty and slippery are the grounds around the Labrador mess that I'm afraid to say what Ginny's dogs looked like lest I skid on some politically charged word and tumble in. Let's say that Merlin had been a big-boned, flashy-looking yellow dog with many titles and tons of charisma. Or let's just say that Ginny loved him a lot.

"I'm *so* sorry," I repeated. Ginny's pain was contagious. I patted my thigh to summon Rowdy and dug my fingers into the depths of his coat. Then I ran my fingertips over his wet nose. The gesture was completely irrational. Rowdy had been bouncing around sniffing tree trunks, lifting his leg, making friends with Wiz, and accepting her drooly kisses. I didn't need to touch him to make sure that he was alive. I felt a renewed urgency about calling Leah. *A mistake*, I thought again, remembering the sympathy card. *A simple error. Not Kimi.*

"Thank you," Ginny said. "People have been . . ."

"It helps," I said. "It helps a little."

"Not really." Cam shook her head. "Nothing does, really."

"It would be worse if no one gave a damn," I said.

"That's how it is for most people," Ginny said. "They can't even talk about it. They're afraid that someone's going to say, you know, 'only a dog.' "

"One thing about this place," said Cam, "is that no one's going to say that. Everyone here understands."

I nodded.

"I was going to bring Merlin," Ginny told me, "and I had to call Maxine and tell her, and then when I got here, she'd left a card."

"In our room," Cam said. "We're sharing." Cam's face and tone lightened. Her smile was wry. "But Max did forget to sign it."

Ginny shrugged. "Maxine's been running her tail off. It's a wonder she remembered at all."

In the couple of seconds since I'd last had my eye on Rowdy, he'd wandered to one of the many covered trash barrels stationed here and there on the grounds. Fastened to the side of each was a big plastic bag that held a large supply of small plastic bags to be used in cleaning up after dogs and then deposited in the big barrels. The barrels were admittedly a sort of tree-trunk brown, and this one must already have acquired the interesting scent of other dogs. Even so. "Rowdy, not there!" I ordered him. His glance called me a fool, but he dutifully lowered his leg. "Good boy." I switched my attention back to Cam and Ginny. "Which cabin are you in?"

Cam pointed. "The first one."

"Oh, I'm next door," I said.

Cam and Ginny exchanged a look I couldn't read. As if first having obtained Ginny's consent, Cam said, "Lucky you."

"To be right on the lake?"

Their expressions changed.

"Am I missing something?" I asked. "That's one of the things Eva was complaining about, that her cabin's in the second row. I mean, it's practically on the lake, but . . ."

Cam shook her head without disarranging a single dark hair. "Met your neighbors yet?" she asked pertly.

"Not really. There's a guy sitting out on the deck, but I didn't meet him. He was talking on the phone. He had a cellular phone. Am I supposed to know him?"

Ginny finally gave me a straight answer. "Don Abbott. You know Phyllis. Phyllis Abbott."

It took me a moment to place the name. "Oh, Mrs. Abbott. The judge. That's right. Maxine mentioned they were next to me. Sure. I've shown under Mrs. Abbott. I stewarded for her a couple of years ago. In Utility." Utility. What is Utility? If you happen to be a Mason, I can explain it easily. It's Third Degree. Really. Three Craft Degrees, First, Second, and Third, leading respectively to the titles Entered Apprentice, Fellow Craft, and Master Mason. Three obedience trial classes: Novice, Open, and Utility; CD, CDX, and UD. UDX? Knights Templar, I suppose. OTCH? Royal Arch. Eerie, isn't it? The Scottish Rite. The York Rite. The Rite of Canine Obedience. "I liked her," I continued. "She was very fair. I'd show under her again. What's wrong with her?"

If a heretofore pleasant and fair obedience judge had turned mean, I wanted to know. I don't believe in paying entry fees to show under judges who make snide remarks or invent their own rules. Neither does anyone else. That's why most obedience judges are terrific. People don't enter under the bad ones, and clubs don't rehire judges who draw small entries. It's a form of natural selection: survival of the fairest.

"Nothing," Ginny said firmly. "It's just that Cam—"

Cam cut in: "It's nothing. Forget I said it. It's not Phyllis, anyway. It's just that Max didn't have to take *everyone* who applied."

"I, uh, have the impression that she more or less did," I said. "It's her first year. I don't think she could afford to turn people down. And what excuse could she give people? 'Sorry, but no one likes you'?"

"There could've been a rule about aggressive dogs," Ginny said.

"Are the Abbotts' dogs . . . ?" I asked.

"No," Cam said. "And anyway, they're Poms." The ideal weight for the Pomeranian is four or five pounds. Toy breeds can be aggressive, but there's a limit to the harm they can do, and, in any case, Pomeranians are sweethearts. "Actually, Phyllis has very nice dogs. And Phyllis Abbott is a good handler. You have to give her that. Ginny means Eva Spitteler. Ginny, just ignore her. Everyone knows what Eva's like. No one pays any attention to her."

"Eva goes around telling everyone awful things about me," Ginny informed me.

Cam sounded impatient. "But, Ginny, no one listens to Eva Spitteler."

"Hah! She lures all those pet people in, and she charges them a fortune. *They* listen to her."

"No one who counts," Cam said. Then she filled me in. "Eva runs a so-called training center. She does a lot of puppy kindergarten, pet obedience, that kind of thing, and she has *no* credentials—no one really knows who she is—but she gets all these pet people, and they don't know any better."

"She's never so much as put one CD on one dog," Ginny said indignantly.

"The pet people don't care," Cam said. "They just don't know. Eva tells them that obedience is some big deal, and they believe every word she says, and then when they hear that she's entered Bingo, they think, 'Oh, wow, an obedience trial. She must be really something.' And she sells dog food and all kinds of dog supplies, and she charges like five percent less than the pet shops, and she tells people she's getting them a special deal on everything. And supposedly she's starting some kind of mail-order business. That's her latest."

"Eva makes a *lot* of money," Ginny commented.

"But she doesn't sell puppies," I said. "She doesn't run a real pet shop."

Cam and Ginny looked suitably shocked. "No," Cam said, "Eva wouldn't do that. As a matter of fact, she keeps people out of the pet shops. That's one *good* thing she does."

Ginny held firm. "The only one."

"Eva does try," Cam said. "Mainly, she's obnoxious. She just isn't cut out to be an instructor. She doesn't have any credentials, but she does try. She goes to workshops and things. It doesn't do any good, but she does go. She just doesn't learn anything. If you ask me, the real problem is her personality. And, Ginny, that's the thing about Bingo. Everyone knows that. Considering what Eva's like, Bingo could be a lot worse."

"There ought to be a rule about flex leads," I said. "I don't mind so much if Bingo is dog-aggressive, but, if he is, he ought to be under control. He should be on a short lead. What happened was that Bingo went flying at Rowdy, and Eva couldn't stop him. If he'd attacked Rowdy, well, Bingo is a big dog, but there wouldn't be anything left of him."

At the sound of his name, Rowdy quit fooling around with Wiz, Ginny's kissy-face Lab, and emitted an elaborate series of northern-breed vocalizations that culminated in a strong suggestion politely intoned as a question: *Ah-roo, woo-woo-woo, woo-woo-woo, roo-roo?* Translation: *Can we get the hell out of here?*

Even without the translation, Cam and Ginny looked startled.

"He needs to finish his walk," I said, "and I have to call home before this meeting. I need to check on my bitch." Real dog people like Ginny and Cam required no explanation, but I couldn't think of a good reason to withhold the real one. "Ginny, the card you got? About Merlin. There was a sympathy card in my cabin, too."

Their faces fell. "Holly, you should've—" Ginny started to say.

"Nothing's happened. That's what's so weird. The last dog I lost was Vinnie, and that was a month before I got Rowdy. Ginny, could I ask you, the card you got, did it have a sort of watercolor scene? With a couple of trees? And something like, 'With Sympathy on the Loss of Your Pet.' In a kind of pale tan envelope."

Ginny nodded.

I said, "I got the same card. I assumed it was some kind of mistake. It probably is. It has to be. Mine wasn't signed, either."

Cam and Ginny both understood: I still had to call home.

Five

THE WOMAN in front of me in line for the pay phone wore a blue T-shirt with a picture of a beret-wearing poodle and the proclamation: *J'embrasse mon chien sur la bouche.* But the dog at her feet was a feisty-looking basenji, and she wasn't kissing him on the mouth, either. She was complaining. "One phone for the whole place isn't *my* idea of luxury. Wouldn't you think they'd have them in the rooms? All these dog people? Everyone's going to need to call home all the time."

The big lobby of the lodge had had its log walls scrubbed and its floor refinished. The furniture had been arranged with such professional skill that the red-upholstered couches and chairs appeared engaged in happy conversation with the consciously rustic end tables, coffee tables, and magazine racks. The sepia-tinted, blown-up photographs on the walls showed grubby, grinning fishermen holding impressive strings of trout. It seemed just as well that the anglers and their catch were now confined behind glass. Sweat, bug dope, and dead fish would have fought the saccharine reek of floral incense, scented candles, and gift-shop potpourri. A mammoth brown trout mounted on a wooden plaque above the stone fireplace paid odorless tribute to varnish and taxidermy. There wasn't a fly rod in sight.

But the renovators had left the original phone booth, a wooden cabinet tucked under the staircase to the second floor. Superman lives. At the moment, though, the hinged door was folded open.

"Just shove it down his throat and clamp his jaws shut," a woman was saying, "and then blow on his nose until he sticks his tongue out, and give him a cookie and tell him what a good boy he is." After she finished, a man in a Big Dog T-shirt interrogated some unfortunate veterinarian about a puddle of perfectly ordinary-sounding vomitus. "Bright yellow and slimy," the man insisted. "You practically wanted to scramble it." Then the mouth-kissing basenji woman reminded someone that under no circumstances was Arax ever to be allowed off leash. My turn finally arrived. Rowdy, of course, did not fit in the phone booth. He had to sit just outside. It didn't matter. I'm not the kind of person who makes the dog say hello.

In the half day since I'd left Cambridge, my cousin Leah had replaced the message on my answering machine with the opening of Beethoven's Fifth followed by a cacophony in which Kimi's *woo-wooing* vied with the loud barks of her friend Jeff's Border collie. The noise abruptly quit, and Leah's recorded voice informed me that I had three minutes in which to record my innermost thoughts. As I was about to do so in rather violent language, Leah came on live.

"Leah, is Kimi all right?" I demanded.

"You don't trust me!"

"I leave you with my bitch in season, and—? Leah, let me tell you, greater trust hath no woman. She *is* all right?"

Although I'm the one who initiated Leah into dogs, she is nonetheless the kind of person who . . .

Although growling and roaring carry poorly over telephone

lines, I hung up reassured about Kimi's vigor, yet in some peculiar way, newly angry about the unsigned sympathy card.

The welcome-to-camp meeting was due to begin in fifteen minutes, and the area between the lodge and the lake, half grass and half pine needles, was already crowded with people and dogs. As Rowdy and I made our way down the stairs to join the group, Maxine McGuire appeared around the side of the building, and I hailed her. Ambling peacefully at her side was the young mastiff I'd noticed earlier, a fawn-colored male the size of a three-car garage and still growing. Max's yellow-gray curls had turned to corkscrews, and her pale face was flushed.

"Maxine, could I have a word with you?" I asked. "Do you have a second?"

"One." She glanced at her watch. "No, two." She raised the hem of her camp T-shirt, pulled out a ragged hand towel caught in the waistband of her shorts, and mopped off the dog's mouth. "If you can't stand drool, don't get a mastiff. Good boy, Cash." She moored the towel back in place. With the giant puppy at her side, Max seemed to have shed some of her earlier nervousness. "What can I do for you?"

"Beautiful dog. Cash?"

"Stud fee," Max explained. "I didn't name him; the breeder did. The deal was that if she kept the pick puppy, she owed the stud fee in cash, and her husband kept telling her, 'Never mind the dog! Keep the cash!' " Maxine let the point sink in. "But she ended up selling him to me. I just got him a month ago. He's only a year. Forty or fifty pounds to go."

Cash stood patiently at Max's side. His ears and tail were motionless, his eyes gentle. By comparison with Cash, Rowdy looked the size of a Pomeranian. He must have thought so, too. The hair on his back began to rise. "Puppy," I told him. Rowdy knew the word, but, for obvious reasons, didn't believe me. Cash stared placidly into space.

"Don't worry about it," Maxine said cheerfully. "Cash doesn't mind."

Confronted with the overwhelming evidence of Cash's total lack of interest—Cash completely ignored him—Rowdy slowly began to lower his hackles. Rowdy is more hierarchical than he is aggressive; if Cash didn't want to play King of the Mountain, neither did Rowdy. Even so, especially because of the subject I wanted to raise with Max, I felt embarrassed. I cleared my throat. "I wondered if there might be some rule or whatever about dogs on long flex leads. People do it at shows, and it can be a problem there—they let the dog out the full twenty-six feet. A while ago, a dog shot out of nowhere and went for Rowdy. Nothing happened. But it made me a little uncomfortable. And I wondered."

Max scowled. "Whose dog?"

"It doesn't matter. It's the general—"

"Eva Spitteler. You ever run into her before?"

"No. Just today."

Maxine drew close. Her breath smelled like candy. "Did Eva bite your head off?"

I live with two Alaskan malamutes, and I'm still here, I wanted to say. I contented myself with a simple no.

"There's a little problem there," Max confided.

"If that big Lab of hers takes on the wrong dog, the problem won't be so little." My eyes darted to the peaceful mastiff. "Even Cash would defend himself."

Max dismissed the possibility. "A Lab'd just bounce right off him. If Eva bothers you, just ignore her. The truth is, I didn't find out about her until she'd already signed up, and by the time I got warned about what a pill she was, it was too late. I put her by herself in one of the cabin units, and all she paid for was a shared double in the bunkhouse, so that ought to put her in a good mood, and no one's stuck rooming with her. That's the best I can do. Sorry, but there's a rotten apple in every barrel."

Without having really addressed the question of keeping dogs under control, Max hastily excused herself to get the meeting started. Rowdy and I followed her. The crowd had grown to about a hundred people and at least that many dogs. I found a shady spot under an ancient white birch near Cam and Ginny. Cam's sheltie, Nicky, was stretched out at her side, his head resting on his paws. Wiz had been lying down, too, but she rose to her feet, licked Rowdy's muzzle, abased herself before him, rolled onto her back, and wiggled. Rowdy sniffed her indulgently. I sat cross-legged on the grass. Rowdy put himself in an alert sit and began a systematic survey of the canine competition. Most of the other dogs napped.

Heather, the self-styled Chief Fecal Inspector, appeared with a small loudspeaker attached to a portable microphone. Maxine took the mike and called the meeting to order. She was no public speaker. The mike squealed. Max shouted a welcome. Everyone applauded. Max said that she was happy to see all of us and excited about camp. She thanked us for having faith in her and for making her dream become a reality. The heat made me drowsy. The temperature couldn't have been above the high seventies, ten or twenty degrees cooler than Cambridge, but in Rangeley, Maine, it must have been one of the hottest days of the year. I drifted.

Max was talking about the contents of the registration packets we'd received when we'd arrived. She held up a red sheet of legal-size paper and said that she was sure that we were just as excited as she was about the courses and the activities. Everyone should take note of a couple of revisions in the schedule. Canine Good Citizenship testing, originally scheduled for Friday, would take place tomorrow afternoon; and Temperament Testing, scheduled for Thursday, would be held on Tuesday. A murmur greeted the announcement. "That shoots that," I heard someone grumble. "Tomorrow afternoon, Teddy's still going to be off the wall." Rowdy already had his CGC and TT titles, so the changes didn't affect me, but I sympathized with the grumbler. Both tests should have been scheduled for the end of the week, when the dogs had adjusted to the novelty of camp.

In response to the muttering, Max said, "I know it's not ideal, but it's very complicated to fit in so many activities, and this is the best we could work out. So bear with it, and I'm sure that the dogs will all do just fine."

"There aren't all that many activities," Cam whispered to me. "Half the time, there's nothing to do. I hope Maxine doesn't totally blow this thing." With her usual superb organization, Cam had brought the long red sheet from her registration packet. She tapped a neatly filed fingernail on the paper on what was evidently a gap in the schedule. "At Dog Days," she said, naming one of Waggin' Tail's competitors, "there's something every second."

Having neither examined the schedule nor attended another camp, I just shrugged. The microphone screamed. Heather moved the loudspeaker. When Max spoke again, her overamplified voice sounded metallic and oddly distant, as if an android addressed us from afar. "Don't forget what we're here for! We're here to get away from it all! So don't push your dogs! And don't push yourselves! This is vacation! RE-LAX!"

The command jolted me and irked me. If Max had ordered us to set high goals for ourselves and to hurl ourselves at the task of meeting them, I'd have been able to rebel by not doing a damn thing. As Max began to introduce the instructors, though, I remembered why I'd decided that camp would be okay. Chuck Siegel, the show obedience instructor, and Kerry O'Brian, the pet obedience person, were supposed to be first-rate. At a show a while back, Rowdy and I had done an agility miniclinic with Sara Altman, who was terrific. When Maxine asked Sara's assistants to show themselves, I wasn't surprised to see that they included Heather. I knew nothing about the people in charge of lure coursing, drill team, flyball, or Frisbee. I'd never heard of the person giving the workshop on pet tricks, but her little shepherd-mix dog established his owner's expertise by dropping to the ground, rolling over three times, leaping up, walking on his front legs, and taking a bow that drew wild applause.

"And our breed handling instructor," Max announced, "Eric Grimaldi." The name was familiar. Max looked around. "Eric? Eric, stand up. Is Eric here? Well, he's here somewhere." The mike echoed tinnily. Max leaned down to listen to someone. "Eric's still trying to get Elsa out of the lake! Chessies are like that. But you'll meet Eric at dinner. And now we have a few very special campers I want to introduce—not that everyone isn't special, but these are people you'll want to be sure you get a chance to know. From *Dog's Life*, Holly Winter, who's brought us our only malamute. Holly?"

I swore under my breath, and popped up and down as fast as possible.

"And we're honored to have a very distinguished couple, Phyllis and Don Abbott. Everyone knows Don, and a lot of you know Don's marvelous book about getting started in the fancy. And Phyllis Abbott, one of our most respected obedience judges. Don and Phyllis?" Don Abbott was, of course, the round-faced man who'd been on the deck when I'd left my cabin, the man who'd been too busy with his phone conversation about AKC politics to give Rowdy even a quick glance. Real dog person. When Mrs. Abbott and her husband stood up, I noticed that she wore a silky-looking blouse and navy slacks that would have been suitable even for the formality of the breed ring. In obedience, it's common to see women judges in informal slacks or warm-up outfits, but when Mrs. Abbott judged she usually wore a conservative suit with a medium-length skirt. By comparison with what Mrs. Abbott wore on judging assignments, then, today's blouse and navy slacks were unmistakably casual.

While I'm on the subject of judges' appearance, let me

mention that I'd love to know the full story behind the AKC guidelines on the matter, which sensibly suggest that women conformation judges avoid short or cumbersome skirts, "noisy, dangling jewelry," and "hats unsuitable for the occasion"; and tantalizingly state that obedience judges "are in the ring to do a job, not to be the center of attention through outlandish dress or bizarre behavior." So what I want to know is, why the guidelines? Damn, I'd love to have been there! I always envision a long-legged female judge strutting into the ring wearing a miniskirt that barely covers her undies and sporting on her head a gigantic basket of fresh fruit that she proceeds to toss—banana by banana, orange by orange, and grape by grape—to the startled spectators. It must have been some show.

Anyway, neither in the ring nor at camp did Phyllis Abbott wear any hat at all. She had pretty hair, carefully styled waves tinted a distinctive blondish-red. She was a big woman with a powerful build, muscular but not fat. The fussed-over hair softened what could have been a stern appearance. When Max introduced her, Phyllis gave the same tense, well-intentioned smile I remembered from shows. The Abbotts didn't seem to mind being singled out. Judges are used to attention—they *are* special. For some reason, however, Don Abbott nodded and beamed for longer than I thought necessary. Maybe he hoped that if he looked like an affable guy, everyone would run out and buy his book.

When the introductions were over, Max turned to the final topic of the meeting: camp rules. We were to clean up after our dogs. We were, of course, allowed to take our dogs swimming, but otherwise, except during classes, dogs were to be kept strictly on lead. We were to observe water safety rules. In particular, we were never to swim alone and never to swim at night. The canoes beached by the lake were for everyone's use, but the paddles were kept in the main house and absolutely had to be returned there. I was disappointed to learn that once we'd started a course, we were expected to stay with it; popping in and out to sample this and that was against the rules. Instructors, Max said firmly, were hired only to teach their courses, not to work twenty-four hours a day. "Please respect their personal time," Max told us tactfully. "Oh, here's Eric! Eric Grimaldi, our breed handling instructor."

The man was fully dressed and utterly drenched. At his side was the beautiful Chesapeake Bay retriever bitch that Rowdy had admired. Eric had obviously found one way to get Elsa out of the lake: He'd gone in after her. He was so wet that it was hard to see how handsome he was. Then Max made a last introduction. "Oh, I almost forgot Everett! Where's Everett? Everett is the one who knows how everything works. If your sink gets stopped up, or if your car won't start, or anything at all, he's the one you ask. There he is! Everett Dow! Don't forget. If it breaks, ask Everett!"

From around the side of the main house appeared a lean, tired-looking man dressed in battered boots, green work pants, and a wrinkled plaid shirt. Although Everett Dow just stood there doing absolutely nothing, hackles rose. As if the dogs had consulted with one another and agreed to act in unison, they leaped off the ground, turned toward the man, and barked a chorus of loud alarm. In my years of dog watching, I'd never before seen so unequivocal a display of apparently unprovoked alarm.

When dogs speak with one voice, dog people listen.

Six

TOURIST BUREAUS in Down East Maine and on the Canadian shores of the Bay of Fundy have a hard time persuading tourists to venture north of Bar Harbor. I don't understand why. When the fog clears, the view of the tiny islands and the healthy green ocean is spectacular, and in mid-August, the temperature of the Atlantic rises to a swimmable sixty-five degrees. The trillions of barely submerged ledges along the rocky, winding coast make for exciting sailing. And the food! Well, you haven't tasted anything till you've sampled pickled whelks. But as I've said, it's still tough to convince summer visitors that the trip is worth it. Directors of visitors' centers must find the situation frustrating. Even the wildlife won't cooperate: The newly emerging puffin-watching industry is hampered by the birds' refusal to nest on the mainland, and the seals continue uselessly to sun themselves on inaccessible rocks instead of flipping out of the water and onto fishing piers where they might productively whirl beach balls on their noses and bark out adorable approximations of spoken English. Historic sites? The event known as the Machias Rubicon simply will not lend itself to reinterpretation as a turning point of the American Revolution, and, in the absence of a snack bar or, better yet, a tiny theme park, there's nothing to do where the incident occurred except leap back and forth across a brook, an aerobically beneficial activity, but not one likely to hold a crowd for long. So all I can say is, thank God for Franklin Delano Roosevelt, who, in an act of awe-inspiring self-sacrifice, came down with polio while vacationing on Campobello Island, thus forever luring tourists to the pond where he is supposed to have contracted the disease.

I thought of the FDR Memorial Polio Pond because it was the last place I'd gone swimming, and I was wishing I were there instead of standing on sharp stones in the shallow water at the edge of this lake listening to Eva Spitteler make fun of Rowdy, who was wading happily enough, but had balked at exposing his belly to water. In all other respects, I should add, the scene was idyllic. Mountains surrounded the lake, which must have been at least a mile and a half across and was dotted with picturesque tree-covered islands. On that hot, windless Sunday afternoon, canoes moved silently, sailboats lay becalmed, Jet Skis zoomed, and water skiers zipped back and forth across the wakes of a few noisy boats. If you looked carefully, you could see quite a few docks and floats on the distant shore, but the houses and cabins were set back from the water, their earth-toned rooftops and stone chimneys visible through the trees. Thirty or forty campers and at least that many dogs were swimming in the cove and frolicking along the shore in front of the resort.

"The big sissy," said Eva Spitteler, who looked even more like a bulldog wet than she did dry. The soaking hair plastered against her head revealed the exceptionally large size of her broad, square skull. Her forehead was flat, her cheeks protruded sideways, and her jaws were not only massive but undershot. In lieu of a bathing suit, she wore green shorts and a long dirt-colored T-shirt. Glued to her torso, the shirt revealed so many rolls of fat on her midriff and belly that she seemed to possess multiple rows of squishy bosom.

I shouldn't have tried to coax Rowdy into the lake, but I'd fallen for the sight of the other dogs. Elsa the Chesapeake kept going after a blue-and-white rubber water-retrieve toy that Eric Grimaldi patiently tossed for her. Joy was gently easing her Cairn, Lucky, in for a dip. Westies played. Cam's sheltie, Nicky, barked and dashed. At some distance from the others, the kissy-face Lab, Wiz, circled Ginny, who swam a smooth old-fashioned sidestroke. A man, a woman, and two English setters peacefully shared one of the resort's red canoes. Am I neglecting the mixed breeds? They were there, too, large, small, hairy, sleek, bony, corpulent, as varied in size and shape as were we campers ourselves. What did me in were two golden retrievers splashing in and out. Goldens were what I had before I lost my sanity. Except to the extent that dog obedience is a sport dedicated to the proposition that any dog can be taught to act like a golden retriever, I'd always loved Rowdy for who he was, a dog who hated water as passionately as my goldens had loved it. It was true that Rowdy chased ocean waves, but only, I suspected, because they represented a particularly aggressive form of what he hated most: water. The time Kimi knocked him off the dock and into my father's pond, Rowdy swam very efficiently. That was true, too. Rowdy raced directly to dry land, where he indignantly shook himself off and tore around in what looked like a frantic effort to ward off hypothermia.

So I should have crated Rowdy in the cabin and gone for a swim by myself. Instead, I'd put on my bathing suit, leashed Rowdy, and led him to the edge of the lake, where he'd moistened the pads of his feet, sniffed, and, having perhaps detected the odor of fish, ventured in up to his pasterns. At that point, when I should have given him the chance to paddle around, I'd stupidly waded out beyond him and tried to sweet-talk him into following me. And Eva Spitteler had listened in.

"The big scaredy-cat," Eva taunted.

Sticks and stones. The shore of the lake offered a great many. I longed to ram every one down Eva Spitteler's ugly throat. But dog people are the best people on earth. No one laughed. No one even smiled. Cam White looked from Eva to Rowdy to me, and moved her head back and forth as if vetoing Eva's existence. Phyllis Abbott, who'd been splashing around with two Pomeranians, one red, one sable, spoke with the same tone of authority she used in addressing the spectators just before she handed out the ribbons: "It's a survival characteristic. In Arctic waters, a dog can die in seconds. It's adaptive behavior." Turning to me, she said, "What a beautiful dog."

I thanked her. Rowdy backed up and shook himself all over. "He blew coat in July," I said. "He's just starting to look like himself again."

"Haven't I seen you in the ring?" Mrs. Abbott asked. She wore a heavily shirred, pastel-print bathing suit with those low-cut leg openings that the L.L. Bean catalog always promises will "provide good coverage in the seat." It's so interesting to see people undressed or even half undressed. At the edge of the lake in her good-coverage maillot with her admirable Pomeranians bouncing around her small feet, Mrs. Abbott remained one of the fancy's perfect types: the great big woman with little tiny dogs. It could truly be said, as the expression goes, that she was "big in toys."

"I stewarded for you a couple of years ago," I replied. "At Cambridge." The Cambridge Dog Training Club's annual trial. Mrs. Abbott knew that. "And I used to have goldens." Before Mrs. Abbott could start encouraging me to train Rowdy, I said, "I still show a little in obedience. Rowdy just got his CDX."

"A CDX malamute!" Although I always try to memorize the heeling pattern a judge is using, I still like to hear the commands ring out clearly. Mrs. Abbott's New York accent somehow helped to project her voice.

His attention drawn to Rowdy, Eric Grimaldi gave me a nod of congratulations, took a second look at Rowdy, and said, "Good-looking dog."

Eric, I might point out, was a conformation judge, and he didn't judge just one or two breeds, either. As I'd learned from Cam and Ginny, he was a Sporting Group judge. Admiring *my* dog. Brag, brag. That the Alaskan malamute belongs to the Working Group is incidental.

I returned Eric's compliment. "Beautiful Chesapeake. I love watching her in the water."

The Adam and Eve of the breed, Sailor and Canton, arrived in this country in 1807 when an English brig went aground on the shores of Maryland. The American ship Canton rescued the passengers, the drunken crew, and the two presumably sober puppies. Ever since, the Chesapeake Bay retriever has been striving to return to the oceanic womb from which it sprang. A good all-around hunting dog and handsome, versatile companion, the Chesapeake is the ultimate breed for hunting waterfowl, and a unitary breed, not split into bench and field lines.

Eric's face showed pride and chagrin. "Once Elsa hits the water, she doesn't come out until she's good and ready." He paused before finishing the Chesapeake-person joke that must date from the arrival of Sailor and Canton. "And," he said, "she's never ready."

When I'd seen Eric at the meeting earlier that day, he'd reminded me vaguely of some old-time Hollywood leading man. Now that he was knee-deep in the lake, I realized that the association wasn't vague at all: Eric Grimaldi looked like an age-ripened Johnnie Weissmuller, Olympic swimmer turned movie star. Weissmuller wasn't much of an actor, but it didn't matter because as Tarzan he usually appeared either half-submerged or swimming a silver-screen version of what my grandmother still calls "the Australian crawl." Like Weiss-muller, Eric was a strapping guy with hard, prominent lats, traps, and pecs, and he had Weissmuller's healthy, friendly face and big features, too.

"I could watch her forever," I told him.

Phyllis Abbott's face lit up. "Oh, Eric has!" she com-mented. "Frequently."

Eva Spitteler had been standing in the shallow water a few yards away from the rest of us. She was alone. Moored to a tree on the bank above the cove, Bingo was barking and yelp-ing. Next to Eva on the edge of the dock lay one of the resort's thick red towels and what I assumed was a bottle of sunscreen. Beach towels were one luxury that we campers were expected to provide ourselves; we'd been asked to bring them, and a politely worded sign in my bathroom had re-minded me that the towels there were not for use in the swim-ming area. I'd complied. So had almost everyone else. The red towel on the dock was the only one in sight. Eva Spitteler reached toward it, picked up the plastic bottle, and poured liquid into the palm of one hand. Instead of spreading the stuff on her skin, she rubbed it on her head and lathered her hair. When she dunked, the clear lake water turned cloudy. Bingo silenced himself. Foam rose, followed by Eva's bulk. She took a deep breath and plunged back in.

"That's disgusting," someone muttered.

"I saw her carrying that bottle of shampoo," someone else reported, "and I wondered if I should say something. . . ."

"Well, you should've."

"Wouldn't you think anyone'd know better?"

"And right here where the dogs are! I mean, it could get in their eyes, and they could all get conjunctivitis!"

Canine ecology.

When Eva surfaced, no one said a word to her. She grabbed the towel, blotted her face, and directed at me what felt like the evil eye. "You ought to just haul that dog right in," she decreed. "I wouldn't put up with that for a minute."

Stimulated perhaps by the sight and sound of Eva, Bingo had resumed his barking. I was tempted to tell Eva that *I* wouldn't tolerate *that* for a minute. I really wouldn't have put up with Bingo's noise; I'd have taken him into the lake.

As placidly as I could, I said, "Rowdy's happy doing what he's doing." Assured that I wasn't going to drag him in, Rowdy was investigating pebbles, pawing at the water, watching people and dogs, eyeing the swimmers, and probably marveling at what fools they were.

"It's very dangerous to allow one of *them* to defy you like that." Eva had swung onto the dock and was dabbing at herself with the red towel.

During our exchange, Eric had used the water toy to lure Elsa toward the shore. I had the impression that the handsome man and his beautiful dog were playing a game that both enjoyed. Moving purposefully, one eye on Elsa, Eric climbed onto the dock, begged Eva's pardon, politely warned her to make way, and called to Elsa. When he reached the end of the dock, he bent down to rap his fist on the wood. Elsa got the message. Her eyes glinting, she veered toward the dock, swam fast, sprang out, and shook off. A Chesapeake has a coat like a duck's feathers, insulating, oily, and water-repellent. In seconds, Elsa looked dry. With a final shake, she became a chocolate-colored streak that sped down the dock past Eva and toward Eric, who was swinging the rubber water toy by a short piece of attached rope. "Elsa, go get it!" he called. He spun the toy and sent it sailing out into the lake. Seconds later, Elsa flew past him and made a spectacular water entry.

Applause broke out.

"Fantastic!" I yelled.

"Any retriever'll do that," Eva grumbled. "You just aren't used to them."

I nearly choked. Not used to them? My parents raised the

golden retrievers who raised me. I all but *am* one. "Oh?" I said. "Well, I haven't seen any of the other dogs dive like that."

Fully initiated member of the Order? Here's a test. What's the one true *diving* breed? Got it. PWD, especially for deep-water retrieves. But camp didn't boast a single Portuguese Water Dog.

"Can't keep Bingo out," Eva told me.

You're keeping him out right now, I thought.

"You wanna see?" Eva asked.

The last thing I wanted to see was Bingo off leash in Rowdy's vicinity. Before I could respond, Eva clambered up the nearby slope, set Bingo loose, then lumbered back to the lake and along the length of the dock. To my relief, Bingo trailed after her. To inspire Elsa's dive, Eric had hurled a toy. To motivate Bingo, Eva shoved Eric aside and, standing at the end of the dock, gave a powerful upward and outward leap, curled her legs under her, held her nose, and executed a cannonball. Her heavy body hit the water as one solid mass that made a loud boom and sent water shooting high in the air. Despite the drama of Eva's cannonball, Bingo stood at the end of the dock placidly regarding Eric Grimaldi and aimlessly wagging his tail.

Cannonballers usually resurface quickly. I watched the water. Maine is not a place where it's safe to dive into unknown water. Submerged rocks hold still. Logs move. "Did someone check that area?" I asked Mrs. Abbott.

Entering the water feet first, Eva would have been unlikely to hit her head on a rock or a log. Still, I felt uncomfortable.

"Eric checked," Mrs. Abbott said. "Before you got here."

But Eva was fine. Instead of bobbing up immediately, she'd swum some distance underwater. Her head now appeared about twenty feet out from the dock. "Bingo!" she called sharply. She was treading water. The surface around her bubbled.

The big yellow Lab continued to stand where he was. In case he headed in, spotted Rowdy, and started trouble, I gathered up Rowdy's lead, edged away from the lake, and prepared to bolt for my cabin. But Bingo just kept standing there.

"Bingo!" Eva yelled hoarsely.

The dog continued to do nothing at all.

I could make excuses for what Eva did next. She'd listened to Judge Phyllis Abbott and Judge Eric Grimaldi admire Rowdy. Bingo had been right nearby, and no one had said a word about him. When Eva had ridiculed Rowdy, Mrs. Abbott had defended him, and, in so doing, she'd given Eva a sharp correction. More excuses? It must be hideously painful to go through life looking exactly like a bulldog, unless, of course, you happen to be one, in which case, it's delightful. But Eva wasn't a bulldog. And Bingo had let her down, or that's how she must have felt. Pride in a dog doesn't have to be justified to be genuine. Eva had bragged about Bingo. She'd wanted him to show off. Treading water harder than ever, she forced her shoulders to break the surface and again shouted the dog's name.

Bingo remained where he was.

Desperate to rouse him, I suppose, Eva kicked wildly, splashed, flailed her arms, and cried, "Bingo, help! Help! I'm drowning! Bingo, come save me!" With that, Eva disappeared beneath the surface. Her feet thrashed and vanished. A waving hand rose and sank. Planted on the dock with his tail drifting back and forth, Bingo regarded the performance with complaisant curiosity.

As I saw it, Eva wasn't playing. Play is joyous. Eva was grim. Eva wasn't practicing water rescue, either. She was lying to her dog. Maybe Bingo thought so, too. Maybe not. In either case, the impression the dog created was unmistakable. Several people commented. I noticed it myself. Bingo looked oddly content to watch Eva go under.

Seven

I HATE TO SEE anyone lose face, even someone cursed with a countenance like Eva Spitteler's. To avoid the inevitable sight, I took Rowdy to our cabin, crated him with a chew toy, and, on returning to the pebble beach, headed directly into the lake. My entry was slow. *Pebble* is a bit of a euphemism, but I've avoided the blunt (or more accurately, the sharp) truth for fear of discouraging tourism. The beach consisted of toe-stubbing rocks and sole-jabbing stones. Wincing with every step, I made my way into the lake until the water came up almost to my waist. At that point, the prospect of the cold lake assaulting my bony rib cage seemed better than the present pain in the soles of my feet. I filled my lungs, plunged, and swam along the bottom. Snorkeling in turquoise waters among coral reefs might spoil me, but on a dog writer's income, I'll continue to love a yellow-green underwater haze seen through unmasked eyes. I even like the familiar shock of passing through the frigid springs that feed a Maine lake. Greater Boston suffers from a summer climate so tropical that displaced Haitians complain about the inescapable heat and humidity. Submerged in the lake, my body felt like an overcharged heat-storage unit mercifully draining itself cell by cell. When the need for air forced me up, I faced the trees on the far shore. As on countless previous occasions, I tried to float. As always, I ended up having to kick my feet and wave my hands to keep from sinking. I used to be irrationally ashamed of my body's rocklike refusal to hover effortlessly at the surface. Then a diver told me that my condition was so ordinary that it even had a name: negative buoyancy. Since I learned that happy phrase, I'm not ashamed anymore. I'd still like to float, of course, and I keep checking up to find out whether my valence has changed, but, until it does, I make the best of my negativity, which is to say that I swim almost exclusively underwater.

Far away, the kind of little outboard favored by fishermen *put-put*ted. Then a Jet Ski whizzed along, drowned it out, and probably scared the fish, too. Or maybe not. In late August, the fish had probably descended to the icy depths, where they could ignore the surface noise and avoid being caught by any method except deep trolling. Deep trolling, I might mention, is perfectly legal but not quite respectable. My father, a *Salmo salar* snob, regards most lake fishing with the eye of Jacques Pepin contemplating a Fluffernutter. Because of some quirky loophole embedded in the arcane laws that regulate social hierarchies among Maine anglers, however, he makes an exception in the case of salmon and trout fishing in the Rangeley lakes, provided, as should go without saying, that it is fly fishing only, preferably for *Salmo sebago*, landlocked salmon, but also for trout, especially if the angler is accompanied by young children. Nothing could persuade Buck to stoop to bass fishing, and he harbors a terrible prejudice against anyone who uses a minnowlike lure in fresh water. The buzz of the Jet Ski faded, and I heard the little *put-put* motor again. It occurred to me that if Eva Spitteler took up fishing, she'd favor the unspeakable: live bait.

After my swim, I fought off incipient hypothermia by taking a hot shower and drying my hair. Then, for once, I worried about what to wear. Ordinarily, I rely on the L.L. Bean catalog's autocratic decrees about what may appropriately be worn when, where, and for what purpose. Unfortunately, I couldn't recall any specific recommendations for dining at a luxury dog camp. Floundering around on my own, I chose khaki pants ("casual" comfort, one Bean-step up from "at-home") and a short-sleeved cotton sweater described, I thought, as "versatile." Neither item, if I remembered correctly, would shame me by having been Bean-relegated to suitability for some ignominious task like cleaning the barn on a cool fall afternoon.

By the time I was dressed, Rowdy was dancing in circles and bounding up and down, and when I opened the closet where I'd stashed his bowl of moistened kibble, he'd reached a state of salivating frenzy. Ever watched a malamute eat? Magic. Truly, ladies and gentlemen, the jaw is quicker than the eye. Nanoseconds after that dish hit the floor, it was empty. Then I took Rowdy for the kind of brief postprandial outing politely known as "exercise." After dutifully cleaning up after him and depositing what I guess ought to be called his aerobic benefit in one of the trash cans, I returned to the cabin, checked my watch, and realized that I had ten minutes in which to look over the material in my registration packet. I upended the big manila envelope over the bed. With the exception of the calendar of events at Waggin' Tail, the contents that tumbled out consisted of a map of the region, brochures advertising local attractions, fliers for restaurants, and other printed matter that Maxine McGuire must have seized in a raid on the Rangeley tourist bureau. The collection bewildered me. Why welcome people who'd just shelled out for Waggin' Tail by hinting that they spend most of the week and a ton of extra money elsewhere? Missing from the packet were what I'd been told were the usual souvenirs and favors provided by

Dog Days and the other competing camps: no penknife embossed with the camp name, no gift certificate for the camp store, no Waggin' Tail ID tag for Rowdy's collar, not even a bumper sticker.

With only a few minutes left before dinner, I skimmed the red legal-size sheet that showed the schedule of activities and quickly picked out agility, advanced obedience, and a workshop on flawless heeling for the competition dog. I intended to take the course on canine first aid and CPR, and I thought I'd let Rowdy try flyball and maybe lure coursing, too. He'd hate nothing more than the daily swimming lessons and the workshop on water rescue, and I'd keep him as far away as possible from herding, which would obviously involve sheep, *live sheep*, of course, unless Rowdy got them first. Hunting was also out. If there'd been any seals around, Rowdy might have located their blow holes, but I couldn't imagine his learning to point to birds for someone else to kill or bringing them back for someone else to eat. Doggy square dancing? Breed handling? Dog tricks? Carting, yes. And definitely the Friday workshop on sled-dogging. No tattoo, though. Rowdy had his AKC registration number on one inner thigh and my social security number on the other. Even my protectiveness had limits.

I'd lost track of the time. I hustled Rowdy into his crate, took off for the lodge, and had the bad luck to arrive at the stairs just behind Eva Spitteler, to whom Joy was babbling about Lucky. "He swam! And he really loved it! I held him, and then Craig called to him, and he swam right to Craig!" Joy's dainty hands mimed the Cairn's accomplishment. Her childish face glowed. "And you could tell Lucky was kind of scared at first, because he wasn't used to it, but he went right ahead! And he was *so* proud of himself! Wasn't he, Craig?" At Joy's side, beaming at his wife exactly as she had beamed at her dog, was Craig, who had the general appearance that Hollywood has persuaded me to associate with F.B.I. agents: the crew-cut blond hair, the cheeks slightly reddened from over-close shaving, the babyish features, and a body that looked artificially enlarged by persistent work with free weights. Craig's head seemed to have been grafted to a big man's neck, and the neck to a giant's body. Joy wore a skirt and her husband wore pants, but their blue-and-rose-red madras plaid shirts were identical. On second thought, maybe it wasn't a razor that explained Craig's red face.

The upper half of Eva Spitteler's compact bulk was shrouded in an unironed man's dress shirt, and as she lumbered up the stairs, I got a close-up opportunity to realize why no one who weighs well over a hundred and fifty pounds should ever wear Bermuda shorts. On her feet were clunky leather sandals evidently fashioned from recycled bits of harness or dog leash.

"Well," Eva told Joy loudly, "at Dog Days, you'd've got a tag for his collar for that. The first time your dog swims, you get a tag. It's got a picture on it, and it says he's a certified swimmer, and it's really cute. You didn't get one, did you?"

Joy's face fell. "No. Should we have?"

"Not here," Eva pronounced. "Too cheap to pay for them."

I felt irked at Eva, who'd succeeded in transforming Joy's pride to a sense of having been shortchanged. The too-cheap crack did, however, point to a unifying theme in the contents of the registration packet: Nothing in it had cost Maxine a dime.

"And," Eva relentlessly continued, "at Dog Days, there's something going on every minute. Here, take tonight. After dinner, there's nothing. We drive all the way here to the middle of nowhere, and then we wait all this time for something to eat, and then afterwards all there is to do is sort of hang around and twiddle our thumbs."

Rangeley was, admittedly, a long drive from New York or New Jersey or wherever it was Eva came from, but it actually was what most other tourist areas merely tried to be: a year-round resort where you could hunt, bird watch, swim, water ski, canoe, sail, sit and enjoy the mountains, hike the Appalachian Trail, or even pan for gold. In winter, Rangeley had sled dog racing and skiing, downhill and cross-country. Spring did, of course, bring black flies, but it also brought fish, and the fall foliage was as good as anything in New Hampshire and Vermont. And the town itself was a beautiful place with a wild streak, rugged and a little rough, not cutesied up, but naturally lovely, set between Rangeley Lake and Haley's Pond. The middle of nowhere, indeed! Furthermore, since dog people are undoubtedly the most gregarious individuals in the world, we do not think of after-dinner socializing as hanging around and twiddling our thumbs because there's nothing to do.

As if to illustrate the sociability of our breed, the people who packed the lodge's reception area and the adjoining bar were all talking and introducing everyone to everyone else. Even without our dogs, by the way, we are often so obviously interconnected as to be recognizable as members of a fraternal and sororal society, but when we're dressed for dinner and not wearing our usual breed-loyal T-shirts and such, you'd have to examine us closely to discover our precise identity. I, of course, have a practiced eye. The designs knitted into Maxine McGuire's cardigan sweater depicted a high jump, a dumbbell, trophies, and other dog-societal symbols, and almost every pair of earrings in the room would, I felt certain, turn out to be a miniature brace of dogs. We were well-groomed and dolled-up. By definition, we love a show, and we sure do know how to put on the dog.

Ahead of me, Eva shoved through the crowd, thus breaking track for Joy and Craig. As they trailed off after her, I squeezed into the only floor space available nearby, a gap between a side table and one of the couches that faced the fireplace. As I was glancing around trying to locate Cam or

Ginny, one of the women seated on the couch suddenly shrieked, "What's *this* doing here?"

From my refuge, I looked almost directly down at her brown curls. I leaned forward to peer at the object of her consternation, which I at first mistook for a tourist brochure like the ones in the registration packet.

The woman next to her said, "It's just another one of those—"

"No, it isn't! What's wrong with you? *Look* at it!" The first woman thrust the shiny folder at her neighbor, who made a noise of disgust and said, "This is gross! Where did you get this?"

"From right there, right on the coffee table. It was sticking out from one of the magazines, and it caught my eye because of the picture of the dog, so I reached for it. And then when I ever saw what it was!"

Well, I wanted to shout, *so what was it?*

As if in answer, the neighbor opened the brochure on her lap and thrust it up to display a brilliantly colored, superglossy photograph of three small satin-lined, lace-trimmed caskets, baby blue on the left, baby pink on the right, and, in the middle, virgin white. Each casket rested on a trestle, and in front of the trestles, three little stands supported ornately embossed grave markers. Before I could focus on the inscriptions, the woman who held the brochure began to read the text at the bottom of the page: " 'Lasting Security and an Eternal Tribute to Your Beloved Pet.' "

"Betty, stop!" ordered the woman who'd found the brochure.

"This really *is* gross," Betty commented. "Katy, listen to this. It says, 'A fitting last resting place for the little one who warmed your heart. The Manson Family understands—' "

"What!"

"That's what it says. It's the name of the company." Betty

flipped over the brochure and pointed. "See? 'The Manson Family, Inc. Loving Attention to Final Needs Since Nineteen Forty-Six.' But listen. This is worse." She turned back to the passage she'd started before. "Where was I? Oh. 'The Manson Family understands the grief of losing the beloved little one whose passing presence here on earth brightened each precious moment. Here at Manson, we, too, have lost small ones—' " Betty broke off. "Don't you get it? Yuck."

"Get what?" Katy demanded.

"Katy, look at the picture! I mean, really look at it. Look at these, uh, whatever they're called. Coffins. Caskets. And that business about small ones and little ones? Just what do you think these are really meant for? And down here, it doesn't even say they're *for* pets; it says '*suitable* for pets.' Right?"

Katy launched herself backward. The couch lurched. She blew out her breath and whispered, "Oh, my God!"

"You see?" Betty said. "Like I said. It really is gross. Pets or babies."

A man sitting in a nearby armchair spoke up. "There's lots more where that came from." He pointed to a magazine rack. "This thing's full of them."

Now that he'd made the conversation general, I joined in. "Are they all, uh . . ." I fumbled for the right phrase. "Are they all the same? All copies of the same brochure?"

"Naw. They're all different," he replied. "Tombstones. Pet cemeteries. Coffins. Urns. All kinds of stuff. You want to see?"

"Not particularly," I answered. "But—"

Before I could finish, the lodge door swung open so forcefully that I had to squish myself against the couch to get out of the way. Brandishing a large greeting card in her hand, Phyllis Abbott strode in and immediately silenced the crowd, less by speaking than by radiating judicial authority. "May I have your attention!" Mrs. Abbott began. Having already obtained it, she lowered the greeting card and, before I could get a look at the picture on the front, gave the card the kind of merciless shakedown that Rowdy administers to play-prey dog toys when he's pretending to break their necks. When she'd finished rendering the card lifeless, she held it in front of her and intoned, "With deepest sympathy on the loss of your pet." Opening the card, she read the following verse:

" 'Your precious pet has gone away.
    I know just how you feel today.
    Dear friend, recall that with the years
    Sweet memories will dry your tears.
    But that is then, and this now,
    When you just heard that last bow-wow,
    When empty dishes on the floor,
    Say your best pal lives here no more.
    You have my thoughts while yours are dour;
    I think of you from hour to hour.' "

Mrs. Abbott whipped the card through the air and deposited it in the hand of her blank-faced husband, who stood a few feet away, as if to disassociate himself from her or perhaps from her performance.

"I have *not* lost a pet," Mrs. Abbott proclaimed, "and furthermore, let me announce to whatever *vile* excuse for a human being has perpetrated this prank that I have no intention whatsoever of losing a pet for a great many years to come! Nigel and Edwina are both young and in perfect health, and if this filthy, vicious act is someone's misguided idea of a joke, I want to make it clear that, far from being funny, it is of the utmost seriousness. The person responsible evidently fails to understand that a judge is a judge is a judge, every minute of every day, no matter where she goes or what she does, and no insult directed toward a judge is *ever* a strictly personal matter, but constitutes a direct affront to the dignity and authority of the AKC. *This*," she added, "will be so treated."

She swung dramatically toward her husband, meaning, I think, to aim a finger only at the offending card. As it was, however, she appeared to be directing the avenging wrath of the American Kennel Club straight toward Don Abbott.

Eight

TWENTY MINUTES after Judge Phyllis Abbott pointed an AKC-authorized finger at her husband, I was seated in the dining room at a round table for eight. Somewhat to my surprise, dinner really was quite formal: white linen, wine, a buffet offering roast beef, Yorkshire pudding, stuffed scrod, scalloped potatoes, broccoli, salad, and, as the brochure had promised, wine, red and white, and not in jugs, either. After the cheapskate packet, I'd half expected to find a genuinely traditional New England Sunday-night supper: hot dogs and beans with ketchup, and brown bread straight out of the can, the ridges still visible, followed by mealy Indian pudding, also canned, but mushed up, heated, and topped with vanilla ice cream, accompanied by the traditional Yankee choice between milk and nothing. Real WASP food is nowhere near as bad as people say; it's much, much worse.

I was sitting with Cam and Ginny, and also with Sara Altman, the head agility instructor, a dark young woman with long brown hair bound back in a ponytail. As I've said, Rowdy and I had once done a miniclinic with Sara, and I'd liked her a lot. Instead of admonishing me to praise my dog while telling me everything I was doing wrong, she'd used positive methods on both of us. Also, when Rowdy had pried the lid off a big metal canister of dog treats and scattered them all over the mats, she'd simply commented how helpful it was in agility to have a dog who was motivated by food. As I've mentioned, that's how agility people are: obsessed. If a falling tree had crushed in the roof of Sara's house, she'd probably have viewed the trunk and branches as an interesting new agility obstacle, and her only worry would have been whether the bark gave proper traction. The others at the table were strangers to me: three women—Myrna, Marie, and Kathy— and a young man named Michael whose left upper arm displayed a still-healing tattooed portrait of his dog, which he said was a cream-colored long-haired Akita named Jacob.

"What a big dope I was." Ginny stabbed her fork into a slice of roast beef. "I'm just glad I didn't go to Max and tell her how touched I was that she'd remembered." Phyllis's dire announcement had somehow cheered Ginny up. The endless braid around her head was still damp from her swim, she'd touched up her tracking tan with a little makeup, and she looked altogether happy to be who she was and where she was. With a smile she added, "Old gullible me."

"I wasn't sure," I said. "Before, it was sort of remotely possible that my card was a mistake, and yours wasn't."

"Come off it," Cam said. "With both of the cards unsigned?"

"Clarity of hindsight," Sara commented.

"Sara," I pointed out, "the other odd thing is all those brochures out there in the lobby, on the coffee table and in the magazine rack. By the fireplace."

"Maxine has a lot of friends here," Sara replied. "She's been coming to Rangeley since she was a kid. That's just her way of showing she's supporting the other local businesses."

With her usual concern for distinctions, Cam, the obedience legal-eagle columnist, said, "Not *those* brochures. The other ones. The ones about gravestones and urns and whatever."

Sara tightened her neck muscles, and her head moved back and upward like a cobra's. "What!"

Cam said, "They were all around, by the fireplace. Holly took them. So nobody'd get upset."

One of the other women at the table spoke up, Myrna or Marie. Neither wore her name tag, and I couldn't keep them straight. They both had short, fluffy hair and heavy New York accents. "Hey," said whichever one it was, "maybe it's a whole new dog activity, right? 'Come on, big boy, for the casket, you like the white, or you want blue? And while we're at it, how about your headstone. Plain old Rest in Peace do for you? Fun, huh?' New dog sport. I mean, why leave him out? It's his funeral."

"Myrna, please," said her look-alike friend, who must have been Marie. "You can laugh, but it's not all that—"

Myrna interrupted. "So what are you going to do? You got some way to keep them alive forever? You lose a dog, and you're a wreck, and you're never going to laugh again, and you're never going to get another dog?" Myrna's raucous style and brassy voice had initially put me off, but when I listened to what she said and ignored how she said it, I admired her attitude. If fate snatched one of her dogs, she'd immediately get a new puppy and thumb her nose in death's face. "So," Myrna went on, "who left that shit out there? Sorry. Marie? Marie, I'm cleaning up my act. No more dirty words until we cross the Long Island border. So who put that stuff out?"

"And who's sending these cards?" Cam added. "And who got them? Ginny. Phyllis. Holly, you did. Did anyone else?"

No one answered.

"I wonder if Eric Grimaldi did," I said. "I was just thinking. When Mrs. Abbott was talking about AKC and being a judge,

I assumed she was taking it a little too personally, in the sense that she's a judge." I lowered my voice. "It did seem to me that she was overreacting. I didn't exactly enjoy getting that sympathy card, but I mostly assumed that I got it by mistake. And Ginny thought hers was real. But even when she found out, she didn't decide that she got it because she's a tracking judge. Did you?"

Ginny shook her head. "I never thought of it. Why would anyone . . . ?"

"I don't know," I said.

"Holly, what about you?" Cam asked.

"Me! Why would I . . . ?"

"In your column. In an article. Somewhere else? Have you written anything that could've made someone want to get back at you? I don't remember anything, but . . ."

"The anti-puppy mill stuff," I said. "The usual stuff about not buying anything from pet shops that sell dogs. But I've been writing that for a long time, and so have plenty of other people. And I'm not AKC's favorite person, but it's no big thing."

In case you don't subscribe to *Dog's Life*, I should mention that I'd written about the miserable conditions of the AKC-registered breeding stock in the puppy mills. In a recent column, I'd discussed a report published in the *Journal of the American Veterinary Medical Association*, according to which the puppies in three California pet shops were about twice as likely to have kennel cough, giardiasis, diarrhea, vomiting, severe gastroenteritis, or some other illness than were pups from private sources. The AKC connection? Every time a puppy mill operator registers a dog, a bitch, or litter; and every time a puppy mill operator transfers a puppy to a puppy broker; and every time the broker sells a puppy to a pet shop; and every time a puppy buyer registers the puppy, the American Kennel Club collects a fee. My great offense, I think, was to point out that in revoking the AKC registration privileges of about twenty puppy mill operators every month, the AKC was actually closing down each month only about .4 percent of the estimated 5,000 puppy mills in this country. I may also have commented that it didn't seem like enough.

Cam looked embarrassed. Her husband, John R.B. White, was an AKC delegate who sat on some committee or other, but his father, Richard Burton White, had been a real power in the fancy and at the AKC. I had the impression that the son had inherited some of the father's clout. "That's not what I was thinking of," Cam said. "It was more like, oh, show reports, something like that. If someone felt slighted, you know, that kind of thing."

"I don't do show reports." I tried to keep my voice neutral. A show report in my own national breed club newsletter reads something like this: *On June 25 at the East Podunk K.C., BOB was CH Wolfwhistle's Silver Dagger, Buzzy, owned by John and Jane Bishop.* It goes on to say that BW, WD was another dog owned by the same people or by someone else; that BOS, WB was a bitch owned by so-and-so; and so forth and so on, all of which is glorious to read if you happen to be John or Jane Bishop, whose dog went Best of Breed, or if yours went Best of Winners and Winners Dog or Best of Opposite and Winners Bitch. Otherwise? Sure, all of us love to see our dogs' names in print, and we want to see how other people's dogs are doing, but what everyone, absolutely everyone, wants to do with show reports is read them or skim them or just know that they're there; there's not a dog writer on earth who honestly enjoys writing them. I mean, you slave over them trying to inject a little spirit, a little dash, a little humor, and what happens? Either no one notices, or someone whose dog just got a plain old mention snubs you or yells at you at the next show and accuses you of playing politics by promoting someone else's dog when all you did was give it an extra two adjectives. So, as I told Cam, I don't do show reports anymore.

"You ever thought about judging?" Ginny asked me, referring, as I understood, to obedience judging. "You judge any matches?"

"No," I said. "I could, I guess, but I don't really have the right temperament. It's not something I've ever wanted to do. I've helped out at a couple of Canine Good Citizen tests, but that's different. I had to fail some dogs, but no one's going to hold a grudge against me for that, and I don't think there's anyone at camp who was there, anyway."

"Actually, I was," Ginny admitted. "Last fall. At Cambridge. Didn't you just do that 'accepts grooming' part?"

"Yes. Yeah, now I remember. But you passed, didn't you?"

"No, as a matter of fact. I had Magic, and you failed her for being too friendly."

"Oh, yeah, I remember. She jumped on me and grabbed the brush, and then she wouldn't let go of it. I had to fail her."

"Look," Cam said, "if Holly didn't remember that Ginny was there, maybe she's forgotten someone else. And Ginny's a tracking judge, and Phyllis judges a lot. So maybe it really is someone with something against the three of you."

"But what?" I demanded. "Obedience judging is really quite objective, at least compared to breed. If your dog refuses a jump or breaks a stay or whatever, there's nothing the judge can do except score you zero on the exercise. And if the dog's perfect, sure, the judge can dock you a few points for supposedly crooked sits and handler errors that no one else saw, and that does happen."

"Does it ever!" Marie groaned.

"Does it ever!" I agreed. "But if a judge is really bad, all the spectators complain to AKC, and if it's just a matter of losing a few points you should've kept, you have to think that the next time, maybe you're going to keep a few points you should've lost. So, if you avoid the really bad judges, in the long run, it all evens out."

"The voice of experience," Cam told Marie. "But what I'm wondering about is Eric Grimaldi, because he's a breed judge, and that's where you're more likely to get exhibitors with real grudges."

True. Obedience and tracking judges follow detailed sets of rules. In contrast, breed judges pick the dogs they like, and that's pretty much it; they're supposed to interpret breed standards, but there aren't any rules about how they're supposed to interpret them.

(*Still* lost? Sorry. Let's get this straight. *Breed:* conformation. How well does the dog *conform* to the breed standard? Like Westminster? On TV? That's breed. In fact, that's a dog show. What confuses newcomers is that obedience trials are often held in conjunction with dog shows, and when they aren't, they tend to be small events that the general public never hears about. And tracking, I'm afraid, just doesn't make it as a spectator sport, because each dog follows a track across a field—and, at advanced levels, through woods—and if the public were allowed to go galumphing after the dog, the scent and commotion would obviously ruin the dog's work. Also, tracking tests have small, limited entries, so the casual visitor who expects anything like Westminster is going be extremely disappointed.)

"Except," I said, "in tracking? TDX tests"—that's Tracking Dog Excellent—"are hard to get into, so it's *possible* that if someone had some problem with a judge. . . ." I faltered. My real source of uncertainty was the high esteem in which I hold tracking judges, who are a remarkably dedicated, fair, straightforward, congenial, and altogether likeable group of people, most unlikely targets for anyone's rancor. I thought, for example, of Ginny Garabedian; it was hard to imagine anyone wanting to do something mean to her. Unless, I suppose, you counted the five dead husbands.

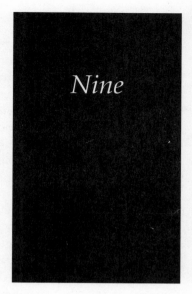

Nine

"WELL, THAT SETTLES THAT." Cam plunked her bowl
of Indian pudding on the table and sat down. Neat and effi-
cient in all things, Cam had cleaned her plate and gone for
dessert while the rest of us were still eating dinner. "Eric
didn't get one."

Or hasn't yet, I thought.

"Cam," I said, "Mrs. Abbott is right about AKC, isn't she?
In theory, if someone harasses an AKC judge in a place like
this, not at a show, is that still grounds for suspension or a
reprimand or something?"

Let me note that a reprimand is what it sounds like—and so
is a fine, another form of discipline. Suspension, however,
whether temporary or permanent, is far worse than it sounds:
It's total excommunication. A person whose AKC privileges
have been suspended can't register a dog, show a dog, or even
set foot on the grounds of an AKC show. For the duration of
the suspension—three months, six months, five years, life—
the excommunicate is dead in dogs.

"It's still misconduct against a judge." Cam dipped her

spoon into the ice cream on top of the pudding and filled the
spoon by pushing it away from her. I wondered whether her
mother had taught her the rhyme about little ships going out
to sea. "And it's obviously conduct prejudicial." The full text:
*conduct prejudicial to the best interests of pure-bred dogs, dog shows,
obedience trials, field trials, or the American Kennel Club.* "And, of
course, once someone prefers the charge, AKC is obligated to
investigate. But even if Phyllis knew who sent that card, the
question would be whether she was harassed in her position as
a judge, I think, or whether it was a strictly personal matter."

"So it wouldn't necessarily be—"

"Well, Phyllis could prefer the charge, but AKC might not
agree. If everyone at camp got harassed, then the complaint
probably wouldn't be sustained, because it wouldn't really
have anything to do with AKC. But she could still prefer
charges, and if the complaint wasn't sustained, all Phyllis
would lose would be the ten dollars it cost her to make the
complaint in the first place."

Michael, he of the Akita tattoo, spoke up. "That's just
judges?"

Almost everyone else answered in unison: "No."

Cam expanded. "In theory, anyone can prefer charges
against anyone. But it has to have to do with shows or whatever—with AKC—which it does if it takes place on show
grounds. Otherwise, it depends. The typical case where
charges are sustained is, like, two exhibitors get in a fight at a
show, or someone gets caught abusing a dog on show
grounds. Or the judge hands out the ribbons, and some guy
who doesn't like how he did starts swearing at the judge and
saying he only looks at faces."

Michael's went blank.

Kathy, a slight blond woman who'd hardly spoken before,
translated: "Human faces. Looks to see who's handling."

"Plays politics," I said. "Cam, is Indian pudding the only
dessert?"

"No, there's chocolate cake."

I carried my plate to a hatch that opened into the kitchen and joined a long line of people waiting for dessert and coffee. My place in line put me right near a table at which Eva Spitteler was addressing Joy, Craig, and some other people on the subject of lure coursing, which, as Eva was explaining, and as I've already mentioned, is a sport in which dogs *course* after a *lure*. As an AKC performance event, it's limited to sight hounds—borzois, whippets, Afghan hounds, and other sight-hunting breeds. Camp offered the opportunity, relatively rare in this part of the country, for dogs of any breed or no particular breed to give it a try.

"Any dog'll do it," Eva proclaimed. "Any dog that'll go after a lure."

The lure, by the way, is artificial, usually a plastic bag. *Field coursing* is another matter. That's the one with live rabbits.

The line inched ahead. A couple of steps placed me in back of Joy, who was writing in what proved to be an address book. She raised her head, shook her blond curls, and handed the book to Eva.

"My catalog's coming out in October," Eva told her. She looked around the table. "Did I get all your addresses?"

One woman seemed to avoid Eva's gaze. Everyone else nodded. I didn't really blame Eva for trying to drum up business. It's hard to make a living in dogs. The small mail-order companies that survived in this highly competitive market did so by providing a narrowly defined clientele—Border collie owners, dogsledding enthusiasts, obedience competitors— with the very best equipment, supplies, books, videos, and odds and ends within a concentrated range of interest. I wondered what specialty Eva could possibly have devised that would interest pet owners like Joy and Craig. A nasty thought came to me: Maybe Eva specialized in clients who didn't know enough to order from someone else.

At the dessert buffet, I ran into Ginny, Michael, and the

three women from my table, who invited me to take my dessert and coffee to the TV room of the lodge to watch Bernie Brown's training tape. I declined. I own the tape, or rather, my cousin Leah does. Leah is a Bernie Brown no-force-method fanatic. I'd watched the tape a couple of times, and I'd heard it in the background at least a hundred times that summer. When I got back to the table with a double serving of chocolate cake topped with a triple dollop of whipped cream, Cam was alone there scraping her bowl clean. With a hard-to-read expression on her face, she turned her head a little, gave a meaningful look at a far corner of the dining room, and asked, "You catch that?"

My eyes followed Cam's. At what was apparently the VIP table, far from the kitchen, near a window that overlooked the lake, sat Max McGuire, Eric Grimaldi, Phyllis Abbott, and three others, all of whom, with one exception, were giving Phyllis Abbott the rapt attention I elicit only from dogs and, even then, only by baiting with liver treats. The exception was Don Abbott. He'd pulled his chair back from the table and was speaking into his portable telephone.

I exclaimed, "But there's a pay phone right out in the lobby! And besides—"

"He always does it. He does it at people's dinner tables. At a show a while ago, I saw him standing right next to a pay phone—a pay phone no one was using!—and talking into his portable one."

"Doesn't that cost a lot extra?" The only thing I knew about cellular phones was that I couldn't afford one. As I've said, it's hard to make a living in dogs.

Cam had the satisfied look of a person getting exactly the response she wants. I almost expected her to tell me what a good dog I was. "Sure does."

"Is he a broker or something?" I clarified the question. "A stockbroker?" Let me amend something else. It's hard to make an honest, self-respecting living in dogs. Brokers—

puppy brokers, the middlemen who buy from puppy mills and sell to pet shops—are the pimps of the American commercial puppy industry and its chief financial beneficiaries. Cam's first take on *broker* would be the same as mine: something that ought to be scooped up, sealed up, and deposited in the nearest trash receptacle.

"Don makes light fixtures. He runs the company. They make industrial lamps, that kind of thing. But that's not what he's doing. What he's doing is, he thinks that if he stays off the phone for ten minutes, AKC'll go kaput."

"On Sunday night? They aren't even open."

"Yes, but the wheels still turn." Cam said it again: "The wheels still turn."

I ate some cake.

Cam spoke into my ear. "Their therapist sent them here. That's what Don's doing at camp, and that's why Phyllis is so stressed out. All that about harassing judges is true, but I don't think that card had anything to do with Phyllis or with Phyllis being a judge, either. She just took it that way. Phyllis is a very sensitive person."

"But why would a therapist . . . ?" I was dumbfounded. My good friend and second-floor tenant, Rita, is a therapist who treats individuals and couples. I couldn't imagine Rita's suggesting joint attendance at dog camp as a way to save a marriage.

"It was part of an agreement they worked out," Cam said. "Some kind of contract. But if you ask me, the only reason Don agreed was the usual."

I felt lost. "I just met him."

Cam's expression became serious. I realized that she'd been fooling around. Now, she adopted a heavy mock-foreign accent and said, "Come the revolution . . ."

"Cam, you've lost me."

"One of these days," Cam said in normal English, "we're going to get rid of all that deadwood at AKC, and Don Abbott knows that, and when it happens, he's going to need Phyllis, who *is* a dog person, and if Don gets really desperate, he might even be driven to getting a dog himself. But in the meantime, he hears what's blowing in the wind, so he needs Phyllis's credentials, and he needs to start looking like he's at least half interested in dogs, of all things, and not just in more playing politics."

It is possible to be in dogs without, in fact, owning a dog. It's even possible to be in dogs without ever having owned so much as a stuffed toy puppy. Anyone at the AKC is, by definition, in dogs; yet there are rumored to be people there who don't live with them. This wasn't the first time I'd heard someone complain about that supposed state of affairs, about which, I should say, I reserve judgment. Among other things, the New York offices of the AKC are at 51 Madison Avenue, and Manhattan isn't a great place to keep a dog. Also, the AKC is a big, complicated organization; maybe it really does make sense to hire superb administrators who don't happen to have dogs. For all I know, the Vatican has dozens of employees who aren't Roman Catholic.

"So here he is," I said, meaning, of course, that here Don Abbott was at camp. As it turned out, though, I'd no sooner spoken than Don and Phyllis appeared at our table. Don must have stashed the phone in his pocket. The only thing he carried in his hand was a wineglass like the ones on our table. Let me say that I'm no expert on wine. We'd had a choice of red or white. But maybe the VIP's at Maxine's table had been offered something special that any oenologist would have recognized immediately, an amber-colored wine that smelled exactly like Scotch. Don took a sip of it and made a big show of greeting Cam and being introduced to me.

"We're in the same cabin," I told him. "I have the other unit in yours, I think." I was, of course, dead certain. Remembering Rowdy's effort to play up to Don Abbott, I said, "I have a malamute."

Quick to address Don's real interest, Cam added, "Holly writes for *Dog's Life.*"

"Maybe you knew my mother," I said. "Marissa Winter."

Don nodded. "Gracious lady."

It was Phyllis who remembered my mother as she would have wished: "*Very* nice dogs. Goldens. So Marissa was your mother!"

God help me, I thought. If Marissa had been an easy mother, maybe losing her would have been a little simpler than it was. Is.

"Gracious lady," Don said again. Then he asked Cam how John R.B., her husband, was, and Cam said he was fine, thank you.

"Not here?" asked Don, draping an arm around a startled-looking Phyllis.

"He couldn't get away."

"Hasn't got dogs on the brain, huh?" Don remarked.

I examined the back of Cam's neck to see whether her short-clipped hair was rising. Neither it nor her face revealed any response. "Like I said, he couldn't get away." Her fingers slowly curled into tight fists.

Don turned to me. "Great guy, John R.B. I knew his father. Gracious old gentleman."

With a nod of approval, Phyllis seconded Don: "*Very* nice dogs."

"English setters," Don told me.

Phyllis frowned.

"Pointers," Cam said. "R.B. had pointers. Elizabeth still does."

At the mention of Elizabeth, whom I presumed to be the widow of Richard Burton White, I could practically see the word *gracious* start to form on Don Abbott's lips. I looked down at my plate, on which remained a half slice of chocolate cake and a big blob of sinking whipped cream that I was saving for last. I felt tempted to mention my father, Buck, who has somehow managed to keep a remarkable number of friends at the AKC and whom the Abbotts probably knew as well. I almost did it, just as an experiment. There are lots of adjectives to be applied to my sire, but no honest man could call Buck gracious. I resisted.

"Elizabeth," Don said. "Gracious lady. Lovely family," he informed me. "R.B. had a farm in Connecticut, gentleman's farm, stables, kennels, twenty-room house, entertained all the time. Course, John R.B.'s kept up the tradition—nice little place he and Cam have. Phyllis and I both admired what they've done with it."

If Cam had been a long-pointy-nails type, the palms of her hands would have been oozing blood. She thanked Don, rose from her seat, and politely prepared to bolt. She'd been up since four A.M., she said; it had been a long day, and she was going to bed. As the Abbotts must have known, Cam was the kind of dog person who thinks nothing of driving eight hours to a show, and once there, spends the whole weekend catching up with people, showing her dogs, and making the rounds of the vendors' booths, and wastes hardly a moment on sleep before driving eight hours home. When no one challenged her white lie, I offered a legitimate version of the same excuse: I really was tired. In the lobby, the Abbotts lingered to talk with Eric Grimaldi. Cam and I walked back to the cabins together.

The night air revived me, and in any case, Rowdy needed a final outing before bed. I leashed him and, after a stroll and cleanup, wandered toward the lake, where the broad white path of beckoning moonlight made Apollo 11 seem like a total waste of time: Swim till you smell green cheese. Rowdy and I clambered down the slope to the dock. I had no intention of violating the ban on night swimming by heading for the moon or even by taking a quick skinny dip; I just wanted to dabble my feet from the end of the dock. As I led a reluctant Rowdy over the wooden boards, my shoes and the pads of his feet thumped the dock. Far out on the lake, a loon suddenly laughed. The freakish yodel echoed over the water.

When we reached the end of the dock, the last echo died. A soft splashing took its place. Someone was swimming a steady breast stroke across the little cove toward the dock. Swimming alone really is dangerous, especially after dark. The swimmers most at risk are those made overconfident by natural buoyancy and long practice. The steady stroke, powerful kick, and smooth timing were the ineradicable marks of hours of drill for competitive swimming. I took off my shoes and socks, sat down, and stuck my feet in the cold water. Rowdy whined. "Settle down," I told him. He lowered his body, rested his chin on the dock, and glowered at me. My belief in the buddy system was one thing I couldn't explain to a creature who'd never voluntarily enter water either alone or in the company of a dozen lifeguards. I stroked Rowdy's head and watched the water. I wasn't sure what I'd do if the swimmer suddenly vanished. Scream for help? The time I'd taken Red Cross lifesaving, I'd flunked out by towing the pretend victims to the bottom of the pool.

Within a few minutes, the swimmer surged close to us, threw out a hand, and grabbed the dock. As I scrambled out of the way, a woman's round-bellied body in a dark tank suit rose from the lake.

"Whew! Caught breaking my own rule!" Maxine McGuire exclaimed cheerfully. "Were you going to snitch on me?"

I laughed nervously. "Of course not. I was just soaking my feet and enjoying the night."

Maxine pattered down the dock, picked up a towel I hadn't noticed, and started to give herself a rubdown. "I never get a chance to swim anymore, but after dinner, ten people started pawing and nipping at me like teething puppies, and I said to myself, 'What the heck! It's my camp.' And I feel a lot better now."

"They were upset about the sympathy cards?"

"Oh, yeah, that and those darned silly brochures. Some joker left a lot of stuff about pet cemeteries and things, all mixed up with the dog magazines I put out. It's just someone's dumb idea of a practical joke. You watch. Next thing, he'll go around short-sheeting the beds. It's camp; you've got to expect it."

"Phyllis Abbott didn't take it quite that way," I pointed out.

Max wrapped the towel around herself. "Well, if I may say so, neither did you. Get up early tomorrow morning, Holly, and let your friend there try lure coursing. It's in the field by the parking lot. Six-fifteen. He'll love it."

Back in my cabin, as I was brushing my teeth and getting ready for bed, I decided to take Maxine's advice. Stupid practical jokes didn't deserve any attention at all. I'd get up early and let Rowdy chase a plastic bag. I was just opening the front window when Don Abbott's voice reached me. It sounded a little thick. The Abbotts, too, must have opened the front window, and Don must have been near it. I couldn't make out his words. He rumbled something, paused, and issued what sounded like a question. I assumed that, as usual, he was using the portable phone. He spoke and paused a couple of times. Then the call apparently ended. A few seconds later, I caught Phyllis's voice. Don replied. His tone was angry and unmistakably demeaning. Until then, I'd heard only speech contours, intonations, patterns. This time, I understood one word. In dog fancy, of course, overhearing the word *bitch* is in itself meaningless. Don Abbott could have been talking about or maybe even to Edwina, the Pom. What gave the word its nasty charge was the way Don spoke it. I was certain he wasn't speaking to or about a female dog. To my ear, he didn't sound like a dog person at all. He just sounded like an ugly drunk swearing at his sober wife.

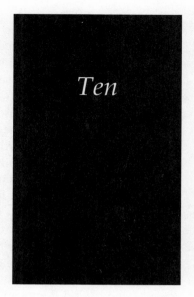

Ten

IN THE EARLY LIGHT of that Monday morning, the elusive white prey that zipped around the green field ahead of wolf-gray Rowdy might have been an Arctic hare, a ptarmigan, or some other little snow-white creature that fled, tarried, veered, zoomed out of reach, slowed to a tantalizing creep, turned a corner, and sped off again. Flashing across the field, hindquarters driving, forelegs reaching, body stretched, dark coat glistening, Rowdy became the soul of dog made manifest: a mythic creature of the Inuit pantheon, Primal Dog, Every Dog, Essence of Dog Itself. The prey at last between his teeth, Rowdy shook his head once, very hard, thus efficiently snapping the neck of the plastic bag.

An hour later, after I'd fed and crated Rowdy, taken a wake-up shower, and observed Elsa the Chesapeake as she intently rearranged the rocks at the edge of the lake, I was sitting in the dining room at a windowside table that gave a great view of the lure coursing. When I glanced out, two basenjis were sprinting around the field giving all the other dogs—and one malamute owner—a little demonstration of precisely how the

sport was supposed to be practiced. I didn't mind. Far from it.
I feel an odd sort of breed loyalty toward basenjis, which in
most essential points of character are small, short-haired,
barkless, curly-tailed African malamutes, creatures that had
once had to fend for themselves.

My breakfast tray contained a glass of orange juice, a big
plate of scrambled eggs, a little plate of giant blueberry muffins, and a cup of not-bad coffee, the entire meal prepared by
someone other than me in a kitchen to be cleaned by someone
other than me and served on dishes to be washed by someone
other than me. I was alone at the table. Neither Eva Spitteler
nor Don Abbott was even in the dining room. The people at
the other tables were strangers to me. I knew them anyway;
they all had dogs. Back out in the real world, some people had
dogs, some didn't, and all too many of those with dogs didn't
actually understand dogs and didn't necessarily give a damn
about them. Here in this little canine ivory tower, however,
every single person had at least one dog, and everyone had
come here, as had I, in a way, in search of dog heaven. I had
the comforting sense of having cracked up and landed in a
specialized asylum in which everyone else enjoyed a form of
madness identical to my own.

On the table in front of my tray rested the Waggin' Tail
schedule, a pen, and a yellow legal pad on which I was listing
activities to attend: agility, advanced show obedience, and, if I
could fit it in, something called jumps chutes that I'd never
heard of and thought we might try anyway. First aid and
CPR? Before and after lunch, I had to steal some time to work
on a column, but then I intended to catch a little of the afternoon's Canine Good Citizen testing, mostly because, like a lot
of other obedience people, I'd initially underrated the value of
the program and now needed to make amends for a couple of
elitist remarks about it in old columns. In the late afternoon,
we'd go to drill team and to flyball. Yes, drill team. Remember
drill team? High school? Brass band music and all. Marching

in formation. With dogs. I hoped that none of my highbrow Cambridge neighbors ever found out, because if caught and convicted, Rowdy and I would find ourselves swiftly deported across the river to Boston. ("You were having *what?*" demands the judge. "This is Cambridge! We expect better than *that!* Anyone can have *fun.*" Bang! goes the gavel. "Guilty as charged!" A gang of Harvard graduates starts pelting us with a weird variety of objects banned within the Cambridge city limits—romance novels, containers of green and blue eye shadow, sharp-edged cartons of flowered wallpaper—as Rowdy and I beat it across the bridge and celebrate our escape by parading along the southern banks of the Charles to the strains of John Philip Sousa.)

And flyball: The dog runs over a series of jumps, gets to a box, and whacks it with his paw, thereby releasing a tennis ball that he catches and carries back over the jumps, at which point the next dog . . . Well, it may sound silly to people, but dogs think the flyball box is the greatest human invention since frozen Bil Jac, and if you don't know what *that* is, I pity your poor canine pal.

Our first postbreakfast activity, agility, took place in what I think was ordinarily an annex to the resort's main parking lot, a large clearing in the woods located at the end of a short dirt road. Let's get the camp layout straight. If you stood facing away from the lake with your back to the big main lodge, ahead of you was the blacktopped parking lot, filled, of course, with vans, station wagons, and other dog-person vehicles, most of them bearing bumper stickers that ranged from the usual loyalty oaths ("I LOVE MY WEST HIGHLAND WHITE TERRIER") and admonitions to tailgaters ("CAU-TION: SHOW DOGS!") to bold declarations of opinion ("ALL MEN ARE ANIMALS, BUT SOME MAKE NICE PETS"). To the right of the parking lot was the field used in the early morning for lure coursing and, later in the day, for drill team and various other activities. At the far end of that field was a big green-and-white-striped tent so festive-looking that I half expected to hear the cries of bar mitzvah celebrants stunned to discover themselves double-booked in the middle of dog camp. As it turned out, the tent was devoted to obedience. To the left, not far from the lodge, was the bunkhouse. The woods began immediately in back of the bunkhouse and ran along the edge of the parking lot to the little dirt road that led to the agility area.

Agility! Of the many orders and allied organizations that constitute the freemasonry of dog fancy, agility alone requires a large and elaborately furnished temple in which to perform its rites. The first-degree rituals of obedience permit nothing more than a dog and a six-foot lead; and, by AKC decree, the regalia used in higher levels of the craft must be of spartan simplicity: flat-white jumps—no gloss, not even semi—relieved only by the stripes of black on the bar jump and the unobtrusive numbers showing the heights of the high-jump boards—black, too, and purely functional.

But every temple of agility represents the glorious and elaborate union of the Tall Cedars of the Obstacle with the Order of the Rainbow for Dogs. Dispersed throughout the big clearing in the woods were an astonishing number and variety of structures not merely painted in brilliant colors, but also trimmed, striped, and embellished in primary green, sunshine yellow, vivid blue, glowing purple, vibrating red, screaming orange, and every other bright color in between. An agility course suggests a schoolyard playground designed by a gymnastically inclined ex-army sergeant turned dog obedience instructor. This equipment looked brand-new. The pause table hadn't even been painted. It sat on shiny metal legs, and the dogs would pause on a top of raw wood. The seesaw was the kind now deemed unsafe for children, except that it was set low to the ground for our group of novice dogs. Also, its board lacked the usual handles, of course, and every twelve

inches or so, a little strip of wood ran across to provide foot-
ing for the dogs. One of the tunnels was a big, tough version
of the long, flexible fabric-covered ones sold for children; the
other was an open barrel with what looked like a gigantic
footless stocking pulled over one end. The dog walk, a canine
balance beam, was a narrow horizontal board with ramps at
each end. Except for the purple, pink, and green stripes, the
PVC bar jumps were identical to Utility practice jumps, and if
I've lost you, imagine a broom handle held horizontal between two vertical supports. What looked like more broom
handles stuck up in rows from metal supports on the ground:
weave poles. Heavy chains attached to sturdy wooden frames
supported tape-wrapped tires from cars and motorcycles.

By far the biggest piece of equipment was the A-frame, a
massive obstacle consisting of two wide ramps, one going up,
the other down; think of an eighteen-foot section of a seaside
boardwalk hinged in the middle and raised at the apex to make
a giant A. Squatting directly in front of the A-frame, blithely
depositing what no one wants to step in, was Eva Spitteler's
big yellow Lab, Bingo. Twenty-six feet away, as far away as a
number 8 flex lead allows, Eva was staring upward in apparent
search of any wood warblers that might be flitting around
high up in the tree canopy. Or maybe she was seeing imaginary creatures in the cumulus clouds, listening to the distant
scolding of a red squirrel, wondering whether to include pew-
ter-encrusted medallions of Saint Francis of Assisi in her catalog, or planning a random act of kindness. I do not know.

Bingo finished. As Eva began to reel him in, I hugged
Rowdy to my left side and quietly delivered an abbreviated
version of the you-buddy-are-not-the-policeman-of-the-dog-
world lecture that opens with a survey of the vile and provoca-
tive behaviors in which undisciplined dogs may engage, moves
to an acknowledgement of the natural wish to impose order
on chaos, and concludes with a happy reminder that sup-

pressing primitive urges is the price we pay for the multitudinous benefits of civilization. Although the lecture is not meant for human ears, my therapist friend Rita once listened in and accused me of stealing it from Sigmund Freud, who, as I was glad to inform Rita, was a devoted dog owner who'd undoubtedly developed these and numerous other ideas in consultation with his beloved chow chow. I mean, if you wanted to understand what Freud wanted to understand—sex, aggression, appetite, rivalry, and house-training, for starters—who'd be the real expert? A stuffy old Viennese doctor? So if you're an academic psychologist hungry to publish, there's a paper in this for you: "The Critical Role of the Chow Chow in the Development of Psychoanalytic Theory: Freud or His Dog? A Controversy Resolved by Reference to the Concept of Castration Anxiety."

When I looked up, Heather was standing next to Eva waving a small plastic bag and pointing toward the A-frame. With a look of baffled innocence on her bulldog face, Eva was shaking her head back and forth. I moved a little closer.

"You're obviously mistaken," said Eva. "It must have been someone else's dog."

"I saw him with my own eyes!" Heather told her. "Not thirty seconds ago! You were looking away."

Eva was indignant. "Bingo hasn't been out of my sight one second! I don't know what dog did that, but it wasn't him, and I haven't paid all this money to come here and spend my time shoveling up shit after other people's dogs, and, if you want my opinion, since you asked for it, for what we're paying here, you ought to be doing it yourself and saying thanks, because if this is how we're going to be treated, no one's coming back! And you can goddamn well tell Max McGuire I said so."

Heather turned geranium red. For a few seconds, she seemed to hold her breath. Then she gave in. "This time," she said, "I'll clean it up. And I hope you understand: Nagging people about this is part of my job. If we leave this place a mess, Max isn't going to be able to use it again, and part of my job, besides agility, is making sure that camp's welcome back next year, okay? So no hard feelings. You ever done any agility before?"

"Not exactly," said Eva, "but Bingo's a natural."

Sara Altman tapped me on the shoulder. "Hey, nice to see Rowdy again. You got food with you?"

Me and American Express. I fished some dog treats out of my pocket.

"Little bits," Sara ordered. Raising her voice, she called, "Could we get together for a minute? Then we'll split up into groups."

All of us gathered at the A-frame. Agility for beginners had drawn a decent-sized group: Eva and Bingo, of course; Cam and her super-sheltie, Nicky; Ginny with kissy-face Wiz; a married-looking couple and the two basenjis I'd seen lure coursing; and dog-tattooed Michael with the real dog, Jacob, a creamy white long-haired Akita. Malamutes with coats like that are called "woollies," and long-haired corgis are known as "fluffies," but as far as I know, long-haired Akitas are just plain long-haired. In malamutes, the long, soft woolly coat is a simple homozygous recessive trait that breeders loathe. You can't show woollies, but in Malamute Rescue, we sometimes have waiting lists of adopters who've owned woollies and won't settle for a dog with a standard coat. (Interested? Alaskan Malamute Protection League, P.O. Box 170, Cedar Crest, NM 87008) Phyllis Abbott had brought her male Pomeranian, Nigel, a handsome fellow who, in contrast to her husband, doubtless refrained from drinking, swearing, and running up big phone bills by talking dog politics. Joy, Craig, and the more-or-less Cairn, Lucky, were there, or perhaps I should say that Joy and Lucky were there and that Craig was also present. Young, blond, and sweet-faced, Joy stood in front of the massive A-frame with the little dog nestled in her arms.

About a yard to one side was her husband, Craig. I had a blasphemous vision of Joy and Lucky as the Madonna and Child posed before the A-frame, their manger. Craig was the awkward, extraneous Joseph, deeply puzzled by miraculous love.

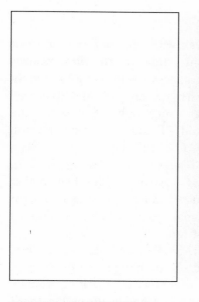

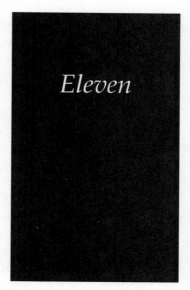

Eleven

"ZONE HABITS!" Sara smacked her open palm on the lower portion of the A-frame, which, I remind you, was like two nine-foot lengths of boardwalk hinged in the middle and raised to form an inverted V. The bulk of the obstacle—and *bulk* is the right word—was painted bright blue, but the lower portion of each ramp, maybe three and a half feet, was brilliant yellow. "This's called a contact zone," Sara told us. "What it is, is a safety zone, and it's on all the go-up obstacles, the A-frame here, and the dogwalk, and the others. And the whole point of it is, if you let the dogs go crashing up onto the obstacles and jumping off, before long, you're going to ruin your dog, because his bones and joints aren't built to take that kind of punishment. Everything's set real low right now, because these guys are beginners, but for competition, the ramps of the A-frame are up about forty-five degrees, and the apex, the top of it's a little more than six feet above the ground." Sara pointed to Rowdy, Bingo, and pretty Jacob. "Take these big guys. You let these big guys go crashing up and down, and in the short term, you're going to have an accident, and in the long run, you're going to wreck your dog, and it might not seem like it, but the same thing applies to the little fellows, too." As if bored with the safety lecture and ready for action, Phyllis's bright-eyed Nigel frisked around and bounced toward Sara. "You want to get going, huh?" Sara asked the Pomeranian. To Phyllis, she said, "Bring him over here. You got food? Everybody got food? Okay. I'll be real quick. Plain buckle collars. No chokes. Go easy, easy. Real gradual. In competition, he's got to put at least one of his feet in that contact zone, and you're going to want that speed, but for now, you want precision, so make sure he's in the contact zone. And keep it fun! Lots of food! And easy does it!"

After the little introduction, Sara quickly divided us into groups. To my disappointment, she took the small-dog group. An instructor I didn't know, another ascetic-looking woman, got medium-size dogs. Rowdy and I ended up in Heather's group, which also included Michael and Jacob; Ginny and Wiz; a sporty-looking couple with the two utterly gorgeous English setters I'd seen in the canoe; and a hefty gray-haired woman and her massive mixed-breed, the two built alike, both on the model of an agility A-frame. And Eva Spitteler. And Bingo.

The small and medium dogs moved toward distant clusters of obstacles. Our group had the first go at the A-frame, the weave poles, and one of the tunnels. We started with the A-frame. At the head of our scraggly line were Ginny and Wiz, both of whom had done a little agility before. Right in back of them were Eva and Bingo. Determined to avoid trouble, I led Rowdy to the end of the queue. We took a place behind Michael and Jacob, who, as Michael assured me and as I observed for myself, was an exceptionally mellow Akita. Akitas, like malamutes, are big, brawny, sometimes dog-aggressive members of the spitz group, and some Akitas are even tougher than the toughest malamutes.

"He won't do a thing," Michael promised. "Jacob is the Gandhi of dogs."

Rowdy is not. His coat is too good. I swear that there's a genetic link. Practically every mahatma malamute I've ever known has been a woollie. That's dog breeding for you: angelic temperament, faulty coat; good rear, east-west front; lovely head, lousy tail; great ears, dippy topline; ideal everything, sound dog, very typey, moves like a dream, and sure enough, one testicle that never drops.

"Well done!" Heather called out. "Praise her! Lots of praise! Good girl. What's her name? Good girl, Wiz. Next?"

Eva led Bingo forward. "This is too low for him," she complained. "He can handle a lot higher than this. This is going to be practically just like walking."

"It's plenty high to begin with," Heather said, "and you want to make sure he gets the idea of the contact zones right now. So you just take hold of his collar, very gently, and you've got your food in your other hand, and you kind of use that to get him right in that contact zone, and when he's there, give him a nice treat, and—"

And before Heather could finish, Eva dashed forward with Bingo at the end of a six-foot lead. On the ground in front of the ascent ramp, the big yellow Lab paused momentarily. Then he bounded up, entirely missing the contact zone, skittered over the top, and leaped off the other side as if he could hardly wait to get his feet back on the ground. "Good boy, Bingo!" Eva screamed. "Good boy! You're a natural! Didn't I tell you? Great, great work. Good boy! With you around, the rest of these dogs look like a pile of giant turds."

Heather rolled her eyes briefly upward, shrugged her lean shoulders, and started instructing the massive gray-haired woman with the look-alike A-frame dog, an Irish wolfhound cross, maybe, an immense creature who turned out to be named Baskerville. Coached by Heather, the woman slowly lured the ponderous dog up and over the ramp. Then the

English setters took their turns. The first was timid and skittish; the second, bold, surefooted, and justifiably proud of himself, a happy dog once again discovering himself good at everything. I'd wanted to watch Jacob, but missed him because just as Michael led him toward the A-frame, Eva and Bingo cut in front of Ginny and Wiz to get in line directly behind Rowdy and me, and I was busy moving Rowdy away from Bingo and trying to size up the yellow Lab's mood.

Then it was our turn. Before we even reached the obstacle, Heather intervened. "You do a lot of obedience," she informed me.

"Yes," I admitted.

"I get *Dog's Life*. I read your column," she said flatly.

I nodded.

"You better start right now getting used to working with the dog on your right," she advised me. "In agility, you've got to be able to work with the dog on either side of you. So get on the other side of him, and put your food in your left hand, and . . ."

Rowdy was already past the yellow contact zone. Tail zipping back and forth, a big grin on his face, he reached the apex.

"Feed him!" Heather ordered. "Lots of praise! And then when he gets . . ."

By this time, Rowdy was in the contact zone at the bottom of the ramp, and I was awkwardly shoving food in his mouth and wondering how I could possibly learn to work with a dog on what was obviously the *wrong* side. The world of obedience, like the rest of the world, is designed for right-handed people. Always, the dog sits and heels at the handler's left.

"Praise him! He did great!" Heather said.

"Good boy!" My words were superfluous. Rowdy had loved the A-frame. For once, he hadn't even been very interested in food. Climbing up and down had been a self-rewarding activity.

"Everyone had a turn?" Heather asked. "Okay, a couple of you keep on with the A-frame, and while you're doing that, I'll get a few people started on the tunnel. Let the Labs try the A-frame again, and the setters, and bring the other dogs over here. And what you want to do with that yellow Lab," she told Eva, "is, you're going to have to slow him down and build his confidence, and even if you practically have to stop him in the zones and at the top of the ramp, that's where you praise him and that's where you give him a treat. Forget speed. All you work on now is correct zone habits."

Again, *zone habits*. I liked the phrase. Erogenous vestments. Panamanian nuns. As I was fighting the dizziness induced by keeping Rowdy on my right—wrong—side, Heather pointed to what agility people call an open tunnel or pipe tunnel, the kind of cloth-covered wire spiral that children use, but, like all agility equipment, very sturdy. Actually, there were two open tunnels, one compressed and fastened with bungee cord to form what was hardly a tunnel at all, the other stretched to a length of eight or ten feet. We started with the hooplike compressed tunnel. Heather held each dog's collar while the handler went around, bent down, looked through, caught the dog's eye, and called. Then Heather released her grip on the collar, and the dog went through and ended up in the handler's arms.

"Hey, these guys are doing just great. Anyone want to try this?" She pointed to the stretched-out tunnel. "You know your own dog best. If he's ready, let him give it a try, and if he's not, just give him a little time, and he will be. Don't push him."

"We'll stick with this," said the big woman. I don't think I ever learned her name. I kept on thinking of her as Ms. Baskerville.

"I borrowed a tunnel from a neighborhood kid," I said. "We've fooled around with it." There are limits to my willingness to brag about my dogs. In fact, the first time I'd borrowed the tunnel, while I'd been busy stretching it out and stabilizing it with cement blocks, Rowdy had gone zipping through.

"Jacob'll watch," Michael said. "Let him see that after you go in, you come out again." To me, Michael added, "He learns a lot watching other dogs."

Michael and the pretty Akita moved to the far end of the tunnel. Heather reached out for Rowdy's lead. I didn't know what breed Heather had. Probably a Border collie, incredible agility breed, fast, accurate, truly agile. Or maybe a mix. Some of the top agility dogs in the country are medium-size, zippy dogs with what mixed-breed fans like to think of as hybrid vigor. Whatever Heather had, it certainly wasn't a malamute or any other breed with Rowdy's power. I'm always embarrassed to tell a real dog person how to handle a dog, but only malamute people understand malamute power. I warned Heather: "Hang on!"

Then I hurried to the opposite end of the tunnel, near where Michael and Jacob had stationed themselves. I hunkered down and peered into the semidarkness. "Let him go!" I called. "Rowdy, here! This way!" I clapped my hands and made happy noises. As Rowdy entered the tunnel, his bulk blocked the light at the far end. "Rowdy, this way! Come on, good boy!" About halfway through, he dawdled. Then he put his nose to the floor, sank down, and settled in, evidently content to take a nap in the middle of what was supposed to be an obstacle.

While I'd been looking in the tunnel, Eva, Ginny, and the others must have decided that they were ready for a new obstacle. I sensed people around. The only voice I heard was Eva's. "Big wimp," she said. "Can't get him in the water, and can't get him out of there."

"Call to him!" Heather instructed.

"Rowdy, here! Hey, let's go! Rowdy, come on!" My whistling, calling, hand clapping, and thigh slapping finally got him to his feet. Once he arose, he picked up speed and flew out of the tunnel so fast that I had to scramble to my feet and step out of his way to avoid getting plowed over. As Rowdy soared past and headed directly for Jacob, I could almost hear the fight begin. I could almost see the hideous tangle of snarling malamute and outraged Akita, the flashing teeth, the terrified efforts to separate the dogs, the unintended bites, the mauled and broken human arms.

But Jacob was, indeed, the Gandhi of dogs. I managed to grab Rowdy's lead. When I hauled him in, away from Bingo, I saw what had delayed Rowdy in the tunnel. Tail soaring back and forth, eyes smiling, Rowdy proudly displayed the treasure he'd found: Clamped between his jaws was a big rawhide chew toy. Faced with a rawhide-bearing male malamute speeding directly at him, almost any other Akita I'd ever known would have gone for the rawhide, and the other dog be damned.

I let out a deep sigh. By now, Michael had moved Jacob a few yards away. "That could've been close," I said.

"What's going on?" Heather asked.

I explained. "That's not, uh, intentional, is it? Leaving rawhide in the tunnel? Because—"

"Hey, we're not crazy." Heather shook her head. "You start some kind of Easter egg hunt with rawhide all over the place, and sooner or later, all you're going to end up with is a fight. Who put that thing there, anyway?" Before anyone had a chance to answer, Heather added, "You know, this is going to be a problem for a while. Every time Rowdy goes through the tunnel, he's going to be looking for more rawhide, and it's going to slow him down. You're going to have to work on that."

"Fine," I said meekly. As I started to ask Heather about the commands to use in telling the dog which obstacle to head for, Eva and Bingo once again diverted her. The diversion was not, I should point out, Bingo's fault. A change in water has that effect on a lot of dogs. Some owners carry a one-liter soda bottle of water with them when they travel, and every time they give some water to their dogs, they refill the bottle, so the dog gradually gets used to the strange water. Or maybe Bingo had a case of nerves. At any rate, he was squatting once again, this time in the woods at the edge of the clearing, and once again, Eva was looking any place and every place else—at Rowdy, at the A-frame, at Nigel, who was making his dainty, precise way down the descent ramp of the low dogwalk toward a happy-looking Phyllis.

"Do you have a plastic bag with you?" Heather asked. "Or do you need one?"

Her mind still elsewhere, Eva watched Nicky, Cam's sheltie, neatly sail through a tire jump.

"You!" Heather was finally losing patience. "Camp rule: Clean up after your own dog!"

"Are you talking to me?" demanded Eva, throwing a stubby-fingered hand across her breast. "He's going in the woods. What's it matter?"

"This has been gone over in detail," Heather replied quietly. "It was in the material you got through the mail, it was in the registration packet you got yesterday, and we discussed it at the meeting yesterday afternoon."

The Leona Helmsley of pooper-scooping, Eva was lofty. "I wasn't there."

"And we just talked about it now, before we got started," Heather persisted. "We leave this place a mess, and camp's not going to be able to come back here. All over camp, there are bags and scoopers and buckets, and if you don't use them, among other things, it's not fair to Maxine. In case you don't know, it's not easy to find a good place that welcomes all these dogs, and part of my job's making sure that when you guys leave here Saturday morning, there's nothing that anyone's going to mind stepping in. Now, do you have a plastic bag, or do you need one? They're right over there by that trash can."

By coincidence, Phyllis Abbott, her hair and makeup fastid-

ious, her white shirt crisp, her white slacks spotless, was heading toward the trash can at exactly the time Heather pointed
to it. As if to model responsible dog ownership, she took a
clean plastic bag and led Nigel slowly along the edge of the
clearing. "Show time!" she told him. "Show time!"

Attracted perhaps by Heather's vehement lecture, the entire
group was gathering around.

"Holly?" Joy asked tentatively.

"Yes?"

"Is this some kind of . . . ?"

"It's nothing," I said. "There was just a little, uh . . ."

"What is 'show time'? I don't . . ."

I'll spare you. Yes, it's possible to teach your dog to elimi-
nate more or less on command, but you can use any word or
phrase you want. Pair it with the act, say it every time the dog
goes, praise him, and before long, you've got a dog that will
relieve himself before he gets into the show ring instead of
right in the middle of the judging. There are other ways to
prevent soiling in the ring, but if you aren't a real dog person,
you've probably lost your lunch already, and if you've managed to keep it, the other ways would bring it up. I limited
myself to assuring Joy that Phyllis was acting perfectly normal. Maybe Eva cleaned up after Bingo as I was watching
Phyllis or talking to Joy. Or perhaps Heather relented. I don't
know; I didn't see.

After that, we again broke into groups and introduced the
dogs to the other obstacles. Because of his background in obedience, Rowdy had no trouble with the jumps, including the
tire jump, or with the down-stay on the pause table, either.
The weave poles weren't a big hit. They're a slalom course;
the trained dog weaves smoothly left, right, left, right, bending his body to speed through. To Rowdy, the poles must have
seemed like a dumb bunch of sticks. We prepared for the
balance-beam dogwalk by using a narrow board so close to the
ground that I couldn't convince Rowdy to keep his feet on it.

With Heather's help, I sent him through the tunnel two more times. The first time, he lingered; the second time, he raced through. We ended where we'd begun, at the A-frame, which was clearly going to be one of Rowdy's favorite obstacles. In fact, by the end of the class, I knew that Rowdy was ready to have the A-frame raised higher. I didn't say so, of course. No one wants to sound like Eva Spitteler, who managed to get into a final dispute with the agility people by loudly announcing her intention of returning to the area, raising the heights of the obstacles, and letting Bingo run the course without what she referred to as Heather and Sara's "interference."

"*No* one," Sara informed her icily, "absolutely no one uses this equipment unsupervised. Got it? No one."

"Oh, yeah?" Eva demanded. "You're here twenty-four hours a day?"

"Everyone!" Sara called. "This is important."

When we'd gathered around her, she tactfully explained that someone had raised the question of whether the agility course was available for practice between classes. The answer, Sara said firmly, was no. We all knew about liability, didn't we? Well, liability wasn't the reason. The reason was the safety of the dogs. "And could everyone get here a little early tomorrow morning?" she added. "We could use a little help moving the obstacles. So get here good and early."

As the group broke up, I heard Eva grumble very loudly, "Good and earlier than you will! How'd one A.M. do? That early enough for you?"

As Cam, Ginny, and I moved out of Eva's range, Cam exclaimed, "Talk about *grating!* That woman makes me feel like a piece of Parmesan cheese, for God's sake!"

In unspoken agreement to get away from Eva as quickly as possible, we gathered up our gear and got our dogs moving, but as we were leaving the clearing to head down the little road and across the field to the obedience tent, Eva and Bingo caught up with us. Even our low-level beginning agility was decent exercise, and the temperature was rising. Besides, Eva didn't look exactly fit. She was panting hard. Hauling Bingo around in front of us, Eva came to a halt, turned to face us, spread her feet apart, and planted herself in the road. Lifting a half-pointing finger and glaring directly at me, she said, "You're a dog writer!"

All I could think of were the old films of the Army-McCarthy hearings. Eva looked and sounded so amazingly like Senator Joseph McCarthy that I was almost tempted to raise my right hand and swear that I was not now and never had been a member of the Dog Writers' Association of America. But D.W.A.A. is a wonderful organization, and I'm not the kind of disloyal member who'd tailor her conscience to fit the fashion of the times.

"Yes," I admitted. "I am."

Twelve

ONCE EVA SPITTELER had decided that I was a lot more important in the fancy than I really was or ever will be, she abruptly cut the nasty remarks about Rowdy and made an ingratiating pest of herself. She loved *Dog's Life*, she loved my column, she loved my articles, she loved not only everything about everything I'd ever written but everything about how I'd written it. To Cam, a more accomplished obedience handler and a far greater legal expert on the sport than I'll ever be, Eva said just about nothing. Ginny's response to Eva was a little hard to interpret. That Ginny hated the sight of Eva was clear. Ginny's friendly, ruddy face hardened and faded into what looked like a death mask. Even the braid around her head seemed to turn to clay. I wasn't sure whether this transformation was merely Ginny's habitual response to Eva or whether it represented a specific reaction to Eva's disgusting attack of writer worship. In any case, Cam and Ginny rapidly made their escape down the road.

Eva's unhappy victim, I remained as pinned as if she'd held a knife to my belly. My cheeks froze in the kind of quirky half-smile that you see on a dog who's just about to vomit. Not content with falling all over me, Eva had to fawn over Rowdy, who will strut, preen, cajole, offer his paw, bat his eyes, sing *ah-roo*s and *woo-woo-woo*s, and, if necessary, fall to the ground and wave his silly big legs in the air to elicit the merest glance of genuine admiration, but who would have nothing of Eva Spitteler and her phony flattery. Bingo, too, was aloof and subdued, altogether a different creature from yesterday's lunger and the past hour's A-frame bounder. Tempting though it is to suggest that the big Lab was sympathetically mimicking his owner's change in attitude, I must report that the real cause of Bingo's sudden transformation was undoubtedly the heavy-duty pinch collar that now encircled his neck. I wondered whether Maxine McGuire or someone else had ordered Eva to keep Bingo under control.

Eva must have followed my eyes. "I never use that thing," she said.

Except right now, I wanted to add. Instead, I said, "I'm not crazy about them, but I use one if I have to." As you probably know, a pinch collar, otherwise known as prong collar, consists of interlocked metal links. When the handler tightens the collar, the points of the links, the prongs, pinch the dog's neck. It's a high-powered and somewhat controversial piece of training equipment, totally banned by some obedience clubs, highly recommended by others. I explained: "Sometimes I help with Malamute Rescue, and if I get a really big, totally untrained dog, sometimes I have to use a pinch collar, or I can't even take the dog for a walk."

"Well," Eva confided, "the truth is that's more or less my situation with Bingo, not that he's untrained or anything—he's really very, very good—but when I got him . . . Really, what he is, is a rescue dog. I had no idea at the time, but the breeder I went to does *not* socialize her puppies, and she breeds dozens of litters, and, believe me, she charges big bucks, too. This woman has a big, big reputation, and I paid a fortune for pick of the litter, and how was I supposed to know?"

I shrugged. The unnamed breeder was, of course, Ginny Garabedian.

Eva resumed: "And right from the beginning, I had to work my ass off trying to make up for what that poor puppy had been through, nobody touching him, nobody even speaking a kind word to him, if you ask me. And I still keep thinking, I should've known, because when I got there, I wanted to see her kennels, and she would not let me back there. And now I know why, because her house wasn't exactly clean, but, back there, it's *filthy*. And from what I hear, nobody but *nobody* gets back there."

Then how did anyone but Ginny know what condition the kennels were in? I didn't ask. "Maybe the breeder's just trying to protect the puppies," I told Eva. "People can track in anything. They don't even have to handle the puppies; they can bring things in on their shoes." Well-meaning visitors can wipe out whole litters by infecting puppies with parvo, distemper, or any number of other diseases.

"Yeah, but that's not why," Eva insisted. "What I know now is, she's got thirty or forty dogs back there, and she never cleans up. What the place is, is just a *puppy mill*."

According to my strict definition, a puppy mill is a wholesale commercial kennel that mass-produces puppies for resale in pet shops. Every once in a while, the fancy discovers in its midst a well-respected breeder whose dirty, crowded, disease-ridden kennel is no better than a puppy mill. Like Masons who find that a member has revealed the secrets of the order, dog fancy henceforth deems such a person, as the Masons phrase it, "devoid of all moral worth." Any brotherhood, any sisterhood, any order, including the fancy, has a few members unfit to be received into the lodge. But *Ginny?* I'd never actually seen her kennels. I had the impression that she bred very selectively, the best to the best. If I'd had to guess, I'd have wagered that she bred only a litter or two a year. But how could I really have defended her? *Ginny is one of us,* I could have said. *And you, Eva, very definitely are not.*

"Bingo sure doesn't look like a puppy-mill dog," I said.

Big mistake. In trying to be kind to Eva, I'd patted an abandoned animal I had no intention of taking home. Eva launched into an intolerably boring and seemingly interminable Bingo-centered monologue that ended only because Rowdy, unassisted by a pinch collar, drowned her out. Malamutes spend hours, sometimes days, without uttering a sound. Old breed joke: They aren't called mala*mute* for nothing. But when they feel like it, they can scream like hungry babies, wail like fire engines, and bellow like moose, all at the same time. I picked up my carrier of scent articles and Rowdy's little canvas travel bag of assorted dog supplies, pointed to Rowdy, mouthed nonsense syllables, and raced off down the road.

The sun had burned off the haze of the early morning. A few white cumulus clouds lingered. Miles up, the air must have been motionless. Just above the asphalt parking lot, it shimmered. Except around the obedience tent, the big field on the opposite side of the blacktop was empty. The breed handling class must have been taking place somewhere else, some place shady. I was sorry to miss it. Also in progress, if I remembered correctly, were doggy swimming lessons or maybe water rescue. Advanced agility would start soon. Jump chutes—chute jumping? Whatever it was called, it sounded like fun. If I could locate it, I'd cool Rowdy down, drench him if I had to, and let him give it a try.

Not for anything, though, would I skip obedience, which is my home within the home of dog fancy and the most comfortingly ritualist of the orders that make up what anthropologists would call a ritual brotherhood but what is, in fact, a sisterhood open to men. A true secret society, we really do have hidden mysteries, not because we try to hide our knowledge, though, but because our craft is damned hard to learn.

Anyway, what's exceptional about us is that whereas almost all other secret societies, from socially valued brotherhoods to notorious criminal bands, from Freemasonry to the Cosa Nostra, are open only to men, our membership consists mainly of women. Also, on a less academic and more practical —not to mention romantic—note, let me add that, far from trying to exclude men, we actively welcome them. For one thing, it's a lot of work lugging around those heavy mats and jumps, and the excess of muscular bulk that results from a lifetime of testosterone poisoning comes in very handy. For another, just as we enjoy having the monotony of all those high-scoring golden retrievers, Border collies, shelties, and poodles relieved by the occasional bloodhound, bullmastiff, Pharaoh hound, or even, God forbid, Alaskan malamute, so too are we delighted to welcome the least traditional of the nontraditional obedience breeds, the human male.

Indeed, to encourage men to participate in our sport, we've even instituted what amounts to an affirmative action program, and in case you think that we lower our rigorous standards in electing men to club offices, making them judges, and hiring them as head trainers, let me point to such gifted males as the late Milo Pearsall, not to mention Bob Self, Bernie Brown, Bob Adams, and the Worshipful Master of our camp obedience lodge, Chuck Siegel, an immensely tall blond guy of forty or so who was standing in the shade of the obedience tent instructing a group of eight women and one man, Michael, in one of the hidden mysteries of our order, namely, the art of spitting food.

I dumped my gear in an out-of-the-way spot at the edge of the tent, opened the canvas travel bag, got out Rowdy's plastic travel bowl and a plastic bottle of water, and let him have a big drink. As he slurped, I filled my pockets with little cubes of cheddar that I'd brought to camp and carried that morning next to a plastic-encased ice substitute that was still cool from its sojourn in my freezer at home. In addition to Rowdy's good wooden dumbbell from Paul's, the bag held his nonre-cyclable white nylon dumbbell, his flex lead with its plastic handle, and a generous supply of plastic clean-up bags, cheap clear ones for when no one was looking, expensive opaque white for public use. The world of obedience is such an eco-logical disaster area that I was surprised to see in the canvas bag one item made of a readily compostable substance, paper, glossy paper bright with the colors of hate-the-planet dyes, I suppose, but paper nonetheless. It proved to be a clipping from *Dog's Life*, an item from what I recognized as our answer to *DOGworld*'s "Science and the Dog" and the *Gazette*'s "Vet-erinary News." On one side of the clipping was a report about the near impossibility of accurately diagnosing Lyme disease; on the other, yet another warning about the hazards on giving human medications like acetaminophen to dogs. I read and even write those warnings all the time; they didn't really worry me. I merely wondered what the clipping was doing in Rowdy's bag.

Popping a bit of cheddar in my mouth, I summoned Rowdy to my left side, joined Chuck's group, and spent a happy fif-teen minutes or so perfecting my aim and Rowdy's attention. The first time I ever saw a handler spit food from her mouth to her dog's, I was totally disgusted. Before that, I'd always imagined that I'd do absolutely anything to get good scores. But *spit? Spit in public?* Well, I felt suddenly liberated, relaxed, relieved to have discovered that there was, after all, a limit to what I'd do to keep a few of those precious 200 points with which every dog-handler team walks into the obedience ring. Shortly thereafter, I happened to be at ringside when that same handler and her standard poodle scored a 199 in Open B, and lost that one point only because the judge lacked the self-confidence to give a 200. As Chuck Siegel told us, "You show me some other way to get a dog's eyes glued on my face and not on my hands and not my pockets, and I'll give it a try, but until we get some kind of technological breakthrough,

spitting's the best we got, so we gotta learn to live with it."
Hear, hear!

Then Chuck announced that he was going to work with
people who were just getting started in Open, people who
were introducing their dogs to the dumbbell and the jumps.
He suggested that the rest of us either practice on our own or
move to the opposite end of the tent, where a tiny little
bright-faced woman named Irma was doing what was billed as
a show-and-go, but turned out to be run-throughs, in other
words, a very informal, for-practice-only version of a trial.
Irma had score sheets fastened to her clipboard, but unless a
handler specifically requested a score, she just made comments and suggestions. Seated on a bench eyeing the run-
throughs were Cam and Ginny. Nicky sat alertly at Cam's
feet. Wiz had half climbed into Ginny's lap. Rowdy and I
settled on the grass at the side of the bench. On the far side of
the ring, Phyllis Abbott and three or four other people exchanged discontented-looking whispers. In the ring, a young
woman called to her high-strung golden retriever. The dog
dashed toward the handler and went directly to heel position.
After Irma had uttered a few tactful words about the hazards
of pattern training, Michael and pretty Jacob ran through the
Novice routine.

"Anyone else for Novice?" Irma called out.

"What is this 'Novice'?" Cam murmured. "This is supposed to be advanced, okay?"

Advanced: Open and Utility. Cam was right. I stood up
anyway. "Sure," I said. With Rowdy, the level makes almost
no difference; the problem is getting him to behave at all.
Recognizing the run-through for what it was, he didn't do too
badly. He crabbed out a little, and his sits could have been
straighter, but when I said, "Heel," he didn't gaze into space
and pretend that he'd never heard the word before; and on the
Recall, he acted as if he'd never once in his life contemplated
the possibility of charging in at ninety miles an hour, hitting

me full on, and knocking the wind out of me. Rowdy treats his creativity like money in the bank. Instead of squandering it on run-throughs and matches, he lets it sit there collecting interest. At the moment, he was saving up for a splurge at our national specialty, where we'd be up against Anna Morelli and Tundra, in whose presence, I felt certain, he intended to blow the whole fortune at once.

"Good attention," Cam commented.

"Thank you," I said. "He crabs out." Translation: Instead of trotting along parallel to me, he heels with his front in close and his hindquarters out.

"Yeah, he does," Cam agreed.

If you don't show your dogs, you might imagine that my feelings were hurt, but except among the very top handlers, and not all of them—Cam, for example—obedience isn't like that, and, especially among owner-handlers, neither is conformation.

I said, "I thought that was the kind of thing Chuck was going to work on."

"It was," Ginny said, "but there weren't enough people or whatever, and so Maxine combined all the show obedience, and he's stuck trying to do everything."

"She did that a long time ago," Cam said. "That's what someone told me. Last winter or spring or something, when Lynette Watson was all set to come and do beginners' and Novice, she got a letter from Maxine saying that, gee, she didn't need her after all, and all about how sorry Max was. And Lynette wrote back and said it was far enough in advance, no problem. Only nobody bothered to tell us."

"Lynette's name was in that stuff that got sent to us." Ginny sniffed. "Not that it matters to me."

"Not that it does to me, either," Cam said. "But what about Lynette? She could've made a stink if she'd felt like it. She lets people take advantage of her."

"Maybe Maxine didn't have much choice," Ginny said.

"Maybe she just wasn't getting as many people as she expected, or there weren't all that many obedience people, and—"

"Which, since you mention it—" Cam said.

"There aren't," I finished. "There aren't all that many of us."

"Open?" Irma called. "Anyone for Open? And could I have some help setting up the jumps?"

Dog obedience shares with other human groups the universal internal distinction between those who pitch in and those who don't. Phyllis Abbott and her buddies continued to talk among themselves while Cam, Ginny, Michael, and I carried out the broad jump hurdles and the high jump. As I was struggling to assemble the high jump, I overheard Phyllis saying, "What a mean thing to do! Losing a dog to bloat is bad enough, but this is utterly inexcusable!"

Bloat: gastric dilatation and volvulus syndrome, killer of dogs, especially of big breeds.

I glanced over to make sure that Rowdy hadn't budged from his down-stay. "Is there a dog here with bloat?" I asked. The condition isn't contagious. To scare me, it doesn't have to be. The word alone makes my own stomach swell and twist.

"No," Phyllis fumed. "Some stupid person has been leaving *printed material* all over camp. And among other things, this individual left an article on bloat in Jennifer's handbag." Phyllis swept a hand toward a sleek, fit, brown-haired woman with an equally sleek, fit Doberman bitch. "And we have been discussing what to do about the problem." Lowering her voice to a level perfectly audible to the Dobermanlike Jennifer, Phyllis added, "Jennifer lost her Samson last spring."

"Bloat," I guessed.

Phyllis nodded.

"I'm very sorry," I said.

"Thank you," said Jennifer. "Whoever this is didn't necessarily mean it personally. It was probably just an accident."

Phyllis pulled herself even more upright than usual. "An accident? Purely by accident, someone is depositing clippings on pet theft and rabies and heartworm and unsafe dog toys? Purely by accident, everywhere we look, we find advertisements for pet loss counseling and brochures on the hazards of shipping our dogs by air? Well, if that's what you think, Jennifer, then you and I have *very* different ideas of what constitutes an accident!"

"No, not that," Jennifer protested. "I just meant that it was an accident that I got that one, the one on bloat. That it was just a coincidence. That it wasn't meant for me *personally.*"

"Well, it doesn't matter one way or the other," Phyllis said.

"We're trying to decide what to do," Jennifer informed me. "We think maybe the best thing is just to ignore it."

"Somebody's just doing it for attention," another woman said.

"Eva Spitteler," someone murmured.

Jennifer nodded. "Trying to feel important. When you think about it, it's stupid. I mean, it's mostly just stuff from the dog magazines. We read it all the time, anyway. And there's no way I'm going to be more scared of bloat than I already am."

I said, "It's like that stuff that was left in the lodge last night, all those brochures for gravestones and things. It's depressing, and nobody wants to think about it, but that's pretty much it. And the sympathy cards. The point is, I guess, to get us worried. But Jennifer's right. We're the people who *do* take precautions. So we're the people who ought to be least scared."

"You're missing the point," Phyllis said. "The point is that we're the perfect targets for this kind of campaign. The reason we take precautions is that we know these threats exist and we know our dogs are vulnerable and we'll do anything to protect them. Is Mr. Pet Owner on the Street worried about kennel cough? Of course not. Mr. Pet Owner doesn't even know it exists, or if he does, and if he's had his dog immunized, he thinks that means his dog's one-hundred-percent protected. Believe me, this is not a campaign to frighten the pet people. It's a campaign directed against *us.*"

"It's just Eva," someone said. "Glutton for attention. Jealous of everyone else."

"Well, I for one intend to ignore it," Jennifer said.

The other woman nodded. I did, too. I disagreed with almost everything Phyllis had said. Although pet people probably weren't as informed as we were, I thought that they loved their dogs as much as we did and tried as hard as we did to protect them; and I saw no evidence of a scare campaign targeted at show and obedience people. Whether Eva or someone else was responsible for the brochures, cards, and clippings, I agreed with the policy of doing nothing. "Whoever's doing this," I said, "wants to make trouble. The best thing to do is not let that happen. Just like training dogs. You make the result interesting, the behavior's going to increase; you make the result boring, the behavior's going to stop."

"It's only serious if we take it seriously," someone said. "We have fun, it's going to stop."

And we did have fun, or at least I did. Watching top handlers work their dogs is always interesting. I returned to Rowdy, released him, and settled down on the grass to watch Cam, Jennifer, and a couple of other people who had a lot to teach me. Cam and Ginny continued to grumble about not getting what they'd paid for, but I felt satisfied to loll in the shade and stroke Rowdy's head while I studied the beautiful handling of the real pros and the almost incredible precision of their wonderful dogs. Top handlers and their dogs move with the control and grace of dancers. Cam and Nicky, in particular, were the Ginger Rogers and Fred Astaire of dog obedience. I wished that Cam were the instructor and that we were taking a course on footwork. On the left turn, you almost never actually see a dog remain in perfect heel position, body parallel to the handler's, every single second. As I watched Nicky, I briefly wished for a sheltie and even thought about asking Cam whether she intended to breed him. On reflection, I realized that if I moved like Cam, I'd give Rowdy at least half a chance to move like Nicky. And if Rowdy had observed the dogs as intently as I observed the handlers, he'd have felt humbled, too. Malamutes jump on power, and Rowdy jumped very well indeed, but when Jennifer's Doberman, Delilah, took her jumps, I caught my breath, cursed to myself, shook my head, and grinned.

While Jennifer and Delilah were working, Phyllis Abbott was warming up Edwina, her Pomeranian bitch. As a team, Phyllis and Edwina, despite the disparity in size, were well matched. Both were bright-eyed, quick, and animated. When their turn came, Phyllis clapped her hands softly. "Let's have fun! Let's play!" she told Edwina.

By the time I was deciding on the color of my Pomeranian, Irma, acting as her own steward, was laying out Phyllis's scent articles at the far side of the ring. The idea of the exercise is simple: There are ten articles—most people use dumbbells—five leather and five metal. Someone, usually a steward, arrays eight of them, four leather and four metal, about twenty feet from the dog and handler, who face away from the articles. The handler scents one of the remaining two articles, which is placed with the unscented ones. On the judge's command, the team turns to face the articles, and the handler commands the dog to find and retrieve the one the handler scented. Then the exercise is repeated with the remaining article. Easy? So you try it! What makes the scent discrimination interesting is that the dog doesn't just zip out and instantly grab the right article. Rather, the dog examines the articles, compares them, checks himself, mulls over his thoughts, and reaches a decision. If you don't believe that dogs *think*, you've never seen a dog work in Utility.

Or that's how it's supposed to be, and that's how it was

until Edwina reached the articles. After one cursory sniff, instead of going about her work, the little dog turned abruptly to face Phyllis and threw her a puzzled and almost startled look, as if to demand what new and weird training trick her handler was trying now. Eager not to interfere with Edwina's work, Irma gave Phyllis a questioning glance. Phyllis shrugged her shoulders and kept watching Edwina, who was now circling the diminutive dumbbells and examining them in a normal, if somewhat suspicious, fashion. After twenty or thirty seconds, Edwina zeroed in on the correct article, a leather dumbbell, but she'd no sooner picked it up than she immediately dropped it. In fact, she didn't just let it fall; she spat it out.

"Something is very wrong," said Phyllis, striding rapidly to the baffled and anxious-looking little dog, who was now scouring her muzzle with her tongue and coughing lightly, as if trying to rid her mouth of a bad taste. After speaking softly to Edwina, Phyllis kneeled on the ground, peered at the articles, and sniffed. Then Phyllis did the sensible, repulsive thing: She picked up one of the leather dumbbells and gave it a light lick. Her whole face puckered. Shaking with rage, she rose to her feet and addressed not only Irma but everyone else under the bright striped tent. "Someone," she announced, "has tampered with my articles. They have been deliberately treated with some bitter substance. This is a vile thing to do to me, and it is a vile thing to do to my dog. And don't you dare try and tell me that *this* is any accident!"

Thirteen

IT HAD ALWAYS SEEMED to me that in the world of, ahem, literary endeavor, my fellow dog writers and I enjoyed the unique privilege of not having to work very hard at what we did. I'd felt particularly sorry for our human-writing brethren, cursed to sweat over so intractably complex a subject as human nature while we got to scribble and jot in effortless celebration of creatures who were simply wonderful. Every time I'd ever tried to plunge out of the genre and into the so-called mainstream of dogless fiction, my tedious human characters would sit around boring themselves and their creator until, against my will and sometimes theirs as well, a dog would suddenly vault in, dig its teeth into my story, and after a tug of war that I inevitably lost, drag me out of the mainstream, where I was drowning anyway, and back to the canine shores where I could breathe again. Years ago, desperate for cash to special a dog, I'd gotten halfway through writing a promisingly trashy and exclusively human romance novel, but then a golden retriever had leaped in and stolen the plot, and I'd given up the project as hopelessly unpublishable. But maybe I was wrong. Maybe there is, after all, more demand for canine romances than I dared to hope.

I threw out the manuscript, but I still have the title, and that's a start.

Heartworms.

All this is to say that at quarter of twelve on that same Monday morning, I sat at the little desk in my cabin, stared at a blank sheet of yellow legal pad, and realized that I had something in common with Phyllis and Edwina: Someone had contaminated my article and left a foul taste in my mouth. I reminded myself that all writing is selective. I rationalized: To write is inevitably to transform. I tried to silence my conscience with scraps of an Ogden Nash verse, something about sins of commission and sins of omission, but either Nash or my own sense of humor let me down. I tried to think that what I wrote didn't really matter, because Bonnie would edit it anyway, and she'd certainly get rid of the pranks, the bad feeling, the gossip, even the loathsome Eva Spitteler.

Immediately after Edwina's unhappy encounter with what everyone suspected was Bitter Apple or a similar antichew product, while Phyllis, Jennifer, Irma, and a few others were discussing techniques for de-scenting scent articles, Eva had barged into the obedience tent, issued loud complaints about the doggy swimming lessons, permitted a wet Bingo to shake off all over everyone, tried and failed to get Chuck Siegel to give her an individual lesson, and then insisted that she and Bingo must do a Novice run-through. Bingo had a trial coming up, she said. Irma capitulated. With no help from Eva, Irma and a few volunteers cleared away the high jump and the bar jump. During the run-through, Irma made the same kinds of tactful suggestions and helpful observations that she'd made to everyone else and that everyone else had accepted with thanks. Eva, however, had already tried everything Irma suggested, wasn't making the handler errors that Irma pointed out, didn't like this approach, rejected that one, and otherwise made an obnoxious fool of herself.

So if you can write up Eva Spitteler as an angel in dog heaven, go ahead. Also try the sympathy cards, so many of which had now appeared that they'd lost their shock value. Scary clippings also continued to appear. We already knew about canine illnesses, hazards in the home, and poisonous plants. We knew not to leave our dogs locked in airless cars on warm days, and we knew that the sweet taste of antifreeze made it an especially deadly threat. Throughout my late-morning course on canine first aid and CPR, I kept reminding myself that I protected my dogs from these and other dangers and that I either knew or was learning what to do if my precautions failed. When I practiced CPR on the canine manne-quin, I made sure that I knew exactly where my hands be-longed and how much force I'd need to use if Rowdy or Kimi ever lay as lifeless as the doggy dummy. Ginny, Cam, and I had a worrisome talk about bloat, for which there is, of course, no first aid. Once a dog's abdomen starts to swell, all you can do is get to a vet. But not every vet knows how to perform the lifesaving surgery. All of us trusted our own vets. Here we felt suddenly unsafe, far from home. Everyone re-minded everyone else always to soak dry food in water and never to exercise a dog just after a meal. That morning, I'd waited until after lure coursing to feed Rowdy. Even so, I listened hard to the reminders and warnings.

After first aid, I'd let Rowdy go twice through the jump chute, which turned out to be a series of bar jumps set at equal intervals along the length of a narrow passageway formed by a tall, thorny hedge on one side and a hurricane fence on the other. The point of the activity, I thought, was to identify and correct jumping problems, especially bad habits that could eventually injure bones and joints. A couple of experts had already assessed Rowdy's jumping for me, and the chute jumping instructor had confirmed their opinion that his form was excellent. But maybe it was Rowdy who'd gotten the real point: Leaping over jump after jump, he'd had a lot of fun.

On the yellow pad, I scribbled, *Jump chutes. Chute jumping? Fun.* Brilliant start. I wasn't even sure what the activity was called. I tore off the page, crumpled it up, threw it in the wastebasket, and began to block out the article about making life easy for judges by understanding the guidelines they had to follow. Sped by the sense of knowing what I was doing, I made swift progress. How, I asked, might exhibitors, stewards, and even spectators inadvertently put the judge in an awkward position? Without actually criticizing clubs for failing to train stewards, I reminded my readers that "under no circumstances may a judge look at a catalog until he has completed judging." In the ring, dogs are, of course, identified only by the numbers of the handlers' arm bands. The catalog would enable the judge to see the names of dogs, handlers, owners, and breeders, information that could bias judging. In reality, experienced breed judges didn't actually need to see a catalog to know precisely who was who, but the ban on looking at the catalog was nonetheless an attempt to minimize politically motivated judging, and I approved of it. And what other options did the AKC have? Were handlers supposed to enter the ring masked and hooded? And what about readily recognizable dogs? If they, too, were disguised beyond recognition, how could anyone be expected to judge them? So, no catalogs anywhere near a judge, and no chitchat that could be misconstrued, either, nothing at all that might appear to bias the judge. Also, exhibitors had to avoid even the slightest appearance of doing the judge a big favor or giving material thanks that might be misconstrued as bribery. No dinners, no flowers, no candy, no liquor, no offer of bed and board, no ride from the airport or to the next show, either, nothing that could compromise the judge's appearance of impartiality. As I refrained from mentioning, the average judge doesn't really care about such inducements, anyway; the real temptation to the typical judge is the prospect of more judging assignments, preferably at prestigious shows in attractive locations.

Then I turned to judicial authority and, specifically, to the matter of what questions it was and was not all right to ask a judge. According to the AKC guidelines, conformation judges "should answer questions, but normally not about their placements and certainly not about a competitor. . . . Judges should never discuss the relative merits of another entry with a competing owner or handler." Obedience judges are "allowed to engage in a discussion on an individual dog's performance with its handler." Forbidden to all judges is any conversation whatsoever with a disgruntled exhibitor. It is fine to request a judge's opinion, but to question the opinion is to make it impossible for the judge to continue the conversation.

I noticed the time, realized that I was ravenous, dropped my pen, rushed Rowdy out for a quick walk, crated him, and headed for the lodge. For once, there were few dogs and few people in sight. At the edge of the woods between my group of cabins and the bunkhouse, the sweet-tempered, long-haired Akita, Jacob, sniffed at a tree stump, lifted his leg, sniffed again, and, evidently satisfied, ambled along in apparent pursuit of new odors to cover. From the human end of Jacob's flex lead, perhaps ten feet from the dog, Michael waved to me. I waved back. Pulling an additional five or six feet of the cordlike lead from the plastic case in Michael's hand, Jacob followed an invisible trail along the rough ground. Patiently waiting, Michael stood still. If I remember correctly, he didn't even move the hand that held the lead—he certainly didn't try to reel Jacob in—and Jacob didn't leap, lunge, or do anything else to strain the cord. To all appearances, it broke entirely on its own. I was amazed. I'd used those flex leads since they'd first appeared on the market, and so had almost every other dog person I knew, including other malamute people with untrained dogs that pulled even harder than mine did. We trusted those leads. You could crack and ruin one by dropping the plastic case on a hard surface; the unwary person who grabbed the cord got a terrible rope burn; and every now and then, the cord would get temporarily fouled up inside the case. But I'd never even heard of the cord, the lead itself, just breaking.

My loose-dog instincts awakened, I got some liver from my pocket and walked smoothly toward Jacob, but as soon as Michael called, the big dog went right to him. When I reached them, Michael had Jacob by the collar. I didn't really expect Michael to know why the lead had snapped. I asked anyway.

"No idea." He offered me the plastic case.

I examined it. It looked exactly like the two I owned, except that the one I'd brought to camp bore a stripe of adhesive tape with "Winter" printed in black laundry marker. And mine wasn't broken. Was it?

"Have you dropped it?" I asked. "Has anything happened to it?"

Michael shook his head.

I said the obvious. "Jacob's a powerful dog. Does he pull hard on it? Put any strain on it?" I don't know why I asked. Kimi routinely strained my identical leads—same brand, same twenty-six-foot length—running around in circles, and she'd never seemed to do them any harm.

"No. All I can think of is that something went wrong inside the case. There's a spring in there."

When the lead had broken, Michael must have been too startled to press the trigger on the handle. The loose length of cord had retracted all the way inside the case. The other end was still attached to Jacob, a short length of ordinary flat nylon lead securely snapped to his collar, then the thin, strong cord, the part meant to retract inside the case. I followed it to its end, held it, stared at it, and wished that I knew something —anything at all—about how to tell whether a rope has simply broken or whether it's been deliberately cut. To my ignorant eye, the cord showed no signs of wear. It certainly wasn't frayed. Except at the end, where it had broken quite cleanly, it looked brand-new.

"Michael," I said quietly, "are you sure that this is *your* lead?"

Fourteen

PROPPED ON AN EASEL at the entrance to the dining room was a cork bulletin board. It displayed a big, bright advertisement for the camp store, an amateurish but enthusiastic-looking reminder about Canine Good Citizen testing, and an unobtrusive announcement of the cancellation of two other events scheduled for the afternoon, something called "Terrier Fun," and a workshop on spinning and weaving dog hair. I didn't really mind missing either. For all I knew, Terrier Fun consisted of coaching bold little scrappers in new and yet more senseless ways to take on malamutes. As for spinning and weaving, Rowdy and Kimi undoubtedly had a greater aptitude for producing the raw material than I did for fashioning it into garments in which anyone might want to be seen. Also tacked to the board was a sheet of white paper that proclaimed in the emphatic red capitals of a felt-tipped pen: "UNSUPERVISED USE OF THE AGILITY AREA IS STRICTLY FORBIDDEN!"

As I started to enter the dining room, Maxine came up in back of me and demanded, "Didn't you just *love* agility?"

Mindful of my instructions from Bonnie, Max's dear friend, I compliantly said that indeed, Rowdy and I had both loved agility and that, if anything, he was having even more fun than I was. That latter part of my remark was perfectly true. The rawhide bone in the tunnel had been an outright treat. Neither the sympathy cards nor the casket and headstone ads nor the scary clippings about dangers and diseases nor Jacob's broken lead had bothered Rowdy at all. He wouldn't have liked having his own scent articles treated with Bitter Apple, but a nasty taste in another dog's mouth was no concern of his.

"It's so *marvelous*," said Max, "to watch all my dreams becoming a reality."

All my dreams becoming a reality? Ever since Rita and I became friends, it has often occurred to me that the average nonpsychotherapeutic person—myself, for instance—lives in what sometimes feels like unremitting need of Rita's professional advice. I seldom have trouble telling whether someone is cracking up; all too often, the break is disconcertingly obvious. What I never know is how I'm supposed to respond. Lacking professional training, I fall back on lies. "It must be wonderful," I told Max. If I'd been Rita, and Max had walked into my office and said that camp was going great, I'd probably have made exactly the same reply.

As I was wondering whether any of the medications in Rowdy's first-aid kit would do as a reality-sharpener for human beings, Eva Spitteler waddled up, planted herself in front of Max and me, and, feet spread, arms akimbo, began to tell Max almost everything I'd kept to myself. "I can take a joke with the best of them," Eva began, "but some of the shit that's going on around here is no joke. Take this." She rummaged around in the pocket of her shorts and produced yet another of the sympathy cards, this one heavily dusted with the residue of dog treats. "It was shoved under my door, and I don't like that one damn bit, and all the other shit about dog funerals and bloat and all that other crap is goddamn depressing; and then on top of it, half of what was in your brochure has been canceled, or it's just sort of disappeared between the time I sent you a fat check and the time I got here. Like tracking. Tracking's not some kind of an *obscure* thing to do with a dog, and it's in the brochure, and I show up here all ready to get Bingo started tracking, and I've got a tracking lead and tracking harness, and I look over the schedule, and well, well, big surprise! No tracking. And instead of advanced obedience, everyone's lumped together, and the whole idea was that we get to try everything, and everyone's giving me this shit about staying with what I started and *not* moving around; and every time I turn around, someone's yelling at me about scooping up poop, and I have really *had* it! Because I did not pay all this money and drive all this way to spend a week sitting around and cleaning up dog shit!"

With that, Eva stomped through the French doors that led to the dining room.

"Her mother," Maxine remarked placidly, "should've taken one look and culled that one."

Cull. In one sense, every breeder does it: separates out the puppies with obvious faults and problems. In another sense, an ethical breeder does it rarely: immediately destroys those pups, the culls. Any good breeder spares a hopelessly sick puppy the agony of incurable illness or pain, and any good breeder removes the culls from the gene pool. A few breeders still follow what used to be a rather common practice of euthanizing any puppy with a show fault: a malamute with a mismark, an Akita with a coat like Jacob's. Neutered, as Jacob was, he obviously couldn't pass along the undesirable trait to any offspring. What a dog like that could do, though, was to advertise the presence of the trait in his breeder's line, announce to other breeders that so-and-so's dogs produced long coats, and maybe make breeders reluctant to pay hefty stud

fees. I shrugged my shoulders, excused myself, and entered
the dining room.

The unappetizing nature of my preprandial reflections was
probably just as well because spread out on a long buffet table
was what extensive experience in helping out at dog shows
immediately led me to identify as the stewards' lunch—cold
cuts, Swiss cheese, thin slices of pale tomatoes, iceberg lettuce, mayonnaise, primary-yellow mustard, soft bread, and
squishy rolls—as opposed to the officials' lunch—chicken, say,
or roast beef sandwiches—and certainly as opposed to the ex-
alted feast of something like lobster salad or the plate of
something hot and delicious that every judge has the right to
expect. We, however—or *they*, the nonscholarship campers—
had paid judges' prices. I filled my plate. The stewards' lunch
was what I was used to, anyway. What really would have
spoiled it would have been trying to swallow it in the presence
of Eva Spitteler. I glanced around and saw her settling her
wide bottom in a chair next to Eric Grimaldi's at a table in the
far corner of the dining room. Eric was sitting right in the
corner, and Eva had every appearance of intending to keep
him there. As I turned to look for a seat far away from Eva,
Cam White appeared at my side. She murmured, "Wasting
her time. Where are you sitting?"

"Nowhere," I said. "I just got here."

"There's room at our table." Jiggling her plate a little, Cam
said, "This is seconds. Hardly worth it, but I'm hungry, and
it's what there is. Come and sit with us. You don't want
to . . ." She turned her head meaningfully in Eva's direction.

"No, I don't," I agreed. Heeling at Cam's left side, I asked,
"What did you mean?"

"By what?"

"Wasting her time."

"Oh, it's just sort of a joke about Eric. He loves to judge,
and he likes to swim, and he doesn't mind working on his tan,
either. He likes California, Florida, and he isn't exactly above

putting up the worst-looking dog in the world if it just so happens that he puts up the dog, and lo and behold, whoever would have guessed, certainly not Eric, the owners turn out to be Mr. and Mrs. President and Show Chairman of the Surf and Sand Kennel Club, which just so happens to need a Sporting Group judge for the middle of January. I don't know what Eva thinks she's doing, but she doesn't even belong to a club, and she's never going to be in a position to get him any kind of assignment, never mind the kind he likes. So like I said, she's wasting her time."

Newcomer to the fancy? The obvious question: Why didn't Judge Eric Grimaldi just write to offer his services to every kennel club in Florida and California? Easy. Masons are forbidden to recruit members; AKC judges, to solicit assignments. And while we're on the subject, let me report that as Cam and I passed by the table where Don and Phyllis Abbott were seated, Phyllis Abbott caught sight of me and exclaimed, "I just have to tell you that I am so impressed by the work you've done with that dog! He really has excellent attention." Touching her husband's arm, she said, "You really must see this dog. It takes a very special person to train a malamute. You deserve a lot of credit, Holly."

"Thank you," said a prominent member of the Cambridge Dog Training Club, just the kind of person who might help the club to select judges for its trials or, at a minimum, to put in a good word—or possibly a bad word—for a proposed judge, for example, Phyllis Abbott. But then, Rowdy and I *had* worked hard, and as for the bit about being a very special person who deserved a lot of credit, the words made me think of Anna Morelli, a very special person in her own right, but also the breeder, owner, trainer, and handler of Vanderval's Tundra Eagle, CDX, a creature of stunning brilliance and commanding presence, and also, as it happens, not that I want to make a big deal of it or anything, not that I'm laying claim to a share of Tundra's achievements, or Anna Morelli's, either, but. . . . Well, let me just mention in passing, simply as a matter of potential minor interest to canine genealogists, that Tundra and Kimi happen to be first cousins. Make of it what you will. Preferably two UDX's, of course, but if you felt like tossing in a couple of OTCH's, too, I wouldn't exactly object, and neither, I'm sure, would Anna Morelli.

When we reached Cam and Ginny's table, I was a little surprised to find Joy and her G-man look-alike husband, Craig, there, too. "They," Ginny said, apparently referring to Joy and Craig, "have a Cairn, and he's been through basic obedience, and he has a nice temperament, and I'm telling them to go ahead and try the CGC test this afternoon."

Cam carefully set her plate on the table. "Sure," she agreed. "You've got nothing to lose, except whatever it is, eight dollars or something. If he doesn't pass this time, you find out what you have to work on, and you go home and work on it, and then one of these days you give it another try."

"Yes, go ahead," I advised. "Nothing bad's going to happen. It should be fun." I finished layering a lot of cheap cold cuts and a great many paper-thin slices of cheese on the bottom half of a roll that looked soft and felt stale. I piled on tomatoes and near-white lettuce, and, on the theory that if you add enough grease, almost anything tastes good, I spooned on a big glob of mayonnaise. I put on the top half of the roll, pressed it down, lifted the sandwich to my mouth, and bit in. So much for the grease theory. I left the sandwich on my plate.

I watched Craig swallow. In spite of the muscles, he had a prominent Adam's apple. He wiped his lips. "Twenty," he said. "Twenty dollars."

Ginny and I exclaimed in unison, "Twenty dollars?"

"For a CGC test?" Ginny demanded.

"That's out of line," I informed Craig. "In fact, I wonder if . . . Cam, does AKC set guidelines for that? For how much you can charge?"

Too orderly a person to consume a messy salad-on-a-roll, Cam had avoided bread altogether and had arranged her food in as appetizing a fashion as the ingredients allowed. She applied her knife and fork to a slice of olive loaf, paused, shook her head, and said, "No, they don't want to. What they say is, whatever you think is fair."

"Well, twenty dollars isn't very fair," I said.

Cam nodded. "Charging a lot violates the spirit of it."

Joy looked bewildered. "So should we not, uh, put Lucky in?"

Cam, Ginny, and I held a wordless consultation. Cam voiced our conclusion. "Go ahead, if you feel like it."

In apparent search of information about her own feelings, Joy looked timidly at Craig, who told her, "What the heck. It's vacation."

I tried to remember the last time I'd heard a man Craig's age use the word *heck*. It occurred to me that Craig and Joy might be churchgoers and that either he or Joy might find a casually spoken *hell* offensive or blasphemous.

"Are you sure?" Joy's manner induced in me what I believe is called a "clang" association: Joy, coy.

Craig nodded. Joy beamed. "I'd better go get Lucky ready," she said.

"Will you excuse us?" Craig asked.

Cam nodded. When Joy and Craig had left, she said, "Nice people. They deserved a decent dog."

"They didn't know any better." I thought for a second. "I hope nobody tells them how awful-looking the dog is."

"Oh," Ginny said, "Eva Spitteler probably has, you know. That's how she goes through life: saying awful things to people. And about people, too. What do you want to bet that's what she's doing right now? I'll bet you anything she's over there with Eric Grimaldi telling him terrible things about me. I'm getting coffee. You want some?"

"Is there dessert?" Cam asked.

"Rice pudding," Ginny said.

Cam had as little interest in rice pudding as I did, but we both accepted Ginny's offer to bring coffee. When Ginny had departed, I said, "You know, Eva really does go around saying awful things about her."

"Eva says awful things about everyone. It's a miracle that no one's taken that woman to court."

"Ginny could probably sue her for slander," I said. "This morning, after agility? I could *not* get away from Eva, and she went on and on about Bingo and Ginny. What she says—and I had the feeling that she tells this to everyone—is all about how Ginny has too many dogs, and how no one sees her kennels, she doesn't socialize her puppies, that kind of thing."

"Ginny does have too many dogs," Cam said.

"She does?"

"I think so, but then probably she thinks so, too. She keeps her old dogs, and she takes her dogs back, and she ends up keeping an awful lot of them. What is true is that—Look, her third husband was a vet, okay? George. Everyone says he was a lovely man, a prince."

"What did he die of?" I asked.

"Heart attack, I think. Anyway, I guess Ginny got used to not paying vet bills."

"A lot of breeders do their own shots," I said.

"Ginny does a little more than that. And she waits a little longer than I'd wait to have a vet take a look at things. She has, uh, a tendency to cut corners. But Ginny believes in OFA. She OFA's all her dogs. I know she does."

OFA: (noun) Orthopedic Foundation for Animals; (verb) to screen breeding stock for hip dysplasia. Buying a puppy? Oh, no you're not! Not until you've seen the *original* certificates attesting that both parents have cleared either OFA or the University of Pennsylvania's PennHIP. Approximate cost of full hip-replacement surgery: two thousand dollars. Enough said?

"How many litters does Ginny breed a year?"

"One or two. Two maximum. Really, she's a very responsible breeder. For all I know, she's as good as most vets. And there's nothing wrong with her dogs."

"Except maybe Bingo," I couldn't help saying.

Cam eyed me. "Holly," she said, "imagine yourself if you'd been raised by Eva Spitteler."

Fifteen

AT TWO O'CLOCK that afternoon, I was sitting alone at a table in the front window of Doc Grant's restaurant ("Half-way between the Equator and the North Pole") looking across Route 4 at the State Liquor Store and the Pine Tree Frosty, and eating two deep-fried fish fillets, a plateful of fries, and a platter of potato skins topped with melted cheese. The fish had come with tartar sauce, the potato skins with sour cream. To make sure I wasn't left starved for carbohydrates or vulnerable to collapse from a deficiency of dietary fat, the waiter brought a little plate on which sat a roll and two pats of butter. I felt happy. The State of Maine abounds in tourist bistros with names evidently inspired by the quasi-artistic productions of children who've learned their colors and their vegetables, but haven't integrated the two spheres of knowledge: The Purple Carrot, The Red Zucchini. Worse, the portions at those places are tiny, and all the food's steamed over no-salt water by anorectic dietitians from out of state. But Doc Grant's? Maine, the way life should be.

At a table not far from mine sat Everett Dow, the camp

handyman, and a blue-uniformed guy with a silver badge pinned to his left breast. On the chair next to him rested a Stetson hat. A patch on his shoulder read: Police, Rangeley. Everett was halfway through an order of fried clams with french fries accompanied by a roll and butter, a bag of chips, and a side of mashed. The cop wasn't eating anything; he was just drinking coffee. In rural Maine, two o'clock in the afternoon is way too late for lunch, practically suppertime. I wondered whether Everett Dow hated olive loaf as much as I did.

Dissatisfaction with the stewards' lunch was not, however, my excuse for driving into Rangeley; and as for my presence at Doc Grant's, if I'd been forced to justify it, I'd have given the Sir Edmund Hilary explanation except that mine wouldn't have sounded quite so silly as his, Mount Everest having been far away and extremely inconvenient to reach, whereas Doc Grant's was a fifteen-minute drive from camp—and on street level, too. In fact, I'd always suspected that when Hilary said, "Because it's *there*," what he really meant was, "Because it isn't *here*." What impelled him to flee his *here* I don't know. Social entropy, perhaps, order turning to chaos. Maybe he couldn't face learning yet one more thing he preferred not to know. Maybe he was starting to hate his own ugly perceptions of people he wanted to like.

Take Max McGuire, to whom I'd been favorably predisposed for a variety of disparate and perhaps senseless reasons, the most imposing of which, literally and figuratively, was her splendid and pacific mastiff pup, Cash. Halo effect: shining Cash illuminates Maxine; radiant Elsa glorifies Eric. Were Chesapeake Bay retrievers granted judging privileges, Elsa, who loved swimming even more than Eric did, would never have compromised the position to which the AKC had elevated her, but would have picked her winners strictly on the basis of their merits. An honest dog deserves an honest owner. Cash. Max hadn't even chosen the mastiff's name. Even so, it now made me squirm.

"Maxine," Cam had said as we were leaving the dining room, "has an unfortunate tendency to get herself in trouble over money."

"With puppy buyers?" I'd asked. It's easy to do, and I'd been eager to overlook misunderstandings about refundable deposits, stud rights, or complex co-ownership agreements. After all, my editor, Bonnie, vouched for Maxine; the two were old friends. Besides, Max was a real dog person, and if you can't trust your own, you can't trust anyone.

"With everyone," Cam had said. "This CGC thing is typical, charging twenty dollars because the pet people are a captive audience, and they don't know better. But what she doesn't take into account is that they're going to find out because we're going to tell them, and they're not going to like it, and the whole thing's going to backfire. And then this stingy lunch after all the hype about gourmet food. Plus the agility people—"

"What—?"

"The CGC testing's in the agility area, so they have to move all the obstacles out of the way. They have to shift them around all the time, anyway, so the dogs don't just run through the same pattern all the time, but they don't normally have to drag everything out of the way. And those things are heavy! The A-frame weighs a ton, and the dogwalk isn't all that easy to move. But the main thing is that Max has drafted the agility people to serve as evaluators."

Canine Good Citizen test evaluators decide whether the dog passes or fails an exercise. Any reasonable person who knows anything about dogs is allowed to be an evaluator, but the task ordinarily belongs to members of the organization sponsoring the test, people who want to make the event a success. It does not usually fall on employees who would otherwise have had time off.

"Why?" I'd asked. "Why the agility people?"

"That's what they want to know. Apparently, it wasn't part

of their agreement. Maxine just sort of sprang it on them: 'And guess what *else* you get to do!' That kind of thing."

"Surprise! Extra work."

"Yes."

"That's stupid, at least if Maxine wants them back again next year."

"Oh, they won't be back, anyway," Cam had said. "They're opening their own agility camp. Don't mention it. Maxine doesn't know. Anyway, what's sad is that it's all so unnecessary, and as usual, Maxine doesn't have any idea that she's doing anything wrong. About anything. The twenty dollars, any of it. Probably she thinks it's a favor to offer the CGC thing, and I'll bet anything she has some rationale for why it costs so much. It's just like that old business with the club funds."

By persuading Cam that I'd never heard anything about any club funds, I learned another thing I'd have preferred not to know. Years ago, it seemed, when Maxine McGuire had been the treasurer of what I'll call the Unnamed Kennel Club, she'd been in charge of a certain Special Fund established for a certain Good Purpose that I shall not specify except to say that said Good Purpose was clearly not to offer an alarming number of no-interest loans to the club treasurer, loans that she was eventually discovered to have taken out and had somehow neglected to repay. And then? Should you have the misfortune to dwell outside the world of purebred dogs, perhaps you will be astonished to learn that instead of venting their collective outrage by promptly dragging Max into court and kicking her out of the club, the members of the Unnamed K.C. viewed Max's behavior as an unfortunate accident, like a puddle left by a puppy that should never have been allowed full run of the house. Incredible? Not at all. Maxine hadn't harmed a dog or broken an AKC rule. Since she'd done nothing unforgivable, the fancy forgave her. She resigned as treasurer, but she was still one of us. Freemasonry, I suspect, handles such incidents in the same way.

As I was working my way through the first of the fish fillets, Everett Dow and the cop were talking about the Celtics and the Bruins, and also those inevitable Rangeley topics, fishing and hunting. Neither Everett nor his companion said anything about Maxine McGuire or Waggin' Tail. I wondered what Everett made of dog camp. I wished he'd say. About the time I finished the fillet, the men stood up to leave. Everett nodded to me. I smiled and nodded back.

For once, I did not clean my plate. I didn't even come close. My stomach pressed up against my rib cage. I felt disgusted with myself for ordering a lumberjack's lunch and equally disgusted with myself for leaving most of it. I paid my bill. I left a big tip. I think I must have been trying to persuade the waiter that despite my wastefulness, I was a decent human being.

When I left Doc Grant's, the sky was the deep slate of an old New England gravestone, the kind that's carved with a death's head and a no-nonsense message about earth and bones, and the recurrent warning, as if the buried dead forever spoke:

> Stranger stop as you pass by
> As you are now, so once was I,
> As I am now, so you shall be
> Prepare for death, and follow me.

I scanned the cloud cover for the shape of a skull or an hourglass or maybe the figure of a scythe-wielding Father Time. I wondered whether I might be getting my period. It occurred to me that some of those unknown Colonial tombstone carvers might have been women with PMS or men with an extraordinary capacity for empathy.

I'd left Rowdy in the Bronco, which was illegally parked in the deep shade under the pine trees by the State Liquor Store. The windows were rolled down enough to give him air, the

temperature had dropped about fifteen degrees since the heat
of the morning, and he had a bowl of water. Even so, I crossed
Route 4 to check on him. Universal dilemma of the real dog
person: You leave the dog home, you worry that something
will happen to him while you're out. You take the dog with
you, you worry that something will happen to him while he's
alone in the car. You roll the windows down a little, you worry
that he won't get enough air. You roll the windows down a lot,
you worry that he'll somehow get out or that someone will
steal him out of his crate. The solution, of course, is to keep
the dog at your side twenty-four hours a day every day, but
then you worry that your constant presence is making the dog
neurotically dependent, and besides, you can't go anyplace
that doesn't allow dogs, so you can't go to work or get your
hair cut or go to the dentist. And then, of course, you feel
guilty because, after all, doesn't your wonderful dog deserve a
better owner than this poverty-stricken, shaggy-headed slob
with decayed teeth? Meanwhile, the dog doesn't worry about
anything. Why should he? That's what he has you for, and for
obvious reasons, he trusts you completely.

Rowdy was fine, if a little disappointed that I didn't immediately let him out of the car, but merely glanced at him and
headed for the Pine Tree Frosty, a dog-memorable establish-
ment that Rowdy had apparently failed to remember from
previous trips to Rangeley. Or maybe he did remember it. He
probably did. How could any dog forget the Fido Special?
Cherry ice cream garnished with dog biscuits. Maine: The
way life should be. Actually, I didn't know what had inspired
the Fido Special—maybe a beloved pet of the owner, maybe
the sled dogs that visited Rangeley for the annual race, maybe
the hunting dogs there for bird season.

Fido Special in hand, I returned to the Bronco and, to avoid
having the interior splashed with ice cream and dog slobber,
led Rowdy to the picnic area at the rear of the Pine Tree
Frosty, a collection of tables and benches on the edge of

Haley's Pond. Habitually fed bits of hot dog and hamburger roll, dozens of mallards clustered around, and as soon as Rowdy had finished his treat, he took a lively interest in them as a possible second dessert. Seated on a bench licking a chocolate ice-cream cone, Everett Dow also watched the ducks and perhaps entertained thoughts similar to Rowdy's. The reflected light of the pond revealed Everett as weirdly old and young. The lines and hollows in his face looked peculiar without the age spots that should have accompanied them, and the hand wrapped around the ice-cream cone lacked the gnarls of age. Even at the temples, his hair showed no gray, and the light-colored stubble on his cheeks was blond, not silver. With a start, I realized that he couldn't be much older than I was. I wondered whether I was seeing the aging effect of poverty or perhaps the impact of a long illness. I felt the impulse to approach him. On my way into Rangeley, I'd thought about getting a present for Steve, salmon flies or, better yet, material for fly-tying or, best of all, if I could afford it, the kind of beautifully carved duck decoy meant to attract aesthetically-minded human collectors rather than feathered prey. If anyone in Rangeley made or sold those decoys, Everett would certainly know.

I was on the verge of stepping toward him to ask when Eva Spitteler, who wore a boldly lettered Waggin' Tail T-shirt, suddenly stomped up to me to demand whether something unspecified wasn't a violation of the health code. Before I could ask what she meant, she announced that Rangeley probably didn't have a health code, anyway. "Jesus," she hollered, "the original Podunk, U.S.A. Wouldn't you've thought Max could do better than this shithole?"

I prayed that the flat waters of Haley's Pond would miraculously rise in rage and gather themselves into a tidal wave that would wash Eva Spitteler from their shores. Alternatively, the mallards could be struck by a sudden Hitchcockian frenzy and leap out of the pond and onto Eva and peck her to death.

Miracles failing to materialize, however, I wished that the ducks would at least quack raucously enough to drown out Eva's horrible voice. *Max couldn't have done better than this,* I wanted to say, *because Rangeley is as good as it gets; there is no better.* All I actually uttered was an inadequate mumble to the effect that I'd always liked Rangeley.

Instead of licking her ice-cream cone, Eva took an aggressive bite that left big tooth marks. The ice cream was peppermint stick, I think, or maybe strawberry or the same cherry that Rowdy had just enjoyed; at any rate, it was something pink with reddish striations. Her bite mark resembled an illustration of what a shark's teeth can do to human flesh.

If I'd been the brave and loyal person that my dogs imagine me to be, I'd have jumped onto one of the picnic tables and belted out an oratorically elaborate, rhetorically embellished tribute to the Town of Rangeley. Failing that, I'd have gone from bench to bench, picnic table to picnic table, to apologize for Eva Spitteler's rudeness and to explain that she wasn't really a dog person at all, but an embarrassment to every one of us, as unwelcome in our midst as she was in theirs. But I'm a coward. Also, I'm slow-witted.

Rowdy, however, is brave and quick. As I was trying to think of a way to make an immediate escape, he glanced from Eva to me. His rib cage began to contract, the telltale smile appeared on his face, and in a heroic act of self-sacrifice, he swiftly deposited the Fido Special on Eva's sandal-shod feet.

Sixteen

DOG OBEDIENCE drill team belongs to the happy class of cultural entities that demarcate the boundaries of the serious by deliberately crossing far, far beyond them. To apply ordinary standards of decorum, restraint, or simple good taste to these usefully ludicrous activities and objects is thus to strip them of their essential function. As the plots of grand opera mock the despair of high tragedy, as the confectionary bride and groom atop a wedding cake deride the solemnity of marriage, as Halloween costumes laugh at death itself, so does marching around with dogs to the strains of John Phillip Sousa ridicule the partnership between us and our animals and thereby define the holiness of the bond.

Now that I've stifled the hoots of Cambridge with that richly Cantabrigian rationalization, let me explain that at Waggin' Tail, drill team took place in the middle of the big field behind the main lodge, in fact, between the lodge and obedience tent, and was taught by a jolly-looking, round-faced woman named Janet, who started the activity promptly at three-thirty by lining us up according to the sizes of our dogs. Stepping back now and then to see how we looked, Janet efficiently arranged us in a long, straight line of thirty-five or so dog-handler pairs, with the toy breeds in the center, a Great Dane bitch at one end, a Newfoundland the other, large breeds next to them, then medium, then small. So meticulous was Janet in assuring that dog height steadily ascended from the center of the line to the ends that I felt almost apologetic about the ups and downs of human heads, as if all of us should have anticipated the aesthetic demands of drill team by selecting dogs according to our own proportions, giant dogs for lofty people, toys for the tiny.

Even if the rest of us had chosen our breeds with a good drill-team topline in mind, Phyllis Abbott would've thrown it off, but in all other respects, she was an asset, and so was little Nigel. Edwina, who'd had the unhappy encounter with the scent articles, was a good-looking bitch and an excellent obedience dog, but Nigel was flashier than Edwina, a sturdy, sparkling fellow with a naturally fabulous, beautifully nurtured coat in a shade of red remarkably like that of Phyllis's hair. Yes! The ovogallinaceous puzzler in cynogynic form: Which came first, the dog or the tint? In either case, the well-matched, soigné pair were a credit to obedience, exactly the kinds of ambassadors we need to dispel our image as the Order of Slobs of The Fancy.

Also, once Janet began directing us, it became evident that Mrs. Abbott knew what she was doing. We started without music. On signal, Mrs. Abbott heeled Nigel forward. Head high, shoulders back, she had a dancer's carriage. When she'd taken about four steps, the teams to her left and right moved forward; and then four paces later, the next two teams, and so on until we were spread out in V-formation, like Canada geese. Reaching the end of the field, our leaders, Phyllis and Nigel, made an about-turn, came to a halt, and waited until, two by two, the other teams executed the same maneuver and thus re-formed a straight line. After that, with Phyllis leading, we again distributed ourselves across the field and performed what in my mind became a rather bewildering series of halts, turns, and forwards, at the conclusion of which we somehow found ourselves back in what had now become a ragged line that eventually straightened out and attempted to rotate itself. Pivoting in place, Phyllis and Nigel acted as a pin that held our center firm, but I'm afraid that those of us at the outer edges created such a straggly effect that, viewed from above, our supposedly precise line must have looked like the melting hands of a Dali clock. I tried my best to do everything at once, but everything proved more than I could manage. I'd take big, fast steps to move us even with the man and the Great Dane bitch at our left, and having positioned us in line with them, I'd discover that we'd forged far ahead of the woman and the big mix-breed to our right. Simultaneously listening to Janet's booming instructions and slowing down to put us even with that team, I'd glance to the far end of the line to discover that our supposedly opposite numbers, Michael and Jacob, weren't actually opposite us at all. Adjusting my pace to make us match Michael and Jacob, I'd lose track of Rowdy, and while bringing him back to heel position, I'd take my eye off the Great Dane, and when I looked toward her again, she'd somehow have ended up way, way behind us. So I'd slow down, thus throwing off the team to our right. And thus it went until, after a great deal of backing up and stepping forward, we ended up exactly where we'd begun, the handlers a little dizzy and out of breath, but so ferociously proud of our performance that we burst into cheers, released our dogs, rubbed their chests, and thus sent them into the leaping, yelping equivalent of our own self-applause.

The second time, we did almost as badly as we'd done the first and congratulated ourselves just as wildly. Thereafter, we became, if not precise, at least a little less sloppy than we'd been. Lost in play, I lost track of time and was amazed when Janet announced the end of drill team by telling us what a great group we were. Tomorrow, Janet promised, we'd add music.

In the past hour, shaded by the darkening clouds and cooled by a sudden steady breeze from the lake, the field had changed seasons from late summer to early autumn. Bare-armed, I needed the sweatshirt I'd left with Rowdy's canvas travel bag; and especially with flyball due to begin almost immediately in the same field, Rowdy needed a drink and a little walk. As I crossed the grass toward the area by the blacktop where most of us had piled our gear and where a crowd had gathered to wait for flyball, I caught up with Phyllis Abbott, who exclaimed, "Now that's what it's all about, isn't it? Fun with your dog!" She repeated, as if reminding herself, "That's what it's all about."

"It sure is," I agreed. When we reached the pile of our belongings, I pulled on a dark green sweatshirt that showed a picture of an adorable malamute of four or five weeks. Above his head was a query addressed to breeders about whether they knew where their puppies were; below, an admonition to support rescue.

"Oh, I *like* that!" Mrs. Abbott said.

Only a few years earlier, I'd sometimes had to explain to disappointed members of the general public that Malamute Rescue does not mean training the breed to sniff out earthquake victims; our dogs have been rescued, and any heroic acts they may subsequently perform are strictly incidental. Far from confusing our dogs with the Search and Rescue variety, a few members of the fancy had seen them as the likely perpetrators of disaster scenes: slavering beasts, their mad eyes fixed on the jugulars of young children. Then all of a sudden, the dog fancy discovered the breed rescue movement and abruptly declared us politically correct. The AKC's stamp of approval hadn't yet paid any vet bills, but cachet was a start. Maybe cash would follow. I wondered whether Phyllis Abbott had ever taken a Pomeranian from a shelter or trained a wild-acting stray to become a civilized pet. When she and Don Abbott were with their AKC friends, did she raise the issue of puppy mills? Or did her support of rescue consist of saying nice things about other people's sweatshirts?

Quite a few people were letting their dogs drink out of a communal water bucket, but I filled Rowdy's own little travel bowl from his own water bottle. When he'd slurped up three or four bowlfuls, I replaced his training collar and leash with his retractable lead, which, I might add, I had examined minutely without discovering any signs of tampering. After taking Rowdy to the edge of the woods for what dogdom persists in calling a bathroom trip, I led him to the big crowd that had gathered for flyball, a sport I'd watched before, but one that neither Rowdy nor I had ever tried. Janet, our drill team instructor, and two other women had set up three flyball boxes, each about the size of a big milk box. Lines of handlers and dogs were already queuing up. The line on the far left was obviously where Rowdy and I didn't belong. Rowdy could easily have cleared the series of low jumps in front of the professional-looking flyball box, but unlike the bouncing, yelping off-lead dogs in that line, he wouldn't have known what to do once he got to the contraption. Should you be as inexperienced as Rowdy was, let me explain that when the dog whacks the front of the box—or in the primitive versions of the apparatus, a pedal at the front—the contraption releases a tennis ball that the dog is supposed to catch. An advanced dog dashes over the jumps, hits the box with his paw, catches the ball, and goes back over the jumps. In flyball tournaments, teams of dogs compete in what are, in effect, relay races. Competitive flyball is simple and fast, beautiful to watch, the basketball of canine sports.

Mainly because Eva Spitteler and Bingo were last in line at the middle flyball box, I led Rowdy to the line at the right. Directly ahead of us were Phyllis Abbott and her male Pomeranian, Nigel; and in front of them, Joy and Lucky. For once, the little quasi-Cairn was standing on his own four feet. Looking bare-chested without the dog clutched to her breast, Joy was engaged in animated conversation with Phyllis Abbott.

I caught the end of something Joy was saying: ". . . from a pet shop. I didn't know any better at the time, and he *is*—"

"Every dog comes from somewhere!" Phyllis interrupted, "and that doesn't mean you love him any less." She paused. "Does it?"

"Of course not!" Joy replied. "It's just that—"

"They don't all have to be show dogs," Phyllis pronounced. "And Lucky has a very sweet face." For that moment, so did Phyllis.

Warmed by Phyllis's praise, Joy made what sounded like a confidence. "And he, uh, he just passed his Canine Good Citizen test."

Considerate obedience judge that she was, Phyllis projected her voice: "Congratulations! That's very special. I hope you're proud of yourself and proud of your dog." What bothered me, I suppose, was a brittle note that made me wonder whether Phyllis's kindness to Joy represented a triumph over some hidden sense of her own fragility.

"Well, all the dogs passed," Joy admitted. "They did the second time." Her pink face reddened. "The first time, they all . . . But then Maxine decided there was something wrong." Regaining her composure, she speeded up. "And so Maxine decided that it wasn't very fair, even though that's what the rules said, strictly speaking, but Maxine decided that's not what the rules really *meant*, because they meant, because what they meant was, uh, a dog you would like to own, really, a dog that *is* a good citizen. And so we all got to do anything we'd failed all over again! And that time, Lucky passed!"

Phyllis Abbott looked as astonished as I felt. The guidelines for the CGC Program are very flexible. The AKC does not, however, even begin to condone the practice of passing all dogs by giving them extra chances at exercises they've failed.

"Really," Joy added, "it *was* fair, because all of them really *are* good dogs."

Phyllis bent down and needlessly fiddled with Nigel's collar. As an obedience judge, Phyllis Abbott was not charged with policing CGC tests. Even so, as my column-in-progress had begun to point out, judges represent the AKC itself and the entire sport of dogs. If Maxine McGuire wanted to keep her campers happy by declaring all "good dogs," whatever that meant, Canine Good Citizens, Phyllis Abbott didn't want to hear about it. When Phyllis stood up, I caught her eye and said, "The dogs at camp are a lot better behaved than the average dog, and the owners are responsible, or they wouldn't be here. And there's probably a lot of self-selection. People probably wouldn't have paid the twenty dollars unless they were fairly sure that their dogs would pass."

"You want to see Lucky's ribbon?" Joy asked. "Craig! Craig! Where's Lucky's ribbon?"

A Nikon dangling from a strap around his neck, Craig was seated on the rough grass, ready, I assumed, to take a picture of Lucky enjoying flyball. Beckoned by his wife, he reached into the pocket of what looked like a government-issue tan windbreaker and produced a green ribbon.

Joy motioned to Craig to bring it to her. Up close, the dark green satiny strip of fabric looked all too familiar. AKC rules about ribbons, prizes, and trophies are clear and rigid. In conformation, dark green means a special prize; in obedience, it's the color of the ribbon awarded to every dog that qualifies. Groups sponsoring CGC tests were, I knew, allowed to give ribbons to dogs that passed. I was quite sure, however, that dark green was not a permissible color, and I was positive that CGC ribbons were not supposed to display the seal of the American Kennel Club. But there it was, smack in the center of the ribbon: three concentric circles, the words *American*

Kennel Club curving around the top of the outer circle, a star fore and aft, the word *Incorporated* underneath; then the circle of little dots; and within the solid inner circle—some mystical significance there, perhaps?—the letters *A K C.* No big deal? Wrong. *Imprimatur:* Let it be printed, the statement at the beginning of books approved by the Roman Catholic Church. Well, the AKC seal is the imprimatur of the fancy, and the AKC is about as happy to see it used without permission as the Pope would be to have the Church's imprimatur casually placed on the masthead of every issue of *Dog's Life*, not that there's anything sacrilegious about *Dog's Life*—for all I know, the Pope may even subscribe—any more than there's anything objectionable about CGC tests. But just as the Pope can't check out every issue of *Dog's Life* before it's published, the AKC can't send a rep to every CGC test; therefore, no imprimatur and no AKC seal.

Appropriately enough, Phyllis Abbott rolled her eyes toward heaven—or maybe toward 51 Madison Avenue. With admirable grace, she murmured, for my ears only, "I am *not* seeing that." She cleared her throat. "I am not looking."

I complied with what I understood as Judge Abbott's request. "Very nice," I told Joy. I pointed out that she was next in line. Taking the green ribbon from his wife, Craig hurried away, hunkered down a few yards from the flyball box, and raised the camera to his eye. The flyball instructor in charge of our group—Betsy, her name was, a wiry woman with weathered skin and deep laugh lines—loaded the apparatus with a tennis ball. With Betsy's help, Joy succeeded in getting Lucky to put his paws on the pedal, but each time the tennis ball flew through the air, the little fellow acted more startled than pleased. At the flyball box to our left, the one manned by Janet, our drill team instructor, Elsa the Chesapeake leaped after a ball, and Eric Grimaldi gave a shout of pleasure. "Good girl, Elsa! Good girl!"

"Let her keep it," Janet advised him. "It's her prize. For now, just let her keep it."

Prancing at the end of her lead, the triumphant Elsa, her catch in her mouth, led Eric to the end of the line. They wouldn't have long to wait. Mainly because of Eva Spitteler's presence, I suspected, their group was small.

While I'd been watching Elsa and preventing Rowdy from finding out whether she'd share that tennis ball with him, Phyllis and Nigel had taken their turn, with what success I don't know.

"And now the malamute!" Betsy called. "Let's see what the malamute can do! What his name? Rowdy? Bring Rowdy up here. All you want to do for right now is get him to get those big paws down here." She pointed to the carpeted pedal that ran across the front of the box. "Can you get him to jump? Bounce around? All we're after now is just getting him to hit it by accident."

Persuading a malamute to clown around isn't exactly difficult. With the big plastic handle of the retractable lead in one hand, I had a little trouble clapping my hands, but my effort, in combination with a lot of excited chitchat, got Rowdy going, and within a few seconds, his forepaws had landed on the pedal and sent a ball flying out of the back of the machine. Clowning around is a virtually universal passion in the breed; retrieving isn't. With Rowdy and Kimi, I'd lucked out. Besides, a lifetime with golden retrievers had trained me to expect demonic fetching from all dogs, and, in part, Rowdy and Kimi had done what I'd expected. When the tennis ball flew, Rowdy took a second to notice it, but then zoomed after it. After a late start, he failed to catch it in midair, but happily snapped it up as it rolled across the grass. When I led Rowdy back to the flyball box and made a big happy fuss that caused him accidentally to whack the pedal, he caught the ball before it hit the ground. Our turn was up. Like Elsa, Rowdy kept the ball he'd caught, and like her, he paraded back to the end of our queue with his prize in his jaws.

As it happens, I have a photograph taken at the exact moment that Rowdy and I took our place at the end of the line. Craig, who took the picture, must have stepped far back to snap it. On the right, Betsy is loading the arm of the flyball box with a tennis ball. Jacob, first in line, is peering at Michael, who is pointing at the box. Michael's mouth is open; he is talking to his dog, trying to entice Jacob toward the pedal. Some of the handlers in back of them are people I remember. Mary wears a cobalt blue Waggin' Tail sweatshirt; Carole, a red anorak. The husband and wife with the English setters are there, the dogs even more handsome in the photograph than in my memory. Baskerville is yawning. Joy has on a fuzzy pink jacket, and adorning her blond curls is a matching pink bow suitable for a child. She kneels down, one arm around Lucky, her hand under the dog's chin to tilt it toward the camera. She is posing; the odd smile on her half-open mouth suggests that Craig may have caught her as she was uttering *cheese* or *pickles* or one of those other words superstitiously believed to confer temporary photogenicity on the pronouncer. Joy does not, however, need to order lunch to look lovely; in the eye of the lens, Craig's eye, she radiates a bride's beauty. Phyllis Abbott's face is turned away, and Joy's body completely blocks the camera's view of Nigel. At the end of the line, at the extreme left of the picture, I am grinning foolishly at Rowdy, who has noticed the camera. Oblivious to the unfortunate state of his coat, he has spontaneously stacked himself for the show ring. As if to brag of his recent accomplishment, he holds his head high and prominently displays the tennis ball in his mouth. My hair looks even worse than Rowdy's coat. His display of pride is unabashed, deliberate. Mine is unintended and entirely unself-conscious. Indeed, I am conscious only of Rowdy and of a thought that is crossing my mind—an unusual thought to cross the mind of any writer, I might add—the thought that—wow!—my editor was right. Bonnie's prediction was merely that and not a calculated injunction after all: I do love camp. And Rowdy loves it even more than I do. We are happy. We miss what the camera saw. Toward the right of the photograph, in the background, a big-boned yellow Lab leaps for a ball.

But the camera does not see all. Or does it? In the picture, Bingo seems to be off lead. He was not. But he might as well have been. A Labrador retriever, young and healthy, if rather beefy, went hard after the ball. And then? I am forced to reconstruct. Eager to let Bingo follow the ball, Eva let him pull out the cord of the retractable lead. Too unfit or too lazy to keep up with her athletic dog, she remained where she was as the cord fed out. By the time I looked, Bingo was twenty feet away from her. At that point, I think, Eva finally pressed the trigger on the plastic handle and hit the little gadget that locks the retracting mechanism in place. His lead suddenly tight, Bingo gave a jolt, then a lunge that tore the handle out of Eva's hands. With its mechanism locked to prevent the cord from retracting, the whole device, handle and twenty feet of thin cord, dragged after Bingo as he began what he must have meant as a game of catch-me-if-you-can. Glancing back at Eva, the tennis ball still in his mouth, he sped headlong and unseeing toward the line of experienced flyball dogs. That he collided with another Lab, Wiz, and with his own breeder, Ginny Garabedian, was a simple accident. Bingo, I am convinced, never intended to knock Ginny to the ground. But mounting Wiz was no accident. Although a gentle, docile creature, the chocolate Lab was nonetheless a female not in season and thus a lady unconditionally unreceptive to the amorous advances of any male. Besides, poor Wiz was terrified. Much smaller than Bingo, unexpectedly jumped, Wiz did her best to fight him off. Clambering to her feet, her face smeared with dirt, Ginny drew on the strength conferred by decades of training, handling, showing, breeding, and just plain bossing around Labrador retrievers. By then, I'd joined the crowd that surrounded the melee. Like almost everyone else who witnessed Ginny's rescue of Wiz, I had the impression that her principal weapon was a tone of voice that brooked no argument. When the crowd around her cleared, Ginny had Bingo sitting really quite nicely at her left side. Having somehow caught hold of the plastic handle of his lead, she held it firmly, the cord now shortened to a few feet. On what looked like a reliable down-stay a yard or so away, Wiz eyed Ginny with well-earned trust.

Making her way through the curious handlers and excited dogs, Eva Spitteler approached Ginny. She reached out for Bingo's lead.

"Sorry about that," Eva blithely told Ginny. "But Bingo just *loves* the girls."

Seventeen

ONE LEAN ELBOW cocked on the bar, Ginny Garabedian spoke firmly: "A Bombay martini straight up with a twist of peel." The spinsterish braid coiled around her head suggested the occasional indulgence in a drop of sweet sherry as a daring alternative to tea. A real bartender wouldn't have blinked. This fellow gaped. I hoped that he stayed away from high-stakes poker.

Impatient, Ginny demanded, "You *do* have Bombay gin?"

"I think so," the bartender stammered. Recovering, he offered to check. I wanted to inform him that Ginny had outlived five husbands.

"Please do that," Ginny said. "If not, Beefeater's will do. And that's *straight up* with a *twist.*"

I ordered a drink I didn't want, a Johnnie Walker Black on the rocks. I wondered why I'd done it. Rita, my therapist friend and tenant, owns so many books that I sometimes wonder how her floor and my ceiling support them. In Cambridge, though, owning a trillion pounds of books is so typical that the building code probably has some special provision designed to protect the citizenry from what would otherwise be daily episodes of lower-floor dwellers being buried like avalanche victims under the descending libraries of their up-stairs neighbors. Anyway, I haven't read many of Rita's books, but sometimes their titles stick with me. The one I thought of was called *The Group Mind.* Maybe it dealt with this compul-sion to order Scotch when all I wanted was a glass of red wine.

When the drinks arrived, we carried them to a little table in a corner of what the resort billed as "The Pub," a room off the big main hall furnished with rustic-looking Rangeley-style furniture, tables and chairs made of white birch with the peel-ing bark left on. As Ginny set her glass on our table, she said, "I hardly ever drink martinis, but I am so mad I could spit." Without so much as a *cheers,* she took a greedy sip, licked her lips, and forcibly exhaled. "Harry had Saint Bernards. He never put barrels around their necks, naturally, but if he had, this is what would've been in them. That's why my kennels are so big, because a lot of them, Harry built for his dogs."

I'd never seen Ginny with any breed but a Lab. After Harry's death, what had she done with the Saint Bernards that had failed to tote Bombay gin? I didn't ask. I tasted my John-nie Walker. One real slug and I'd be asking Ginny how many litters she bred a year and whether she ever permitted visitors to see the kennels where Harry's Saints had trod.

Before I had a chance to ask anything, Ginny transferred her glass to her left hand, made a tight little fist with her right, and punched the air. "Eva Spitteler is not allowed to breed that dog without my written permission. It's right there in my contract."

Reputable breeders have what always strikes me as a touch-ing faith in the power of signed contracts to regulate the be-havior of puppy buyers. Breeders rewrite those contracts, add new clauses, and explain all the provisions to all their puppy buyers. According to the typical contract, the buyer promises to take great care of the dog, swears to get the breeder's permission before breeding the dog, or, in the case of pet-quality puppies, promises to have the pup spayed or neutered. If the owner ever decides to get rid of the dog, the animal returns to the breeder. A few breeders add special requirements: The dog lives in the house, and once a week, he has a bath and gets his nails trimmed. The hitch? Envision the diligent breeder who, in the course of her weekly visits to the homes of every puppy she's ever sold, is shocked to discover that whereas all her other buyers have been following her contract to the letter, young Fido's owners have reneged on the promise to trim his nails and, indeed, report themselves unable to wield the trimmers themselves and unwilling to pay a groomer to do so. Can you hear it in court? Moral: A contract is no better than the breeder's ability to monitor and enforce it. So what's a breeder to do? About nail trimming, nothing. About breeding?

I spoke hesitantly. "You didn't think about limited registration?" A limited registration wouldn't have prevented Bingo from pouncing on bitches, but in making his offspring ineligible for AKC registration, it would sure have neutered Eva's breeding plans.

"Well, of course, now I wish I had, but I have . . . had, I should say . . . Well, I still have a hard time shaking the idea that when you buy a dog, you *buy* him. And I know. Limited registration doesn't change that. But I've just never done it that way." Liquor and anger, which should have aged Ginny, had had the reverse effect: Her eyes were clear, her expression unguarded, her face fresh.

"Ginny, you ever thought about trying to buy Bingo back?"

Ginny drained her glass and ordered another martini. "Let me count the ways. I started offering half the purchase price. Then the full purchase price. After this mess at flyball, I even said I'd give her double."

"And?"

"And I will not repeat what she said. Obscenity is one thing that has no place in dogs." Unspoken words formed on Ginny's lips. When she spoke again, she said, "You know, Holly, that was a lovely, lovely puppy. It makes me sick to see him so fat, and I know he's not getting any exercise—look at him! And it would be bad enough if she left him home, but every time she takes him anywhere, I feel like crawling into the ground. *You* know what it's like! Eva lets him get away with murder, and then all everyone says is, well, he came from *my* breeding. Have you ever seen one of my dogs act like that?"

"Never," I said. "But you're right. People are going to say that. They always do. Instead of always asking 'Where did he come from?' they ought to stop and think about where he went and what's happened to him. They should, but they hardly ever do." And that's the truth. The only people in this country who take even more unfair blame than mothers do are diligent, ethical, hardworking breeders of purebred dogs.

I was saying as much to Ginny as we left The Pub and entered the main hall, where hungry campers were filing into the dining room. Stuck in the bottleneck, I glanced at the bulletin board, still propped on its easel. Prominently displayed at the top was a copy of Waggin' Tail's release and waiver of liability. In the ones mailed to us, however, the sentences about Maxine's right to expel a camper for almost any reason had not been highlighted in bright yellow. The board had another change. The announcement of CGC testing had been replaced by a big red-lettered list of the new Canine Good Citizens and their presumably proud owners.

Stepping up behind me, Heather, our Chief Fecal Inspector, murmured, "What bullshit! Passed! *Bought* it is more like it."

As the line moved, Heather expanded on the topic by citing examples of dogs that finished their AKC championships because their owners hired professional handlers and entered the dogs hundreds of times, if necessary, until the judges got so sick of looking at the same awful dogs that they put them up just so they'd never have to see them again. As I was about to pipe up in defense of judges, Eva Spitteler came barging up, shoved ahead of me, and accosted Ginny with, of all things, the suggestion that they sit together at dinner.

"Miss Social Skills," I whispered to Heather, who grimaced. At a normal pitch, I said, "Look, I agree that titles shouldn't be up for sale, and, yes, there are a few people who abuse the system—"

Before I could finish, Eva butted in. "A few? The whole thing stinks. Hey, Holly, you ever thought about writing about that business with fixing gay tails? Because if you ever want to do it, I can tell you—"

As I've admitted, my Danny had a gay tail, one that's carried above the horizontal, a position that's fine in some breeds, faulty in others. The malamute's glorious over-the-back plume could, I suppose, be considered the ultimate in canine caudal gaiety, but the dog person who says "gay tail" is usually talking about a golden retriever or maybe a Chesapeake with a tail carried too high for the breed standard. As published exposés had reported, a few sleazeball professional handlers would perform surgical butchery to correct the fault; and according to widely-circulated rumors, so would a few AKC judges. They'd do it for less than a vet would charge, and they'd leave no written record, of course. Anesthesia? Hey, forget it. After all, these are just dogs we're talking about, right? Show dogs, which is to say, objects brought into this world to do one and only one thing, and that's win, win, win.

"People have written about that before," I told Eva. "I've heard rumors—so has everyone else—but you can't publish rumors."

Eva leaned so close to my ear that for a crazy second, I thought she meant to kiss me. "Eric Grimaldi," she whispered. "Eric Grimaldi."

Almost like a vision, Elsa's image appeared to me, the joy in her eyes, the beautiful head, the deep chest, the powerful shoulders and hindquarters, the whole put-together look of a very typey bitch, and that ultra-Chesapeake expression that always seems to me to indicate an exceedingly high and perfectly justified regard for the intelligence and judgment of the Chesapeake Bay retriever and a correspondingly low opinion of everyone else's. Oh, and Elsa's tail, too. Elsa's correct Chesapeake tail.

"Eva," I said, "I've been in dogs my whole life. And one of the things I've learned is that if you listen long enough, sooner or later you're going to hear everything about everyone, including yourself."

I must have spoken more loudly than I'd intended. Myrna, the raucous New Yorker who'd been at my table the night before, caught my words. "You can say that again," she boomed. "Half of what you hear from some of these people," she added, glaring in Eva's direction, "half of it, you gotta take with a grain of salt."

Yes, I thought. *But which half?*

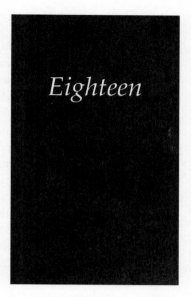

Eighteen

THE MASONIC SHTICK is no joke. Take blackballing. As I understand it—maybe I'm wrong—in Freemasonry, *blackball* is no figure of speech. If you want someone in, you cast a white ball; if not, black. That's *cast* as in *cast a ballot*, or so I assume. As far as I know, in casting their secret votes, the members just slip table tennis balls, white or black, into some sort of container, probably something more or less like a flyball box stripped of the pedal and the resulting ball toss, of course. Unless I've been seriously misinformed, the poor applicant doesn't have to sit on some specially designated ceremonial seat in the middle of the temple and get pelted, pro or con, by member after member of the entire elected assembly. All secret societies play games of one kind or another, but the exclusion-inclusion game is inevitably more complicated than either Ping-Pong or flyball.

As I look back, though, I realize that if we'd wanted to find a considerate way to deny Eva's bid for admission, we might as well have placed her on a hard-backed chair in the center of the dining room and taken turns slinging scraps of rejected food in her bulldog face. Would I have participated? Certainly not. Neither would any of the rest of us. Or so I like to suppose. I want to think that we were and are civilized, and I persist in believing that what characterizes civilization is something other than the refinement of cruelty.

As it was, I cast my vote quite discreetly. When Eva reached into the pocket of her mud-colored, grass-stained jacket, produced a brochure for her kennel-supply and dog-training enterprise, and thrust it at me, I did accept the thing. Before shoving it in my own pocket, I even gave it a cursory look. Perhaps I shouldn't have. The name of her business infuriated me. "High In Tail," she called it. If you're active in obedience, you'll understand why I thought then and still think that "High In Tail" was a shameless rip-off. If you're not? Because High In Trial, *T-r-i-a-l*, is a well-established, well-known, reputable, and otherwise altogether estimable mail-order supplier of leather leads, dumbbells, scent articles, practice jumps, harnesses, and other goodies used in obedience, herding, tracking, Schutzhund, and plain old having fun with your dog. If I'd shown any sense, I'd have realized that the people at High In Trial were capable of looking after themselves; they didn't need any help from me. It might also have occurred to me that even a language as rich, diverse, and wondrous as that of my own community offered only a limited number of word plays and catchy phrases that might suitably be dogtrotted out into the dog-eat-dog free-market economy of canine commercial enterprise. In brief, had I paws'd to reflect—see what I mean?—I'd have kept my mouth shut.

But this is a story about how things were, not about how they should have been. In what was probably a nasty tone of voice, I said, "High in Tail? You're not calling the *catalog* that, are you?"

"It's my name," Eva said. "It's what I use."

"Well, I don't think that's very fair to High In Trial."

"My catalog's not like theirs. It's nothing like theirs. They aren't going to mind. You'll see. I've got a lot of good stuff lined up. New. Not like what everyone else has." After that, Eva tried to worm my address out of me. It seemed to me that she almost tried to buy it. Her exact words were: *Ten percent off for my friends.* So I told her that she could send me anything she wanted in care of *Dog's Life.* As I didn't tell her, I failed to understand why she'd want to bother, because there were scads of kennel supply and dog training businesses all over the country, and the existence of hers wasn't going to merit so much as a sentence in my column. I want to admit, though, that my response was petty. Stupid, too. If you're in dogs, your address is no secret. Whenever you enter your dog in a show, your name and address appear at the back of the show catalog. Furthermore, dog people are dedicated joiners. I, for example, belonged not only to a great many clubs in which I had an obvious personal interest—my obedience clubs, our national breed club, the Dog Writers' Association of America, the Alaskan Malamute Protection League—but to numerous others, including two organizations for fanciers of breeds I'd never even owned . . . or not yet, anyway. Dog sources failing her, Eva could have looked me up in the Cambridge phone directory. But would I *give* her my home address? No. So you see? A forkful of pot roast or a lump of lobster in her face might have been a kinder blackball than the one I hurled.

That was the choice, supposedly, anyway. Some choice, pot roast or lobster Newburg, except that whereas everything else was self-serve, the lobster, if you could call it that, was doled out onto toast triangles by an unfortunate and probably generous-hearted young fellow stationed behind an industrial-size chafing dish containing liquified cheese so free of *trayf* that a Hasidic rabbi could have lapped it up in good conscience.

The Orthodoxy of the dish did, however, enable me to escape from Eva Spitteler, who lingered in fierce dispute with the cheese-sauce server while I fled. Hailed by Maxine, I had the good fortune to end up at her table with the VIP's—Eric Grimaldi, Phyllis and Don Abbott, Sara, Heather, Cam, and Ginny. Eric was, of course, a Sporting Group judge; Phyllis, an obedience judge; Ginny, a tracking judge. Sara and Heather were extremely well known in agility. Cam was there partly because she was married to John R.B., an emerging AKC pooh-bah in his own right and the son of the legendary R.B., and partly because she wrote her column, showed a lot, won a lot, and knew a great many people, most of whom liked her and respected her judgment. I was there as a representative of *Dog's Life*, thus as the recipient of the courtesy owed to my employer, and as a stand-in for my editor, Bonnie, who was too good a friend of Max's to publish anything really negative I might write about Waggin' Tail, anyway. Bonnie, however, couldn't spice up my article with the authentic zing of first-person enthusiasm that my inclusion among the notables was probably meant to inspire.

My luck, though, consisted less of finding myself in elevated company than in discovering myself protected from the food-griping that would dominate the conversation everywhere else in the dining room of Waggin' Tail. Not that dog people are picky eaters. Far from it. The food at most dog shows makes lunch at the typical American high school cafeteria taste like a banquet at the Tour d'Argent. But we do want value for money. A few bucks for a plastic-encased ultrasoggy tuna on dry-roasted cardboard was one thing; gourmet-crustacean prices for Welsh rarebit were quite another. My position at the VIP table had another bonus, or so I imagined: Since my place was the last vacant one, there was no way I could end up having to endure yet more of Eva Spitteler, or so I was assuring myself when an unseen force slamming against the back of my chair sent me lurching forward so hard that my solar plexus collided with the edge of the table.

"Hey, sorry about that!" The voice drowned out my involuntary moan. "You wanna move so I can get in here?"

I'd been right: Eva and I wouldn't be at the same table. Instead, we'd be back to back.

"Shit!" Eva exclaimed. "Shit! You guys got real *lobster!* I'm going back." And away she stomped.

Across the table from me, Maxine blithely raised her fork toward her mouth. "Just ignore her!" Balanced on the tines of Max's fork was what my Maine-bred eye identified as a chunk of tail meat. "She has done nothing but complain about everyone and everything. Some people are never satisfied."

Phyllis Abbott, who was seated to my immediate right, charitably opined that Eva was a very unhappy person. At my left, Eric Grimaldi gave what I took to be a grunt of agreement. Maxine leaped on the idea. "Sara? Heather? Now, you heard that! Does that make you feel better?" Before either could reply, Max addressed the table at large: "There was actually an attempt of sorts to lodge an official complaint."

"About us," Sara explained.

Heather corrected her. "More about agility. The obstacles weren't quote sufficiently challenging unquote for somebody's quote natural unquote at agility, and they better be raised pronto, and . . . Holly heard her. What she intends to do is to go and use *our* equipment when we're not there. She said it this morning when everyone was there, and when Sara ran into her this afternoon, Eva—this is unbelievable!—she made a pretend gun out of her fist, and she pointed it at Sara, and she said, 'One A.M.!' Is that childish? Like it's the OK Corral."

"Also," said Sara, "she complained to Max that we were 'surly.' Surly! Hah! All we did was remind everyone not to use the equipment when we weren't there. We didn't single her out. What we should've done was toss her out on her ear."

Heather said damningly, "That's one person with what I'd call zero aptitude for agility. The dog, maybe you could work with. But her? Forget it. The whole problem is that she just does not understand dogs."

"If that, uh, basic affinity simply is missing," pronounced Phyllis Abbott, "there really isn't a great deal to be done."

I found my eyes fixed on Don Abbott, who was alternately pouring down wine and picking at a big helping of pot roast.

Eric spoke up. "You're born with it or not. So I've always claimed. Genetic. You have it or you don't."

Maxine nodded. "Just wait till they finally finish cracking this DNA code. You'll see! It'll be right there next to eye color or whatever, just like color blindness—dog blindness! So it really all depends on the roll of the dice. You luck out, you love dogs; you don't, you don't."

In other company, I'd have spoken up as Nurture's lone defender, albeit a rather weak one, because I certainly agreed with the proposition that loving dogs had a strong genetic basis. I disagreed only in believing that the potential was universal, waiting there in every human infant's DNA, but activated only in the fortunate by a powerful environmental trigger, a crucial childhood experience that allowed the genes to express their full potential, a sort of all-determining Primal Woof. Think of the implications for therapy. So you see? There's hope for everyone.

Or almost everyone. Events at my own table and at the one in back of me suggested two exceptions. The first, the subject of discussion amongst Phyllis, Don, Eric, and Cam, was a woman I'll call Lizzie Nopet, who was the head of a certain animal-rights group and the person whom the fancy most loved to hate. If we'd held an election for a sort of un-president—the last person on earth we'd have chosen as our leader —Lizzie, as everyone called her, would've been assured a unanimous victory. I was as sickened as everyone else by what the fancy viewed as Lizzie's twisted vision of a dogless, catless, loveless future, a sort of Black Mass utopia in which domestic animals would return to the disease-ridden wild, thus abandoning us with nothing to pat and train except one another. At the risk of jeopardizing my own position in the fancy by suggesting that I was soft on Lizzie, I'll argue, however, that as the ultimate outcast, Lizzie did a spectacular job of bringing us together.

Unfortunately, though, almost everything to be said about Lizzie had already been said so many times that, as a topic of conversation, she soon left our table in a silence that was filled by the second exception to my hope-for-everyone credo, namely, Eva Spitteler, who could be overheard loudly lecturing to her tablemates, that is, the people on whom she'd managed to force herself. A glance over my shoulder revealed Myrna, Marie, and Kathy, the women from New York; Michael; and Joy and Craig, none of whom, I thought, would have chosen Eva's company. The object of Eva's present pontification, the eighth person at the table, was a pleasant-looking midfiftyish woman I'd seen here and there around camp with a big tan shaggy dog, a bouncy fellow of unguessable but obviously amiable parentage.

"Nothing to it!" Eva bellowed. "All you do is get an ILP on him as an otter hound, and who's going to know?"

I turned my head, the better to listen in.

"Well, *I* am, for one!" the woman replied.

Undaunted, Eva jabbed a thumb toward Michael. "Well, yours looks as much like an otter hound as this guy's looks like an Akita." After a moment's pause evidently devoted to gathering her thoughtlessness, she added, "And these people here've got what's supposed to be a Cairn, came from a pet shop, and it's got papers, but ask anyone! It's no Cairn; it's nothing. It'd no more get an ILP as a Cairn than . . . than *I* would!"

As a bulldog, she might've stood a chance. The AKC grants ILP—Indefinite Listing Privilege—registration to dogs of unknown origin that are obviously specimens of AKC-recognized breeds. In other words, if you adopt what's obviously a Lab, a malamute, a Gordon setter, or whatever from a breed-rescue group or a shelter, and if you do what you should do anyway, namely spay or neuter your pet, you can apply for an ILP number. Why bother? To show in AKC obedience trials, among other things. And that's what Eva had in mind.

"I don't know how else to say this," the woman told Eva, "but I just don't believe in it. If I wanted a purebred dog, I'd get one! Buddy isn't, and I have no intention of saying that he is."

As soon as the woman finished her dignified defense of her own integrity and her dog's, too, everyone at both tables broke into cheers. Everyone, that is, except Eva Spitteler.

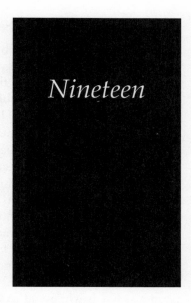

Nineteen

IF YOU'RE A REAL DOG PERSON, you'll join me—and not for the first time, either—in reflecting on the vast superiority of the average dog to the average dog owner. Consider Rowdy and me, not that Rowdy is even remotely *average*, of course, but then neither is any other beloved dog in the eyes of his companion biped. So, failing a truly ordinary dog, I'll offer him up, and myself, too, such as I am, which is to say, except in the dog-trivial matter of vision, virtually senseless by comparison with Rowdy, who, in any case, cares little for how things *look*—how they appear to be—but zooms in on how they *are*—how they reek and ring and vibrate, where they've been, and what they portend. Although my auditory and olfactory senses function adequately for those of a mere human being, compared with Rowdy I hear almost nothing and suffer from advanced anosmia, my nose dead where his is quick, my brain, too, as slow as my feet. And in matters practical—food, hierarchies—he outruns me every time.

By comparison with dogs, you see, every human being has profound special needs, and every dog is an assistance dog, a hearing dog, a smelling dog, but most of all, a superb guide to uncommon sense. I have lived with dogs all my life, yet learned pitifully little from their example. In my place, for instance—my place at the table—Rowdy would have kept his priorities straight: First, he'd have cleaned his plate. In fact, if he'd actually been sitting next to me in the dining room watching me attend to human blather while neglecting my food, his patience with human senselessness would have run out, and he'd have leaped up in front of me and wolfed down my untouched dinner. But as I've said, Rowdy is no average dog: He's an Alaskan malamute. Food thief? Now and then. But a rotten little *sneak?* Never. Besides, if Rowdy waited until I turned my back, how could he be sure that he'd succeeded in teaching me the lesson in survival that I so obviously need? Kimi teaches the same lesson, the legacy of the Arctic: Food is precious. Eat it while you can.

With Rowdy and Kimi in mind, I thus turned to my cold and glutinous Newburg, and was inserting a glob into my mouth when the unseen force struck again, this time leaving my midriff unharmed, but driving my fork and its contents dangerously close to the back of my throat, as if Eva Spitteler were practicing a sort of reverse first aid: Having already performed a crude Heimlich maneuver, she was only now going to make me choke. In fairness to Eva, though, let me point out that strife among dog people would be greatly reduced if some of us, myself included, were thus randomly yet regularly rendered speechless. The intervention could, of course, be milder than Eva's, and the agents of the talk-stopping squads could be perfectly polite. Indeed, courtesy to the silenced would be an essential part of their AKC training. Upon graduation, they'd get official badges—logo and all—to wear while walking their beats at dog shows, pausing briefly here and there to tickle eyelids and ears, stopping now and then to clamp mannerly hands under exhibitors' jaws, thus subtly reminding us of what to keep open and what to lock firmly shut.

I'm serious. Those know-nothing know-it-alls who stand out-side the rings saying awful things about other people's dogs? There's got to be something to do about them! And now there is. Squads. AKC delegate, are you? Propose the plan at the next meeting. And if you're embarrassed, explain that it wasn't your idea. Blame it on me. I'll take full responsibility.

In this case, however, Eva had reverse-Heimliched the wrong victim: I wasn't on the verge of saying anything about anyone or about anyone's dog, either. The probable trouble-maker was, of course, Eva herself, who might've repeated the ugly rumor about Eric's butchering dogs with gay tails, or might have come right out and accused Ginny of running a puppy mill. More likely, she'd have got in a few sneaky digs at one or both of them; Eva was no malamute. In one respect, however, she acted as Rowdy or Kimi would have done: She took off in search of food, in this case, dessert.

Shortly after Eva's departure, while Maxine and the Abbotts were going for dessert, and people were milling around from table to table, Michael appeared beside me. Looming over me, he said, "Could I ask you a question?"

Michael was a sweet guy, and not bad looking, either. "Sure," I said. "Pull up a chair."

Cam, Ginny, and Eric scooted over to make room. When Michael had eased a chair and then himself between Eric and me, he gestured toward Eva's empty place. "You heard some of that, right?"

"Yes," I said. "Ignore her, okay?"

"The thing is," said Michael, "I've got Jacob entered."

"Good. This your first trial?"

"Yeah."

"Good!"

"But the thing is," Michael repeated, "is anybody going to give me a hard time? About, uh, Jacob? Whether he's, uh—"

Want to get a man where it really hurts? Forget the all-but-painless knee in the groin. What you do is insult his dog. Model Mugging, are you listening?

"Look," I said, "in obedience, for all the judge cares, as long as Jacob's AKC-registered, he can have purple ringlets. Obedience doesn't have anything to do with the breed standard."

Unconvinced, Michael said, "Yeah, but—?"

"Maybe the judge might ask about his coat, but it'd probably be just, 'Hey, I've never seen one before.' And even if—"

By now, Eric, Cam, and Ginny were listening in. Cam picked up for me. "Even if your judges wonder if he's purebred, the worst they're going to do is report it to the trial secretary or the superintendent, and somebody who knows Akitas is going to say he's an Akita, and that'll be it. But that's not going to happen. The most that's really going to happen is that a judge is just curious, that's all." Cam brightened up. "So where're you entered?"

"Long Trail. It's on the way home."

The famous Green Mountain Circuit is in July, of course, but because of certain dog-political controversies dating back so far that no one remembers what they were, the Long Trail Kennel Club does not participate in the cluster. Instead, it holds its show and trial in September, making it one of the last outdoor events of the year.

"Who's the judge?" Cam asked.

"Mrs. Abbott." Michael sounded as if he'd finally spat out what *the thing* really was. "Can I just make sure she knows he's an Akita?"

"I wouldn't," said my mother's daughter.

"Oh, for heaven's sake, why not?" Ginny exclaimed. "Go ahead! Or don't. Phyllis'll know, anyway."

I hesitated. "Discuss a dog with a judge you've got him entered under? This close to the trial date? I don't know. I just wouldn't." In response to Michael's guilty expression, I added, "It's okay to *talk* to her. Anything's okay, really. I'm just . . . The only thing you really can't do is to show under a judge who's your instructor."

Eric, who'd been quietly listening, said, and said wisely, "If everybody who became a judge had to drop out of dogs to avoid hearing anything, there'd be no judges left. What happens is your friends show under you. So do your enemies. So do a lot of people you've never seen before and you're never going to see again. You look at 'em all, you nod your head, and then you get down to business, and you've got enough to do looking at dogs without wasting your time on who they belong to."

"Well spoken," said Ginny Garabedian, active breeder and exhibitor of Labrador retrievers, to Eric Grimaldi, who just so happened to judge her Group.

"So you see?" Cam said lightly. "Eric's a judge, and Ginny's a tracking judge, and we treat them just like normal people!"

Ever the irrepressible educator, Marissa's daughter, I said, "Cam's half serious. When you walk into Mrs. Abbott's ring, you don't have to pretend you've never seen her before." Catching myself, or rather, nabbing my mother, I added, "And then when she gives you a two hundred and you end up High in Trial—"

Michael got it. A perfect score—the legendary 200—going for a first Novice A leg? Dream on! Well, maybe it's happened, but if so, I'm willing to bet that the dog wasn't an Akita. Or a malamute, either. Regardless of the breed of dog, most first-time handlers are ecstatic just to survive the experience without requiring immediate psychiatric hospitalization or gastrointestinal surgery. High in Trial doesn't require a 200 score, of course; it means more or less what it sounds like, the highest score at the trial in Novice, Open, or Utility, the regular classes, not Brace or Graduate Novice, which maybe I should point out are called "nonregular" rather than "irregular" classes, there being nothing shady, fishy, ill-fitting, or second-rate about them. Anyway, HIT doesn't require a 200. Empirical observation indicates that what it really requires is a golden retriever or possibly a Border collie or a sheltie, at any rate, not a first-time-in-the-ring Akita with a rank-novice Novice A handler who needed all the encouragement he could get, including my dumb effort at a joke about going High in Trial, and who did not need, I should add, the kibitzing of Eva Spitteler. Insinuating herself into our group, she interrupted me: "And after you go High in Trial, don't go and offer the judge a ride home, either!"

In case you haven't been preparing to write a column on the AKC regulations and guidelines pertaining to judges, let me explain that Eva was and wasn't correct. The guidelines for dog show judges—conformation judges, people like Eric Grimaldi—explicitly forbid judges to "travel to or from shows or stay with anyone who is likely to be exhibiting or handling under them." Obedience judges are just advised to be "particularly judicious in the manner in which they conduct themselves in the world of dogs," in other words—how the AKC loves to hammer in a point!—as befits judges, they are supposed to conduct themselves . . . well, judiciously. Lest it be thought that in issuing specific vehicular and social guidelines solely to conformation judges, the AKC adopts a who-gives-a-damn attitude toward their obedience counterparts, let me quote from the regs for obedience judges: "A judge who has a shadow of doubt cast upon any of his decisions has caused his integrity, as well as the integrity of The American Kennel Club and of the Sport, to be compromised." The AKC always talks like Cecil B. DeMille handing down the Commandments to Charlton Heston. And, indeed, in the *Sport*, in *The Fancy* itself—the voice of the AKC really is the voice of God. So, while those poor rigidly regulated breed judges are, if necessary, trudging from show to show on foot to avoid creating the slightest impression of personal bias, are the wildly overindulged obedience judges encouraged merrily to hitch rides to and fro all over the place with their exhibitors? Don't ask me; ask the AKC. I've quoted the guidelines. Your conclusion? Mine, for what it's worth, is that the AKC takes an inexplicably authoritarian approach to disciplining breed judges, but when it comes to obedience judges, suddenly goes all permissive and guilt-tripping. "A shadow of a doubt . . . the integrity of The American Kennel Club." A breed judge riding in an exhibitor's car? Forbidden. But when it comes to obedience judges, the vehicle that the AKC has in mind, I guess, is an old Chevrolet, and specifically, the back seat of an old Chevrolet: Use your own judgment, dear. Mommy and Daddy trust you completely.

Twenty

DOGWORLD, Doberman World, Whippet World, Golden Re-
triever World, Dog Fancy, Dog's Life, Dog News, The Canine
Chronicle, Front and Finish, Off-Lead, Gun Dog, Northwest K-9
Connection, Northeast Canine Companion, New England Obedi-
ence News, Groomer to Groomer, Good Dog, Bloodlines, Pure-bred
Dogs/American Kennel Gazette, Dogs in Canada, The Borzoi
Quarterly, The Boston Quarterly, The Bull Terrier Quarterly, not
forgetting, of course, The Malamute Quarterly, The English
Cocker Quarterly, The Gordon Quarterly—Gordon setters—or
The Rhodesian Ridgeback Quarterly, The Labrador Quarterly, The
Irish Wolfhound Quarterly, The Corgi Quarterly, The Corgi
Cryer, The American Airedale, The Courier—Portuguese Water
Dogs—and not omitting Northland Shepherd News, German
Shepherd Dog Review, The Shepherd's Dogge, Chinook World,
Beagle Tails, or . . . well, I could go on and on, and will pro-
ceed to do so: Ilio and Popoki: Hawaii's Dogs and Cats, The
Rottweiler Quarterly, The Shar-Pei Magazine, The French Bully-
tin, Newf Tide, plus, of course, Working Sheepdog News, Ameri-
can Border Collie News, The Northeastern Sheepdog Newsletter,

Dog Sports Magazine, The Guardian, The Barker, and *The Newsletter of the Society for the Perpetuation of Desert-Bred Salukis. That'll Do!* Meaning I'm done? On the contrary, meaning *That'll Do: A Journal for the Canadian Stock Dog Handler.* And will *that* do? You're kidding. Why, I haven't even mentioned Cornell's dog-health letter, and I've skipped over most of the breed quarterlies, and I haven't had a chance to mention dozens and dozens of wonderful all-breed, single-breed, national, regional, and local, weekly, biweekly, monthly, and annual magazines, tabloids, bulletins, and newsletters. Enough? Really? Well, if you insist. Let's just say that here in dogs, we like to stay in touch.

And let me brag a little. Amateurs and professionals alike, from the volunteers who sit at their kitchen tables hunting and pecking out the club newsletters on battered Royal portables to the big-city editors of the high-circulation color glossies, we maintain remarkably high standards of careful, ethical journalism. Amazing, isn't it, that this periodical cornucopia of dogs-in-print should, week after week, month after month, year after year, abundantly spill forth a fresh and tasteful harvest? And in its sumptuous midst, but a single rotten fruit.

Strictly between us? Remember, I've got a mortgage to pay; a high-mileage Bronco to replace; two big dogs to feed, groom, show, immunize, train, and entertain; and myself to nourish, more or less, and to clothe, too, albeit not in great style, but decently, okay? So if anyone asks, *I'm* not the one who said it, or at least I'm not the one who said it first, except that, come to think of it, my opinion is identical to everyone else's, so maybe it doesn't matter after all, and desperate though I may become to supplement the pittance doled out by *Dog's Life*, I hope I never have to stoop to scandalmongering for the outrageously gossipy, wildly irresponsible yellow-dog rag known as *Dog Beat: The Pulse of the Fancy*, the name of which turned out to be weirdly appropriate: In listing Phyllis

Abbott as a deceased judge, *Dog Beat* came close to giving her a heart attack.

We learned about the error, hoax, or what-have-you at the end of dinner, when Don Abbott was called from the table to take a phone call. The caller, we later heard, was a guy named Robert Russell, a fellow pooh-bah of Don's who'd just received the latest issue and, having talked to Don a few dozen times in the past couple of days, had brilliantly decided either that Phyllis was still alive or that Don had been too preoccupied with AKC politics to notice his wife's radical drop in body temperature. Panting heavily, Don returned to break the news to his spouse with the subtlety and tact he'd no doubt perfected in his many years of power-playing. "Phyllis," he bluntly announced, *"Dog Beat* says you're dead."

Phyllis did what most of us, I suspect, would have done in that situation. Instead of sensibly placing a hand on her wrist or breast to locate a familiar, contradictory throb, and instead of drawing the obvious Cartesian conclusion from what looked like intense cogitation, she screeched, "What! Let me see!"

"Bob's faxing it," Don told her. "It'll be here in a minute."

Lowering her voice, Phyllis asked Don what may sound like a strange question: "Dead?" she said. "Dead in what way?"

How many ways are there? From Phyllis Abbott's viewpoint, there must have been two: the usual dull way, for one, and then the really alarming way—dead in dogs. I thought then and still believe that when Phyllis grasped the true nature of the report, she was momentarily relieved to find that the life she was supposed to have departed was merely the biological one. On the pulp pages of *Dog Beat*, she hadn't, after all, lost her AKC privileges and, with them, her license to judge. Scary there for a minute, but—whew!—the important part of who Phyllis was, the *Judge* in Judge Phyllis Abbott, still existed.

Once recovered from the initial shock, Phyllis passed beyond relief to real anger that none of us succeeded in tempering. While Don went back to the resort's office to get the fax of *Dog Beat*, Ginny, unasked, fetched a small medicinal dose of brandy for Phyllis, who tasted it, made a face, thanked Ginny, and drained the glass. Eric Grimaldi reminded Phyllis that only a few years earlier, the *AKC Gazette*, too, had listed a judge as deceased and had then had to report the mistake.

"This is not the *Gazette* we're talking about!" Phyllis had indignantly replied, as if it were one thing to find herself reputably, if falsely, demised in the *Gazette*'s prestigious pages, but quite another to discover herself shamefully defunct in the scandal-ridden sheets of *Dog Beat*.

In unwitting testimony to his genuine efficiency and organizational ability, Don Abbott soon returned bearing not only the fax of the entire offending issue, minus the ads, but ten neatly collated and stapled photocopies that he handed around to the people at our table and to some of the others who'd been drawn by the hubbub. Seated right next to Phyllis, I managed to snag a copy. I'm not usually greedy, but as a dog writer, I felt that my profession entitled me to first grabs. And I did share my copy with Cam and Ginny.

"It's probably just some ordinary snafu," proclaimed Maxine, looking up from her copy. "Unfortunate. But there you have it."

"We," I said, royal *we*, meaning *Dog's Life*, "check with the family, and I think the *Gazette* does, too. Standard practice is that you prefer to hear from the family, and at a minimum, you double-check."

"Is anyone finding anything else in here?" Ginny asked.

"Drivel," said Heather. "I've never seen this thing before. It's really a piece of junk."

"It's for show people," I told her. "Or supposedly, anyway. It started out mostly reporting show results and running ads and things, but it couldn't really compete with *Dog News* and the other biggies, so it degenerated into this. First, it started running gossip columns like the normal ones—who wore what, best-dressed judge, whose birthday was celebrated, who was at fund-raisers—but then it really couldn't compete that way, either."

"This is trash," Sara snapped. Proudly raising her chin, she added, "In agility—"

I interrupted. *Dog Beat* was garbage, but in a disgraceful sort of way, it was part of the fancy, and I felt compelled to explain that the show people didn't approve of it any more than Sara did. "Well, for what it's worth, the one rumor that *Dog Beat* won't publish is that it's supposed to be in big financial trouble. People think it won't be around much longer."

"Well, Max got a plug," Don Abbott remarked.

Max groaned. "Oh, God, what've they said about me?"

"They wish you luck," he told her.

"Well," Maxine said, "I find that slightly ambiguous, don't you? Luck? Not best wishes? As if I *needed*—"

"No, it's a real plug," Don said. "Second page."

Finding herself ignored, Phyllis said, "Donald, this is a matter that I take very, very seriously. Someone has done this to me!"

Rather gruffly, Eric said, "You know what, Phyllis? There's something off here."

"Off?" she demanded. "They say that they're sorry to hear that I passed away, and you find that—!"

Eric was calm. "Naturally. But it's not like you and Don are hard to get hold of, and it's not like you've been in hiding. You've been out there."

"Good point," Don agreed. "We both have. Phyllis's been visible enough. And lately, too."

"All summer!" Phyllis said. "Ever since . . . We were in Boston—Ladies' and Essex County. When was that?"

"Around Memorial Day," I said.

"And you judged Passaic," Eric reminded her.

"That was mid-June," said Ginny.

Barging in, as always, Eva Spitteler added, "Yeah, Passaic.

Cam and Nicky went High in Trial. I watched 'em in Mrs. Abbott's ring. I was there."

My reflexes took over. To be precise, two of them did. I rejected Eva Spitteler's bid for inclusion just as automatically as I congratulated Cam. "Cam, that's great! That's a very competitive—"

"You know," Cam said, "if there's this thing about Phyllis here, I wonder if any of the rest of us . . . Has anyone found anything about the rest of us? Besides wishing Max luck?"

Almost simultaneously, Phyllis addressed her husband. "Donald," she demanded, "would you please put that telephone to good use, and find out exactly *who* has done this to me!"

It was an odd little episode. Even for a handler like Cam who was used to being in the ribbons, High in Trial at Passaic must have been special. Furthermore, nothing in the guidelines for obedience judges would have prevented Phyllis from commenting on Nicky's performance. Having awarded Nicky the score that put him High in Trial, Phyllis could have stood behind her own judging by saying how good he'd been. Both Cam and Phyllis, however, had changed the subject. It crossed my mind that Phyllis could have given Nicky a perfect score and later regretted that 200. A perfect score—that legendary 200—is, by AKC decree, "extremely rare if the Regulations are followed." As the AKC goes on to warn judges: "When the owner of a dog which has received a perfect score feels that the performance deserved only 197½ points and knows just where the dog should have been faulted, it is evident that the standards of Obedience have been lowered by the judge." Some judges never give perfect scores; the rest, almost never, and when they do, they do it very, very carefully. I wondered how close to perfection Cam and Nicky had really come at Passaic. Oh, and, of course, I wondered exactly what their score had been, but that means nothing. Obedience addict that I am, I always wonder what people's scores are—except, alas, my own. Those I know by heart, and all too well.

Eva's scream interrupted my thoughts. "Oh, shit! Listen to this!" She brandished one of the photocopies. Lowering it to eye level, she read, *"Black ribbon.* What the hell does that mean?"

The term isn't all that common. I started to explain: "A tribute to a dead—"

"Black ribbon," Eva repeated indignantly. "Listen to this! It says: *Condolences to Eva Spitteler on the sudden loss of her three-year-old Labrador retriever, Benchenfield Farmer's Dog."* Eva's voice dropped. "That's Bingo."

"No kidding," someone muttered.

Eva resumed her reading. *"It's always sad to report one of these, especially when the tragedy could so easily have been prevented."* Eva's face, never exactly attractive, was contorted with rage. "What the shit's that supposed to mean? That I left him shut up in a hot car? What the—"

When my mother died, all the dog magazines wrote about her, and every time I came across the words of sympathy, I felt as if I'd just heard news that couldn't possibly be true. Again and again, I'd read, "With the passing of Marissa Winter, the Fancy mourns the loss of a great lady," and I'd want to shout, "No! Not true!" But then my eyes would fill with tears, and time after time, I'd learn of her death for the first time. The death of a dog, of course, is like the death of a mother, but simpler, therefore much worse, like the death of a child, pure grief. After my last golden, Vinnie, died, every card, every note, every phone call, every hand on my shoulder broke the news again. What truly consoled me was Rowdy, a dog totally different from Vinnie, but a dog, even so. And Marissa? Many dogs, one mother.

Eva's rage? The familiar outrage: *No! Not MY dog! It's a hoax! It's a cruel hoax.* In Eva's case, it really was a hoax. The feeling, I thought, was identical.

Looking down at the photocopy on the table, I scanned for familiar names. Mine, maybe? Not that I could find. But Don Abbott's was there, and so was John R.B. White's. I put my finger on it and asked Cam whether she'd seen it. She nodded. The item was trivial. According to *Dog Beat*, John R.B., her husband, was widely considered a young Turk at the AKC and a threat to conservative types like Don Abbott. If so, *Dog Beat* wondered, why had John R.B. and Don Abbott been spotted together at so many shows this year? The only noteworthy feature of the item, I thought, was the absence of any reference to Phyllis Abbott's supposed death. But the inconsistency wasn't surprising; *Dog Beat*'s editing was always lousy.

Cam turned a few pages and asked, "Did you see this?" Her perfectly filed nail tapped the paper midway down the page.

"No," I said.

"Well, read it."

Most of *Dog Beat*'s columns appeared under pen names. No self-respecting writer would want to admit to having produced such trash, but then no self-respecting writer would have thought about contributing to *Dog Beat* in the first place. I suspected that the real purpose of the pseudonyms wasn't so much to let the writers save face or to let them escape responsibility for what they wrote as it was to fool the readership into believing that *Dog Beat* employed a multitude of contributors. All ten or twelve toxic columns, I thought, actually oozed from the slimy digits of only two or three people. In truth, what offended me about *Dog Beat*, in addition to its viciousness, was its blatant failure to fill what I've always perceived a major gap in the dog-writing market. Aspiring canine journalist, are you? Well, the next time you find yourself stuck in line at the supermarket, run your eyes over the racks of tabloids, and read therein your own future. Indeed, *The Canine Enquirer!* Really, consider the possibilities. Each issue would practically write itself. *Day-Old Siamese-Twin Basenjis Whelp Litters of Three-Headed Pups. Amazed owner says, "And they're just the sweetest little bitty things you ever saw.*" Basic tabloid Elvis reincarnation and miracle-cure story, with dog, of course: "*Jailhouse Rock*" *Crooning Coonhound Cures Caddie Dealer's Cancer.* More? *Brave Brittany Battles Alien Captors, Saves Self and Cairn Companion,* except when you read the story, it turns out that the whole thing happened in 1932, but it did happen, right? That's what counts. The Royals: *Queen's Corgis, Caught in Secret Love-Nest, Snub Di.* That one's a little disappointing, I'm afraid. The so-called love nest was just an ordinary cedar-filled dog bed; the breeding was, in fact, carefully planned; dogs being dogs, it didn't take place in any kind of bed or nest at all; and the corgis, sensitive to their owner's true sentiments, had never much liked Di to begin with. Oh, and don't neglect celebrities. *Exclusive Poolside Photos Show Latest Lassie's No Lady.* None of them have been, actually— male collies have better coats for the role—but the pictures'll be a real plus, good and graphic, blurred, too, obviously shot from the depths of shrubbery.

Anyway, the column to which Cam directed my attention— "Nose to the Dirt," this journalistic gem was called—appeared under the shamelessly plagiarized nom de plume of Snoopy, according to whom—*Dog Beat*'s, not Charles Schultz's—Sara Altman and Heather Richards were starting their own agility camp next year. Had Max McGuire heard the news? And if Waggin' Tail made it through its first year, would Max have any staff left? Not according to the rumors that had reached *Dog Beat.*

Maxine must have read the item at the same time I did. "Heather," Max demanded shrilly, "is this true?"

Heather, who'd supplied herself with coffee, took a casual sip. "It's just something we've discussed."

"Well, not with me!" Maxine snapped.

In what I took to be an effort to deworm Max's mood with a purgative dose of reality, Eric reminded her that *Dog Beat* wasn't exactly a reliable source of information. Phyllis was obviously alive, he pointed out. So was what's-her-name's dog. But as Max correctly told him, Heather and Sara hadn't denied the rumor. Far from it! Hadn't Eric just heard . . . ? Was that what *he* called loyalty? Was it *his* idea of loyalty, too? Maybe Eric was *also* planning . . .

Eric spoke calmly. "Max, running a camp's not on my agenda." He excused himself from the table and rose. In a huff, Max followed him. Don and Phyllis, who'd been muttering about who at *Dog Beat* was really to blame and how best to deal with the situation, were now giving voice to long lists of people they needed to call. With Don stating that he'd track the damn thing down, they departed. Everyone else was leaving, too. I'd had all the human company I needed for one day. I started to slip out of my chair.

In back of me, Heather addressed Eva Spitteler: "*You* did this, didn't you? I know you did."

Sara, chiming in, said, "*All* of it! The cards, the scary stuff, everything! And you know what? Everyone knows you did it, too, because you're the only one here who's mean enough. You just can't stand to see anyone else have fun, can you?"

For the third time, the force hit the back of my chair, but I'd just squeezed out, and I escaped the impact. As I crept away, Eva was loudly defending herself. "You know what you're doing? You're scapegoating me! And the reason is, you're just jealous, is all, because you're all trying to make a living in dogs, and not one of you's got a clue of how to do it. Let me tell you something. The real problem here isn't me; it's Maxine. She's greedy, and she's stingy, and she's not even good at covering it up. She doesn't know the first thing about running a business or about allocating resources. She can't plan, she can't make decisions, she can't follow through. And she's stupid: She made a whole lot of promises she couldn't keep. This whole damn camp is completely disorganized. But, hey, everyone's buddy-buddy with good old Max. So who gets the blame? *Me.* And I paid good money to be here, and all I've got for it is your shit."

What popped into my mind was, of all things, a line from a poem I'd had to memorize in high school: "The world is too much with us; late and soon. . . ." Wordsworth. I remembered his first name: William. His country: England. England, fair England, where the official church is the C of E and the true religion is the worship of dogs. Not just England, either! Taken together, the British Isles constitute a devout Bible-belt of fervent canine fundamentalism, country after country, county after county, district after district pledged to the Irish setter, the Irish wolfhound, the Scottish deerhound, the pointer, the foxhound, the Border collie, the Welsh corgi, both Cardigan and Pembroke; terrier after incredible terrier, Irish, Welsh, West Highland White, Norwich, Norfolk, bull, Bedlington, Dandie Dinmont, Staffordshire, Kerry blue, soft-coated wheaten, Skye, Sealyham, Manchester, Lakeland, and the others, present and past; the Old English sheepdog, of course, and the collie, smooth and rough, the Shetland sheepdog, and the toys, too, the Yorkie, the English toy spaniel, and, speaking of spaniels, the Sussex, the Welsh springer, the English springer, and . . . Well, if I haven't gotten to your breed, sorry, but the list is almost endless and, even if complete, wouldn't tell me what I didn't know, which was, of course, the particular breed favored by Wordsworth, he of late and soon. But I knew what mattered: I knew that when Wordsworth wrote, "The world is too much with us; late and soon," he meant that he'd had it with human beings and was desperate for the company of dogs.

As was I. I almost ran back to the cabin, and as soon as I got inside, I practically yanked the latch off Rowdy's crate in my eagerness for contact with his pure-hearted goodwill. Never lived with a malamute? Well, according to the official standard, the Alaskan malamute is "playful on invitation, but generally impressive by his dignity after maturity," a description that illustrates the divergence of Dog English from what is absurdly called Standard English, as if there were anything normal, or, God forbid, desirable about stripping the language as a whole of the rich phraseology of the fancy. But as always, back to the Alaskan malamute, Rowdy, in this case, quintessence of the standard, "playful on invitation, but generally impressive by his dignity after maturity," meaning in Standard English, that *after* maturity, which is to say, in advanced old age and beyond, he'll display an air of noble reserve, but that until then, he'll fool around at absolutely anyone's invitation, including his own, which is to say that Rowdy bounded from his crate with a furry toy whale in his mouth, gave it a hard shake, dropped it, rose on his hindquarters, rested his snowshoe paws in my outstretched hands, and cleansed my face and soul of that icky residue, the grime of too much with us, late and soon.

"You want to go out?" I asked him. "Go for a walk?" Rowdy doesn't fetch his leash the way Vinnie did, but he understood what I meant and headed for the door. I snapped on his flex lead.

At the end of the dark afternoon, the sun had set by swelling to ten times its former size, turning a garish shade of raspberry, and exploding into the tops of the mountains like a flambéed dessert blowing up in the faces of the gods. Now, hours later, the moon's balm soothed the burns. Low to the ground, twin sets of lights twinkled, nighttime safety collars around the necks of what looked like little phantom dogs. The air was fragrant with pine. Enforcer of the buddy system, I wandered to the dock, led Rowdy to the end, looked, listened, and nowhere found a sign of a swimmer. Strolling toward the main lodge, I saw the burning cigarettes of three or four people sitting on the stairs. Like a patriotic cartographer intent on charting unknown land and claiming it for his own, Rowdy marked tree after tree.

"Could we get down to business here, buddy?" I asked him.

"Be a good boy! Hurry up!" Code words, those. Kimi obeys them. Rowdy does, too, but not at the cost of cutting short a good walk. Or maybe he knew that there was no real hurry. He wasn't due in the show ring, and my only appointment was with a soft pillow. I liked the feel of the night air, and I liked letting Rowdy mark his trees. He was a dog being a dog. Maxine passed nearby, the massive Cash on lead. I said hi and moved on. Here and there, other dog walkers meandered, some in silence, some in small murmuring groups. I missed Kimi. With only one dog, I felt unbalanced, incomplete. But I missed no one's company but hers, not even Steve Delaney's. When Rowdy had charted our route away from the lake and back to the wooded stretch that separated the cabins from the bunkhouse, I heard a couple of cabin doors bang lightly. A distant voice said something I couldn't really hear.

The next sounds I couldn't miss: the yelp of a dog in sudden pain, a female scream of fright, and the unmistakable cursing of Eva Spitteler. The light outside her cabin, hers on one side, Joy and Craig's on the other, showed something of a classic postdogfight tableau, two groups, each bending over to check the wounds of the canine combatants. At the first sound of the fight, Rowdy had yanked out the entire length of the retractable lead and, convinced that he was missing the greatest camp activity yet, a spectacular dog battle that he'd undoubtedly win, had tried to haul me into the center of the fracas. You know who Carol Lea Benjamin is? That's not a digression. Really it isn't. Carol Lea Benjamin is a genius dog writer who captured in a few words the whole point of the Alaskan malamute from the breed's own point of view, and I quote her: "The Malamute, the one with the big 'S' on his chest." Rowdy doesn't need a phone booth. He doesn't believe in kryptonite, either.

By the time I'd hauled him in, Bingo was quiet, and so was Joy's little sort-of Cairn, Lucky, who, to my amazement, had inflicted the only visible damage. In the light from the cabin and the beam of Eva Spitteler's flashlight, I could see blood flowing from one of Bingo's ears. Little Lucky, though, was unscathed. From the cock of his head, he was pretty proud of himself. The dogfight was over. The human fight was just beginning. It, too, ended quickly.

"Bingo's bleeding!" Eva yelled. "He's going to need plastic surgery, and you're going to pay for it!"

With boldness as surprising as Lucky's, Joy replied, "It was *your* fault for dropping that food right in between them. If you didn't have to go around all the time stuffing your fat face—"

Craig tried to intervene: "Joy—"

"You bitch!" Eva shrieked. "Look what that little rat of yours has done to my beautiful show dog!" Lowering her voice only slightly, she added, "Vicious little pet-shop mutt."

How to hurt a man? How to hurt a woman, too. Joy scooped up Lucky, hugged him, and began to sob. Craig wrapped protective arms around both of them. From the opposite side of the circle of light, Maxine McGuire suddenly spoke. "Eva," she said, sounding as calm as Cash looked, "that will do. You are out of line. You can stay here tonight, but in the morning, you pack up and get out. This is my camp, and I want you out of here by eight A.M. Read your contract. Out you go."

"Not on your life," Eva screeched.

I missed whatever followed. I didn't want to hear it. With the dogfight over, Rowdy had lost interest. We went quietly to our own cabin. As I stood on the deck trying to regain the peace Eva had spoiled, I heard Phyllis Abbott. She was using that distinctive voice that people reserve for the telephone. "Greatly exaggerated?" she asked with outrage. "Why does everyone keep saying *greatly exaggerated?* It's a total fabrication!"

Twenty-one

EARLY THE NEXT MORNING, the unseasonably hot sun beating on the dead-calm lake inspired me to join Eric Grimaldi and Elsa the Chesapeake for what proved to be a frigid swim. Impervious to the cold, Eric stood waist-deep in the water and kept tossing out Elsa's blue-and-white rubber retrieve toy. To generate internal heat, I engaged in hot competition with Elsa, racing her for the toy, losing, and again pitting my inadequate flailing against her effortless surge.

Heather and Sara may have made their discovery as Elsa and I were sprinting toward the rubber toy. Perhaps it happened while I was clambering over the sharp rocks at the edge of the lake in a dash toward my towel. Maybe I was standing terry-wrapped on the dock, smirking at Eric's efforts to bribe Elsa out of the lake with a dog biscuit and at her gleeful refusal of what she clearly saw as a bad bargain. At about the same time that I was fooling around with Elsa, Sara and Heather made an early check of their colorful canine playground in the woods, where they discovered a body pinned beneath the collapsed ramps of the massive A-frame. The fallen ramps covered the head and torso, but the clumsy sandals could have belonged to no one except Eva Spitteler. No one else would have worn the clunky things at all, certainly not over camouflage-patterned socks. The ugly military-green trousers were recognizably Eva's, too. Touching the flesh between a cuff and a sock, Sara felt no warmth. Even so, she and Heather decided to apply their strength to shifting the heavy ramps. As Sara told me, "We're athletes, just like our dogs. It didn't seem right to leave her lying there, especially . . . Well, just in case. Really, we knew, though. But at the time, it seemed like we had to try. It was our equipment; it felt like our responsibility. And, of course, she'd threatened to go and use it. She kept saying one A.M. We could've stayed out there all night. I could've—I've got a tent with me. It would've been no big deal."

Too late to save Eva's life, Sara maintained a civilized vigil over the pieces of the A-frame and the body they had crushed. Heather went to summon help. If I hadn't bothered to dry my hair and if I'd crated Rowdy without giving him a little quick-leg-lift trip outside, I might have been sitting at breakfast when Heather arrived at the main lodge. I'd have been at a table eating eggs and muffins when she dashed in, found Max, and broke the news about the accident. I might even have been among the campers who followed Heather back to the agility area, maybe one of the people who made an effort to straighten out Eva's twisted body. People shed their jackets and sweatshirts, I heard, and placed them over Eva's battered corpse as a sort of makeshift crazy-quilt shroud. The body shouldn't have been moved, covered, or even touched, but the massive obstacle had landed directly on Eva's head. I wouldn't have been able to keep looking, either.

Because I lingered in the shower and dutifully took Rowdy out, I learned of Eva Spitteler's death when I arrived at the main lodge, where Chuck Siegel, Cam, and a couple of other obedience people were ordering Maxine to call the police.

Instead of responding, Max caught my eye. With un-characteristic solemnity she said, "Holly, the most awful thing has happened. Eva Spitteler has had a terrible accident."

With an exasperated sigh, Cam said outright that Eva was dead.

"You're positive?" I asked. "Because—"

Cam shook her head. Her face was pale. "She never stood a chance. She must've been trying to raise the height of the A-frame, and she was underneath, fixing the chains, I guess, when the whole thing collapsed on her. Her head must've been right under one of those support beams. It's like . . . It's like somebody picked up the A-frame and hit her over the head with it."

Let me explain the construction of an A-frame. Each ramp is three feet wide and nine feet long, and when they're joined together, they're held in place at the top—at the peak of the *A* —by a couple of hinges. If the A-frame were raised to compe-tition height—a bit over six feet above the ground—with nothing to link the ramps but the hinges at the apex? And then a big dog raced up and over? WHAM! So there have to be additional supports of some kind, for instance, in the case of Heather and Sara's A-frame, a pair of chains. On that kind of A-frame, the chains are like double crossbars on a capital *A* —what makes the A-frame an *A*, and not just an upside down *V* that would fall apart if it took any weight. Okay so far? If so, it's obvious that every time you raise or lower the height of the obstacle, you don't just move the hinged ramps up or down; you also have to reset the chains. Still lost? Draw a tall, skinny capital *A* and then a short, fat capital *A*. Look at the crossbars, one very short, the other very wide. And to set the chains? You have to get under the obstacle, where the chains hook to the ramps.

"Cam," Max said sharply, "it was a terrible *accident.*" There were bright spots of color on her cheeks.

"Of course it was," Cam said, "except that she had no business being out there, and—"

Chuck tried to break in, but before he could succeed, a plump, prosperous-looking man with an air of authority—the manager of the resort, I assumed—approached Maxine and announced that someone named Wayne was on his way.

"That's Wayne Varney," Maxine explained to us. "Well, that's all right. Wayne will know what to do." After Chuck had asked just who Wayne was, she said, "Oh, he's Rangeley Police, and I think . . ." Addressing the plump man, she asked, "Is Wayne still a deputy, too?"

The man nodded.

The city kids probably expected to see the lodge doors swing open to admit a six-gun-toting clone of Charles Bronson. Law enforcement people in the State of Maine are, of course, armed—so, for that matter, is the bulk of the citizenry —but sheriffs and their deputies carry up-to-date weapons in ordinary holsters, as do the state and local police. County sheriffs and deputies are important in Maine because—believe it or not, New Yorkers—up in the wild woods, there's mile after beautiful square mile of sparsely-populated land divided into what the tax bills call "unorganized territories," areas with names but no governments, and entities marked on the maps only by abbreviations that must mystify the tourists, T3 R 13 WELS—Township 3 Range 13 West of the Easterly Line of the State—Big Ten Township, Rainbow, Redington, and plantations, too, in all of which, there being no local police to call, you holler for the deputy, who may, as in the case of Wayne Varney, also be a police officer in a nearby town. All that's assuming that you haven't had a boating accident, which would be Fish and Game's business, or . . . Well, you get the idea. And Eva Spitteler clearly hadn't had a boating accident. In fact, soon after the pale blue Chevy Caprice cruiser pulled into the parking lot of the Mooselookmeguntic Four

Seasons Resort Lodge and Cabins, Wayne Varney refused to assume that Eva's death had been any kind of accident at all.

I heard the siren in the distance and saw Varney's cruiser pull in because I was on my way to the agility area, not to gawk at the death scene, and certainly not to get a close look at Eva Spitteler's body, but to rid myself of the insidious suspicion that Eva Spitteler's supposed death was nothing but one more hoax. It took me a second to identify the big man who emerged from the cruiser as the same guy I'd seen in Doc Grant's, the cop who'd been drinking coffee while Everett Dow ate. Today, he had on big, ultradark sunglasses, and when he stepped out of the Chevy, he put on the hat I'd noticed the day before, a dusky blue woven-straw Stetson with silver braid trim. On the left breast of his uniform was a silver badge; on the right shoulder, a little American flag. Fastened to his belt were a set of handcuffs, a miniradio, a sidearm in a holster, extra clips, and so many other tools of his trade that at the guess-your-occupation booth at a country fair, he'd have been a sure loser. Maxine, who must have heard the siren, came dashing from the main lodge, approached Varney, and like a dog offering its paw, raised a hand and rested it on his sleeve. In return, he gave her shoulder a few gentle thumps.

I can only reconstruct what happened after that. Maxine, I'm sure, tried to get Varney to treat Eva Spitteler's death as a simple accident. One look at Varney, though, should've told anyone, even an amateur guesser of occupations, that this guy was a law enforcement professional who took that profession in earnest. Within minutes of his arrival, he'd radioed for backup, ordered a surprisingly large crowd (of people and dogs) out of the agility area, obtained what was probably a cogent account from Sara and Heather, and let it be known that the State Police were on their way.

When I entered the dining room, I was a little surprised to discover how many other people had also shown up for breakfast. Although I hadn't eaten anything, I wasn't hungry.

Rather, I suffered from a distinct sense of unreality for which food, I thought, might be a cure. After I'd eaten, I was going to make a quick call home. Then I intended to groom Rowdy, not to work on his appearance, I should point out, but to clean up my own emotions and, I think, to try to clear my conscience.

As I sat alone eating my eggs and toast, I had the eerie feeling that the dining room was haunted by the ghosts of mean things I'd said and done to Eva Spitteler, the shades of cruel thoughts I'd had about her, the spirits of my own unkindness. Was Eva Spitteler the only person who'd ever wanted a plug in *Dog's Life?* The only person whose chair had ever collided with mine? And if she'd perpetrated the dirty tricks? So what! I'd heard her accused and convicted on the basis of no evidence, and I hadn't felt even a twinge of objection. Eva's wants now seemed pitifully simple: She'd wanted to be liked. She'd wanted to feel important. In the matter of her death, I had perfect confidence in my own innocence; I suspected almost everyone else; yet I was the one who felt guilty.

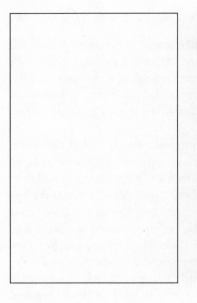

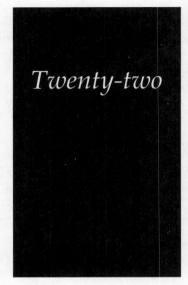

Twenty-two

IMAGINE THAT YOU WANTED to summon death, to grab it, to hold it, and to force it even momentarily to do your bidding. I'm serious: If you decided to lure it in, trap it, and boss it around even for one single fleeting moment, where would you begin? With an enticing bait, with an irresistible snare: life itself, and lots of it. *Whose* life? Anyone's, everyone's. Death cares not at all. Bankers will do, clerks, plumbers, salespeople, hairstylists, writers, dog trainers. Taken one by one and considered dispassionately, we—any and all of us —are a motley, humdrum lot, unprepossessing, weak; and when considered as potential raw material for any sort of spiritual purpose or higher goal, worse than unpromising, in fact, hopeless and helpless. And that's true! When it comes to snagging death, we're no good one by one. But occupations jettisoned, appearances discarded, our very individuality cast aside? Herein lies the power of the secret society: Banded together, spirits summed, essences merged, we're the bait that death can't resist. Tempted, allured, ensnared, death squirms, struggles, lashes out, takes the blows, cringes, and submits, the captor captive, the victor victim, the predator at last the prey.

Metaphorically so, of course, or so I'd always been told. As I understood it, for instance, initiation into Freemasonry represented the strictly symbolic enactment of a battle, an ordeal, a test that pitted life against death, a *ritual* trial, its outcome predetermined, endlessly repeated, death and rebirth, death and rebirth, not even a fair fight, really, just an elaborately, if credibly, staged wrestling match in which a paid-off death invariably agreed to take the fall. But not this time! What fools we'd been! What dupes! How could we have been so stupid? How could we have trusted him? Had we honestly expected Death not to cheat?

Behind the glass door of the old-fashioned phone booth tucked away at the back of the lobby, I nervously dialed my own phone number, listened with irritation to Leah's recorded greeting, waited for the beep, and was starting to leave a worried, angry message when I heard her groggy voice.

"Leah, haven't you let Kimi out yet?" I demanded.

"An hour ago," she said.

"You *did* wait for her."

"Yes, yes!"

"And you are remembering—"

"Everything! And just in case you wondered how *I* am—"

I felt a pang of remorse. "Leah, I'm sorry. Everything here is . . . How *are* you? Is everything going okay?"

"Fine, except that last night, Jeff brought over a pizza, and Kimi stole the whole thing, and by the time I got it away from her, she'd eaten half of it and slobbered over the rest of it, and then she grabbed the carton and ran into your bedroom and hid in that little space under the headboard of your bed, next to the wall—"

"That's where she always takes things," I said placidly, "because—"

"You're not listening! I'm not done. It gets worse. So by the

time I finally got her out, she'd chewed up most of the cardboard, and then after Jeff got back with the second pizza, she
went into the bathroom and—this is *really* disgusting—she
went into the bathroom, and she came out carrying—"

"I don't want to hear about it," I declared. "Are you sure
she's all right?"

"*Kimi* is just fine. She's right here. *I* nearly died of embarrassment."

"Don't say that!" I explained about Eva Spitteler. I also
gave Leah an assignment. "Check *Front and Finish*," I told
her, "and the *Canine Companion*. They might have something.
But I think our best bet is *Dog News*. It seems to me that they
really covered Passaic—I think there's a whole article—and
also check their gossip column, okay? And anything else you
think of. Just scan as much as you can." I finished by dictating
a list of names: Max McGuire, Eric Grimaldi, Don and Phyllis
Abbott, Cam and John R.B. White, Ginny Garabedian,
Chuck Siegel, Sara, Heather. "And Myrna," I concluded.
"How many people are there named Myrna? She's from New
York or somewhere near there. And Jennifer something. She
has a Doberman—working in Open, I think. Anything about
Waggin' Tail. And anything at all about Eva Spitteler. Or her
dog." I spelled Eva's last name and told Leah to look for ads
that Eva might have run for High In Tail; for Bingo's name—
either the call name or the registered name, Benchenfield
Farmer's Dog—and also for oblique references to an unnamed yellow Lab. "The whole thing may be a waste of
time," I warned Leah.

I hung up with the intention of going straight to my cabin.
But I got waylaid before I'd even left the main lodge and
ended up back in the dining room, where Maxine was making
an announcement to as many campers as she'd been able to
gather.

"Purely as a formality," she was chirping, "Officer Varney
has decided to call in the State Police, which will, I'm told,

mean a rather large number of people *descending* on us, and something called a Crime Lab that's apparently a van of some kind, but the point is, as I've explained to Wayne—to Officer Varney, that is—that we will go ahead with our plans as much as we possibly can in the face of this terrible, terrible tragedy, which is, and I'm sure you'll all agree, exactly what Eva would have wanted us to do."

Reluctant to reenter the dining room, I'd stationed myself against a wall just inside the door. Next to me, Myrna was whispering loudly to Marie: "Can't you just hear Eva if it'd been someone else? If they'd canceled agility so they could get the body out, she'd've been screaming for a refund for the time she'd missed."

"Myrna, for God's sake," Marie murmured. "She's dead, all right?" She looked ill.

"Yeah, well," Myrna replied, "if it'd been someone else, she'd've been the first person to throw a shit fit." After a brief pause, she added, "So who do you think finally had the guts?"

With genuine shock, Marie cried out, "Myrna, really!"

Undaunted, Myrna replied, " 'Really' yourself! I wonder if it was her dog. It could've been, you know. I mean, we just had to put up with her at shows and stuff; poor old Bingo had to live with her, and if that wouldn't drive anyone to murder, I don't know what would. It's a miracle he didn't—"

"Oh, honestly," Marie said.

"Honestly! Think about it. She must've had him off lead, right? Why not? In the middle of the night? No one around? So she leaves him on a sit-stay or a down-stay, and she goes crawling under the A-frame, and what's he going to do? Break, right? Same as ever. So there she is, under the A-frame, and he breaks, and as soon as he goes charging up on it, the whole thing comes crashing down on her! And if that's not how it happened, then you tell me—"

"But not on purpose!" Marie countered fiercely. "Yeah, maybe Bingo did go and jump on the A-frame, except that those things weigh a ton, and it could've just slipped, but even if he . . . Myrna, even if he landed on it, it was just an accident! He didn't murder her! Honestly, what an awful thing to say about a dog!"

With a triumphant smirk, Myrna shot back: "Yeah, well, so if he's innocent, how come he took off, then? Huh? You see? He murdered her, and then he fled the scene of the crime."

"You know, Myrna, it's really not funny." Marie's eyes were blazing.

"So if he's not, uh, what do you call it, fleeing the long arm of the law, then where is he?" Myrna demanded.

"Where any other dog would be," Marie said. "He got loose, and he took off. For God's sake! He probably just took off after a bitch in season."

Marie's frivolous-sounding guess eventually proved correct. The myths of the fancy, of course, abound in stories of death-denying canine devotion to deceased masters. According to legend, for instance, and as far as I know, according to fact as well, for nine years after the death in 1925 of Professor Eisaburo Ueno of Tokyo University, his loyal Akita, Hachiko, went daily to the railway station to meet the train of a man whose terrestrial commuting days were over. Instead of meeting trains, Hachiko might have staged a series of howling concerts at his master's grave. Vocal gifts failing him, he could always have refused to taste a morsel of food offered by a hand other than his master's, thus hastening his celestial reunion with the professor. When you think about it, he had a lot of options. What's clear, though, is that if the sport of dog agility had existed in 1925, and if Professor Ueno, having taken it up, had had the bad luck to perish under one of the obstacles, the faithful Hachiko would have stuck around.

Hachiko was the stuff of legends. Bingo was not. A healthy, young, hormone-driven male, he was discovered in the yard of a neat little white house near the center of Rangeley, the home of a golden retriever in her first heat. According to

Ginny, who'd organized the search for Bingo and who'd also been the one to locate him, the bitch's owners had been really quite nasty about the whole thing—and stupid, too. Desperate to rid themselves of Bingo before he could destroy the screen door at the front of the house, these ridiculous people had demonstrated their fathomless ignorance of the Labrador retriever by turning a hose on him! Could I believe it? Indeed I could, I told Ginny. People went out and bought malamutes, I said, and then had the audacity to turn around and complain —complain!—when their arctic bulldozers pulled, of all things! So if people thought that water would repel a Lab, it didn't surprise me at all.

"And instead of thanking me," Ginny reported, "they actually tried to get me to pay for replacing the screen on their door! Ignoramuses! The bitch should be spayed, anyway; she's definitely not of breeding quality. Among other things, I didn't like the looks of her hips one bit, and I told them so, too."

We were just outside my cabin, where I'd been peacefully grooming Rowdy when Ginny and Wiz had appeared and Ginny had begun to tell me all about finding Bingo, who now occupied Wiz's crate in the room that Ginny and Cam shared. Wiz herself had exchanged sniffs with Rowdy and dropped to the ground in a quivering mass of ingratiation. With what must have been Rowdy's implicit permission, she'd then risen to her feet and was now adding to my grooming efforts by vigorously scouring his muzzle with her pink tongue.

Idly raking out undercoat, I said, "Well, at least you found Bingo."

"And none too soon! These people were *so* stupid! I don't know why they didn't just grab him and tie him up! If I hadn't been there, they'd have bungled everything, and sooner or later, he'd have gotten to that bitch! And these were just the kinds of people who'd've put up a sign at the side of the road and given the puppies away to anyone who stopped."

Although I hadn't met the people, the assumption seemed unwarranted. Also, I felt pretty sure that Ginny had made just as poor an impression on the golden's owners as they had on her. Among other things, she was wearing what I think is called a crusher hat, a funny-looking green felt thing that rested absurdly on top of her basketlike coils of thin braid. Everyone in dogs was used to her appearance, and none of us would have been startled by a spay-neuter lecture. In the outside world, though, people must have considered her something of an eccentric.

Pulling the undercoat rake through Rowdy's tail, I said, "Well, I am glad that Bingo's safe. That tear on his ear and the scratches on his muzzle happened last night, you know. He got into a scrap with that Cairn—or whatever he is. Lucky. Otherwise, Bingo's okay?"

"By some miracle," Ginny said. "You know, that woman really was an idiot."

"The woman in Rangeley who—?"

"That Eva Spitteler! Going out in the middle of the night and fooling around with that damn equipment! I mean, what kind of judgment does *that* show? The poor dog! God only knows how long it'll take me to rehabilitate him."

Sensing a tremor in my hand, perhaps, or a change in my breathing, Rowdy fastened dark, questioning eyes on my face. I spoke hesitantly. "Ginny, I know it's always hard to remember, but, uh, legally, dogs are property, and—"

"Oh, that's strictly a nonissue," Ginny said blithely. "No one else is going to want him. And I have right of first refusal. It's in my contract." Breeders, as I've mentioned, place great faith in those documents. In a satisfied tone, Ginny repeated what she'd just said: "Right of first refusal. It's in my contract."

Twenty-three

"I COULD NOT HELP overhearing."

Phyllis Abbott spoke what I took to be the literal truth. She'd been sitting on her side of our shared deck doing what I'd been doing, grooming a dog and wondering what to do with herself, or so she confided to me. "I must say," Phyllis continued, "that if you didn't know Ginny, you'd be bound to think, 'Well, what a heartless response!' Really, it's just shock. Ginny's not a young woman, you know, and she was worried sick about the whole situation with Eva Spitteler and that dog, and then worried sick when the dog disappeared. Ginny really hasn't had time to absorb what's happened. Once she does, she'll feel just as dreadful about it as all the rest of us. What a terrible, terrible tragedy!" Phyllis swept the air with a tiny slicker brush.

Uninvited but not unwelcome, Phyllis was joining me in an impromptu grooming workshop. Rowdy was resting in belly-up nirvana on a beach towel while I used a porcupine brush on his inner thighs. Phyllis had coopted the steps that led up to my part of the deck as a makeshift grooming table.

Handsome little Nigel stood patiently as she systematically back-brushed layer after layer of his lovely coat.

"Grooming is so therapeutic, isn't it?" Phyllis remarked softly. "What on earth would we do without our dogs!"

"Yes, what on earth?" I agreed, momentarily interrupting my work on Rowdy's coat to run my fingers down his neck.

The exchange led us into a discussion of antidog legislation. Like virtually everyone else in the fancy, we opposed breed-specific legislation. One personal source of my opposition was stretched on the ground having his tummy brushed: The town that begins by outlawing pit bulls may soon create a list of prohibited breeds, a list that eventually includes the Alaskan malamute. Furthermore, as Phyllis understood, legislation forbidding the ownership of specific breeds sets a precedent for global legislation forbidding the ownership of any dog at all.

Lifting Nigel and turning him around, she asked whether I happened to know whether the town of Rangeley had enacted any such legislation.

"Not that I know of," I said. "I'd be amazed. I can't imagine . . . If anything, Rangeley seems like a very prodog place. There aren't a lot of show dogs, maybe, but almost everyone hunts, so a lot of people have gun dogs, and there's sled dog racing, pets . . . Besides, people around here are big on individual freedom. I can't see them supporting legislation that would threaten their right to own dogs."

"That's a dangerous assumption!" Phyllis warned me. "We absolutely must not underestimate the strength of antidog sentiment anywhere in this country!" Still diligently brushing Nigel, she added, "Take what's just happened here. Now, on the surface, it certainly does appear to be a terrible accident, plain and simple, and *nihil nisi bonum* and so forth, but an accident that reasonable judgment and basic safety precautions could have prevented. But if the police feel otherwise

. . . We'll see, I suppose. If that's the case, I can't help wondering. . . ."

The idea felt totally loopy. I just couldn't see Rangeley as a hotbed of antidog activists, one or more of whom had snuck into camp and somehow caused the A-frame to crash down on Eva Spitteler. As it turned out, though, I'd initially misunderstood Phyllis. What she had in mind wasn't an unnamed member of some hypothetical antidog conspiracy. The person she raised questions about was Everett Dow, who, I learned, had a reason to be hypersensitive about the whole subject of dogs. Furthermore, as Phyllis informed me, Everett had built the A-frame.

"Well, you see," Phyllis explained, "Maxine has taken him up as a sort of pet project of hers. She's known him since I don't know when. His father was the caretaker of her parents' cottage. And then a couple of years ago, his wife—this one's wife, not the father's—was very, very ill—she had ovarian cancer, young woman, too. . . . Well, so, on some sort of misguided impulse . . . What happened was that he was in Augusta or Bangor or someplace, and he was walking past a pet shop, and on one of those horrible impulses that get people in so much trouble, he wandered in and bought a little Yorkie puppy. A present, you see—therapy for his wife's morale. She was bedridden by then, you see. And it worked! For a day or two. I gather that she took one look, and she fell madly in love with the little dog, kept it with her . . . Well, you can imagine. And then after only a few days, the vomiting and the diarrhea started."

"Parvo," I said. Parvovirus.

Phyllis nodded. "And at first, they just thought, well, an upset stomach, whatever. But it finally dawned on them that something was very, very wrong, and he got the dog to the vet, and they went through what sounds like a heart-wrenching experience. The puppy'd begin to rally, then the whole thing would start up all over again. But in the end, the puppy didn't pull through."

"The poor people!"

"Wait! And a week later, the wife died. She'd been very, very ill—but this terrible experience probably did hasten her death. *We* know what it takes out of you to lose a dog! At any rate, at that point, the poor man fell completely to pieces. If it hadn't been for Maxine . . ."

I found it hard to imagine what anyone could have done to help. "What did Maxine . . . ?"

Phyllis's voice became light and brittle. "Well, this Everett started drinking quite heavily."

I hadn't seen Don Abbott take a drink in the daytime, but evenings were another matter.

Skipping quickly on, Phyllis added, "You can hardly blame him, after what he'd been through, but there you have it. And then he got himself fired from his job. And as if that wasn't enough, he got drunk one night and drove all the way to this pet shop, wherever it was, and started throwing bricks through the window! Not that they didn't deserve it for selling him that sick puppy, but someone saw him, and he got arrested. And that's when Maxine came in like a guardian angel. She got him a lawyer, and she got him into counseling, and she really grabbed him by the bootstraps and hauled him back on his feet!"

I made the obvious comment: "That was very kind of Maxine."

"It was also very ingenious," Phyllis said. "Who else would've thought about getting him hooked up with the agility people? She got him some other work, too, handyman things here and there, work here at the resort, but, you see, he'd been building things his entire life! Docks, picnic tables, benches, all sorts of things like that! And what Maxine realized was that this man could make A-frames and dogwalks and so forth, which really aren't all that different, at very, very competitive prices."

"And Maxine knew the people who'd want them."

"Precisely."

"But," I said, "it doesn't . . . It doesn't exactly sound as if Everett has a reason to hate dog people, does it? He could hardly hate Maxine, could he? And agility? If anything, you'd think he'd be all for it."

"Yes, of course," Phyllis conceded. "Even so, it's something to think about, isn't it? And you *do* remember what the dogs thought of him, don't you?" She stroked Nigel's head pensively. "They rose against him. They were obviously trying to tell us something. But perhaps it'll all turn out to be just what it seems. What a terrible, terrible shame." She shook her head.

"I wish I'd been kinder to Eva," I confessed. "All I can think of now is how desperately unhappy—"

"—how unhappy she made everyone in her vicinity!" Striding up from the direction of the main lodge, Don Abbott finished my sentence for me.

"Donald, really!" Phyllis protested.

Conflict interests Rowdy. In fact, he's a connoisseur. Within seconds, he was on his feet. Although Phyllis was the last one who'd spoken, Rowdy stared at Don, who said, "The damned shame of it is what this is going to do to Maxine." Lowering his voice, he added, "The truth is, this is nothing short of disaster for her. The economic consequences of this are going to be something even Maxine just can't get herself out of." Eyeing both Phyllis and me, he said sourly, "But that's going to be the last thing to cross the feminine mind."

The blood rose to my face. I live in Cambridge; I'm spoiled. Cambridge is a place where an African-American Jewish lesbian octogenarian encounters no discrimination at all— provided, of course, that she speaks in an educated voice and unfailingly remembers to renew her subscription to *The New*

York Review of Books. You think I'm joking? I'm serious. I love Cambridge. It's a place where we try hard not to go around making the blood rise to other people's faces. The surprise I felt was a great luxury.

Jabbing a well-manicured hand in the direction of the lodge, Don said, "There's a hullabaloo up there about some pins."

"Pins?" I asked. "Oh, hinge pins." The feminine mind at work. A man, of course, would immediately have thought of sewing pins. "They secure the hinges," I told Don. "They're sort of thick, heavy pins that go through the hinges." He still looked bewildered. "At the top of the A-frame."

"Well, these agility women are all agitated about it," Don said. "They got taken out of there for some reason or other, and there's some question about where they found these pins —whether they would've slipped out when this thing collapsed on her."

"Or?" I asked.

"Well, what it boils down to," Don said, "is basically that. Did they fall out? Or—"

"Or," I said, "were they pushed?"

Twenty-four

AFTER EVA SPITTELER'S DEATH, my sense of time became a luckless accordion squeezed and stretched by the protesting hands of some phantom child whose parents believed he had talent and who was determined to prove otherwise. The same grubby little fists that stretched minutes into empty hours would suddenly slam together, wrenching discordant seconds out of lengthy intervals.

I assume that the grooming session, my therapy hour, lasted the usual length: fifty minutes. By lunchtime I longed for the resumption of regularly scheduled activities, which, by Maxine's decree, had been canceled for the morning "out of respect for Eva" and would resume in the afternoon—here I again quote—"because Eva would have wanted it that way." Hypocrisy? Not exactly. Respect for Eva hadn't taken a posthumous upward zoom; what drew genuine awe was death itself. As for Eva's presumed wishes, it seemed to me that if she'd been in a position to survey the situation, her primary concern would have been her own demise; all else would have felt trivial.

When lunchtime finally arrived, the dining room presented a depressing scene. The walls and ceilings that had previously absorbed sound now sent it bouncing and jingling throughout the room so that everyone seemed to be either whispering or screaming. When Ginny bustled past me, her face grim, I pondered the husbands and, for the first time, took the matter seriously. Cam, who'd been Ginny's almost inseparable companion throughout camp, was nowhere in sight. My old friends weren't there, my new friends seemed like strangers, and the real strangers felt like people I didn't want to know. Banded together in what sounded like law-school study groups, people with tense shoulders and low voices mumbled about contracts, refunds, and waivers of liability. An independent student, I'd already consulted the camp contract, most of which consisted of waivers and releases so all-encompassing that in signing the document, we'd practically granted Maxine complete impunity to go around bludgeoning campers and dogs or to toss all of us in the middle of the lake. Absent from the formal contract was any mention of Maxine's obligations. Having spent long hours grinding away at the University of American Motion Pictures and Television School of Legal Studies, I concluded that the combination of campers' canceled checks and the written promises Maxine had made in the brochure and elsewhere probably added up to a contract. So if people packed up and departed, were they entitled to partial refunds? At a guess, no. If camp ended early? A moot point. No matter what, Maxine wouldn't send people home, because canceling camp this year would, in effect, mean permanently abandoning the enterprise. If this year's campers had paid mightily for a few days of camp followed by a fiasco and an early dismissal, who'd sign up for next year? Another moot point, perhaps. Alive, Eva had seemed like an especially crabby rotten apple. Equally rotten, however, was Maxine's ability to run the camp. In saying so, Eva had been dead accurate.

But the legalities were no concern of mine. I had no reason to sue Maxine; and having paid nothing, I clearly couldn't ask for a refund. Furthermore, even if every other camper decided to go home, Bonnie might expect me to demonstrate loyalty to her old friend Maxine by sticking around for the entire week. And at the end? When I finally got back to Cambridge, I'd have to sit down and write about the nightmarish days alone with Maxine as if camp really had been dog heaven with no bad dreams. If everyone else really left? Actually, I had a plan. Broke and disheartened, in no condition to care for a dog, Maxine would go away, leaving me in charge of her peaceful and charming young mastiff, Cash, whom a miraculously transformed Rowdy would immediately accept as a valued member of our little pack; and with the lodge, cabins, and lake to ourselves, the dogs and I would have such a great time that I'd only have to inject a few fictional human campers to make my article the literal truth.

Fantasy, yes. Reality: Yesterday morning, I'd sat at a table in this same dining room to watch swift dogs course after lures. If I sat at the same table today, I'd have a view across the field toward the parking lot, where an ominous-looking blue van had joined the cruiser. So, instead of filling a plate from the spread on the buffet table, I quickly assembled a sandwich, wrapped it in a napkin, left the lodge, wandered down to the dock in front of my cabin, and made my way past Heather and Sara. They were lying flat on the dock as if they'd intended to sunbathe, but had forgotten to undress first. Heather, lean and fit, now looked thin and pinched. The effect of the bright sun and the lake's glare on Sara's face reminded me of one of those wildly unflattering photographs of what people look like before cosmetic surgery. At the end of the dock, I removed my shoes and socks, sat down, soaked my feet in the lake, and ate food I couldn't taste. Also, I eavesdropped. I'd previously heard Heather and Sara hold a few minor debates about matters related to agility, for instance, whether a dog was or wasn't ready to try something new. Otherwise, they'd spoken with one voice, Sara's soft and warm, Heather's a little sharp, perhaps, but one voice nonetheless. Now, however, they were engaged in disjointed argument.

Heather's voice had lost its occasional edge to become steadily acerbic. "Look, Sara, face reality!" she demanded. "It was a booby trap, okay? Nobody goes out in the middle of the night to work a dog; you don't, I don't, and Eva Spitteler didn't, either. What she was out there doing was trying to rig the A-frame so it'd collapse under the first dog—or the first big dog, anyway. She hated me, she was jealous of both of us, and she wanted to make us look bad."

"But *nothing* would have happened," Sara insisted. "The fact is that the first thing we would've done would've been to check the obstacles. One of us would've found out! Okay, so maybe there's a remote possibility that it might have collapsed on, or more likely under, one of us, if we hadn't actually looked at the hinges. But there wasn't a chance that a dog would've been hurt. Not a chance!" she finished breathlessly.

"You're missing the point. We know a dog wouldn't've gotten hurt. But Eva didn't know that! And what if we'd—"

"We wouldn't have. We always check."

"Sara, yesterday, after the Canine Good Citizen test, we started moving things, and it's just remotely possible, you know, that this morning we would've said, 'Well, the A-frame's okay, because we just checked it yesterday afternoon.' "

"You know what, Heather? I don't know! All I really know is that those pins didn't just jump out of the hinges! They didn't slip out, fall out, drop out; they were in tight. How they ended up on the ground is one thing. But how one of them ended up *under* her . . . But if she was stupid enough to go under the A-frame and undo the chains, maybe she was stupid enough to—"

Heather snapped, "Remove the pins from the hinges and

then go under it? And then stand with all that weight over your head and undo the chains and try and move it? Nobody's that stupid. But maybe . . ." Her voice trailed off.

The two women fell silent. One of them sighed. In muted tones, they began to discuss their plans for next summer. Sara pointed out, correctly, I thought, that in agility, a reputation for unsafe equipment was a disaster. No matter how much people respected or liked the instructors, no one would take a chance with obstacles that might injure a dog.

After that, I caught only the occasional stressed word: *safety, reputation, liability*. And again and again, *competition*.

In the hope of finding the calm and solace that nature is reputed to offer, I studied the lake, but found nothing soothing. Two approaching Jet Skis buzzed like chain saws. From a tree at the edge of the lake, a belted kingfisher swooped out and dove at the water, its flight jerky, its rattling call dry and cruel. Making my way past Sara and Heather, I left the dock and went to my cabin, wherein lay nature's true source of peace and comfort. What's wrong with mountains, lakes, trees, kingfishers, and all those other supposedly restorative elements of the wilderness—or for that matter, of the cosmos —is that no matter how intensely you stare at them, admire them, venerate them—no matter how much you love them, they'll never love you back. But a dog? A really *good* dog? It's like the Miracle of the Draught of Fishes. You're Simon, the fisherman, and you spend all day casting your net into the water without catching so much as a minnow. And then along comes Jesus and tells you that you've got to try again, and you do: You catch such a multitude that your net breaks. In other words, hanging around in nature's vicinity is a waste of time until love and faith come along. And when they do, you get back more than you can handle: draughts of fishes, Alaskan malamutes.

And that's how I spent the next hour: handling Rowdy. Or trying. In obedience, almost all of us handle our dogs ourselves; it's an amateur-dominated sport and none the worse for it, because, except among the top handlers, it's as competitive or noncompetitive as you choose to make it. Conformation, however, is the hardball of the dog show game. That's why I hire a professional handler to show Rowdy in breed. If the dog-eat-dog breed competition depended strictly on the merits of the animals, I'd be spared the expense; but as it is, Rowdy deserves a better breed handler than I'll ever be.

That Rowdy and I ended up in Eric Grimaldi's breed handling class is thus testimony to my respect for the authority of AKC judges: Eric gave me an order, and I obeyed. Eric didn't phrase it as an order. What he said was that Maxine McGuire was the best of the best, and that if Maxine wanted him to do a breed handling class, he was happy to oblige. Like all other activities scheduled for the morning, breed handling had, of course, been canceled. For reasons unconnected to Eva's death, however, the afternoon schedule contained numerous gaps. The carting workshop was off; according to rumor, Maxine had had some sort of financial dispute with the instructor. The people running the Temperament Testing had phoned to report that their van had broken down on the Maine Turnpike. The last-minute cancellations seemed to me to confirm Eva Spitteler's analysis of Maxine's deficiencies as camp director.

"We can't let Maxine down," Eric told me. "What we all need to do is pitch in and try to salvage what we can. You're not doing anyone any good hanging around here with a long face, are you?" I admitted that I wasn't. "Come on!" he said. "I was counting on you to be a good sport, Holly. And you'll like it. It'll be fun."

The class took place in the same big field we'd used for lure coursing and obedience, but at the end near the main lodge, as distant as possible from the police van and the cruisers clustered near the little road that led to the agility area. Because of Eric's determination to recruit participants and thus to create a semblance of normal camp activity, he ended up with about twenty people, five or ten more than he probably wanted. Although conformation is, by definition, open only to purebreds, a few campers showed up with what I think I'm now supposed to call random-bred dogs, mixes, crosses, and anybody's guesses owned by people who wanted to find out what breed handling was, I suppose, or by people who just wanted something to do. Jacob, the long-coated Akita, couldn't be shown in breed, but Michael brought him, anyway, for the socialization, I suppose. Maybe Joy and Craig brought Lucky for the same reason. I certainly hoped that they didn't ask Eric's opinion of the little dog's merits. To support Eric, I think, Phyllis Abbott showed up with Nigel, who really was a show dog, as were quite a few of the others gathered near the two baby-gated rings that Everett Dow was setting up. Today, the dogs ignored the handyman. At the last minute, Cam and Ginny turned up, Cam with Nicky, and Ginny, to my amazement, with a highly subdued Bingo.

Let me remind you that Eric Grimaldi was a handsome man with an appropriately judicial air of authority. He started the class by assembling us in one of the rings and explaining what we'd try to accomplish. We'd begin, he said, with a review of a few basics: the correct collar position, the appropriate position of the dog, the stand. Then we'd break into groups. Eric would work first with the real beginners; meanwhile, the rest of us could observe or, if we liked, practice in the other ring.

Rowdy sat at my left side with his eyes fixed on my face. When he's with his breed handler, Faith, he knows not to sit, and he gaits for her without twisting his head to watch her face. I had to remind myself that in taking Rowdy to a single breed handling class, I wasn't going to confuse him; plenty of dual-ring dogs had the same handler in breed and in obedience. In fact, I paid more attention to Rowdy than I did to Eric, who was delivering a little introductory lecture about the artificiality of the show pose. "The natural look isn't what we're after here," he told us. When Eric switched to the topic of collar position, I followed his instructions, moving the collar to Rowdy's jawline, tightening it there, and making sure that the dead ring was just below Rowdy's right ear. Glancing around, I noticed that, for once, Craig was working with Lucky, stooping down and running unfamiliar fingers around the little dog's neck. When it came time to pose the dogs, I mechanically followed along with everyone else. Rowdy, however, who'd evidently grasped the purpose of the class, got a glint in his eyes and not only stacked himself to advantage, but went to great lengths to wag his tail with eye-catching enthusiasm.

"That's a real showman you've got there," Eric commented.

I nodded. To Rowdy, I said, "Happy now?"

Soon thereafter, Eric asked the experienced people to leave the ring. To what was probably Rowdy's disappointment, I led him out. In other circumstances, I'd probably have gone to the second ring to practice almost anything. Instead, I stood outside Eric's ring and listened to him address the beginners. "The first thing you have to ask yourselves is: What is your intention here? If you're here to have fun, that's fine. If you're here to socialize your dog, that's fine, too. If you're here because you're thinking about trying to finish your dog, I'll give you my opinion. But if you ask for it, there are a couple of things you have to bear in mind. First of all, it's just my opinion, you asked for it, and you do what you want with it—keep what you want, throw out the rest. And second of all, don't ask if you don't want to hear."

Stepping rapidly up to me, Joy asked, "What's he talking about?"

"*Finish* means finish a championship," I said. "Some of the people might want to know whether their dogs might be worth showing, and he's offering to give his opinion, but just if it's helpful, just if people want to hear."

Joy burst in: "Well, I hope he doesn't say anything awful about Lucky! Because that's the last thing Craig . . . *I* understand, and I really love Lucky, and I don't care, but . . . I don't know why Craig insisted on coming to this. We really don't belong here. We don't belong at this camp at all. I wanted to go home this morning, but Craig said we'd paid our money, and we were going to stick it out."

"If Craig asks, Eric will be tactful," I said.

"Not like Eva. . . . Was that the most awful thing? Everything has been awful since practically the first second we got here, but last night was *the* worst." Joy paused. "But do you *believe* what Lucky did?" When Ginny came striding up with Bingo, Joy's pride evaporated. "Oh," Joy said softly, "here comes that horrible dog. But at least today he's wearing a muzzle."

"Rowdy, down!" I ordered. "Stay!" I bent over to give him the signal, my flat palm in front of his face. When I stood up, Ginny and Bingo had reached us.

"That's not a muzzle," I informed Joy. "It's a training halter."

And in combination with Ginny's in-charge manner, it worked very well indeed. When Ginny told Bingo to sit, sit he did, and promptly.

"Eva," Ginny announced with glee, "was planning to open a dog camp! Next summer! That's what she was doing here all along, the little sneak—trying to find out about what they were like. She'd been to *two* others this year."

"Yeah," Joy said vaguely. "That's why she was getting people's addresses. She asked us not to mention it, because Maxine might not understand. And Eva said she wasn't inviting everybody—just a few people she liked."

I ignored Joy. "Ginny, where did you hear that?"

"Oh, it's definite. I talked to her brother-in-law, just now.

Max gave me the sister's phone number. Eva'd listed her sister as her emergency contact, and I had to arrange things about Bingo, not that they had much choice, but I wanted it settled."

"And?" I asked.

"Oh, it's going to cost me," Ginny said, "but I was prepared for that all along. They're not dog people—the sister and the brother-in-law—and no one else in the family is, either. They don't want him. We settled for the purchase price. With me, you know, he's been perfectly okay. The Halti's just in case he forgets who's who. And I've been thinking: I'll get this blubber off him, give him some exercise, get him in shape, and . . . Well, we'll see, but I think maybe I can finish him."

At my side, Rowdy stirred. "Stay!" I reminded him. To Ginny, I said, "So this business about Eva's camp . . . That explains a lot. The sympathy cards, the gruesome stuff, the troublemaking."

"The police found a dozen more cards in Eva's room," Ginny informed me. "Clippings. Lots of stuff."

"So we were right all along. She must've arrived here ready to—"

"To ruin Maxine's camp," Ginny said. "To kill the competition."

Twenty-five

"I'VE JUST STARTED going through the magazines," Leah reported. "I haven't had time."

"Leah, you know, I don't ask you for all that many favors, and—"

"But I have the Passaic catalog," she replied smugly. "That's what I've been doing all this time. Or doesn't that interest you?"

"Of course it does! But where . . . ?"

"Faith Barlow."

As I've mentioned, when I show Rowdy in conformation, I use a professional handler: Faith Barlow. Faith shows a lot. She shows her own dogs and other people's. She hits so many shows up and down the East Coast and is such an avid collector of show catalogs that as soon as Leah spoke her name, I felt stupid. Leah never tries to make me feel that way. Far from it. She achieves the effect by assuming that I'm as quick as she is. In her place, I'd have started by poking through dozens of recent issues of dog publications. Leah, however, had gone straight to the point, or to one of the points, anyway. She'd still have to look through the magazines, but in getting hold of the show catalog, she'd obtained a complete list of everyone officially connected with the show: the officers of the Passaic Kennel Club, the judges, the stewards, even the vendors and the official show veterinarian, as well as the name of every dog entered, and the names of the dog's breeder, owner, and handler, too. Leah was about to start her freshman year at Harvard. I wished Harvard luck.

"Oh, Faith Barlow, of course," I remarked, as if the need to call Faith had gone without saying. "You went out there? How'd you get there?"

"Borrowed Steve's van. Does it ever smell like dogs!"

"He's a vet," I said. "What do you expect it to smell like? Did you take Kimi?"

Faith has malamutes. With the Alaskan Malamute National Specialty coming up in October, Kimi—in season or out—needed all the exposure to others of her breed that we could provide.

"Yes," Leah said. "I fed her chlorophyll and sprayed her with Lust Buster, but the males were interested anyway."

"And how'd *she* do?"

"Okay."

"Meaning?"

"Meaning I did what Anna Morelli said to do. I put Kimi on a down and—"

"Yeah, well, Anna Morelli's one of the people we're going up against, you know, and Tundra is so good with other animals—"

As a reminder to myself that an exceptionally brilliant and intense malamute can, in fact, be trained to behave herself in the presence of other animals, I'd placed a framed photograph of Anna and Tundra on the windowsill directly in front of my computer, where I had to look at it every time I sat down to work. Also present in the picture was, of all things, a ferret, which lay spread out on Tundra's neck, its head peering over the top of hers. In case you know anything about malamutes, I should add that, remarkably enough, the ferret was alive and that, rather than attempting to kill it, Tundra was making intelligent and peaceful eye contact with the camera. Anna was smiling joyfully. And for good reason.

"Stop!" Leah demanded. "I know all about the ferret! I've seen the picture. And if you expect me to go out and get some ferret so that Kimi can learn . . . Holly, it's a *malamute* specialty! There aren't exactly going to be a lot of ferrets—"

"It's important to proof against all possible contingencies," I said blandly.

"So are you interested in this catalog, or would you rather nag me—"

"Leah, I'm sorry. What have you found?" I rested a little notebook on a shelf under the pay phone and prepared to scribble.

"Okay. Um, Mrs. Donald Abbott judged Novice A and Open B."

"You have the catalog there? Where are you in it? At the beginning?"

"Yes. Where it lists the rings. You want me to read it to you?"

"Yes. Just the relevant parts, not everything."

"Okay. 'Ring eleven. Judge: Mrs. Donald Abbott. Stewards: Mary Ellen Fisher, John Greely, Trudy Parker.' "

"Never heard of them. Go on."

" 'Nine A.M.' I'll just summarize this, okay? Twenty-four Novice A entries. Lunch at noon. Then twelve-thirty, Open B had fifteen entries, and the stewards were, uh, Eileen Alberts, Ann Hull, Joseph Weiss."

Again, unfamiliar. "Now look at the entries, okay? Toward the back—"

"I know! Just a minute. Okay. Novice A—"

"See if she had a dog called Benchenfield—"

"Benchenfield Farmer's Dog," Leah said. "Yes. The

breeder . . . This is one of the ones you gave me. The breeder is Virginia Garabedian. That's Ginny, isn't it? The one with the skinny braid all wrapped—"

"Yes. Where'd you meet her?"

"Hockamock."

"So, keep reading."

"Labrador retriever. And the owner is Eva J. Spitteler. You want me to look up the addresses?"

"Yes," I said. "Before we hang up. For now, just scan the rest of Novice A, and see if you see any of the other names." I waited. Leah found none. She turned to the page of Open B entries. "This is one of them," she said. " 'CH OTCH Windemere's Nickum.' "

Owned, of course, by Camilla White. I recognized a few other names of people who'd had dogs in Open B, but no one from camp. In case you don't show your dogs . . . Well, in fact, if you don't show your dogs, consider taking up the sport, huh? It's a lot of fun. But, as I started to point out, if you don't show, you may not realize that you don't just turn up at the last minute. You mail or fax your entry weeks before the show, and definitely by the closing date, after which time the show-giving club prepares the catalog. Consequently, unless there's been an error in the printing of the catalog, every dog actually shown is listed under the class in which he's entered.

When we'd finished reviewing Open B, Leah turned to the last pages of the catalog and consulted the index of exhibitors, looked for names, and gave me a few addresses. Maxine McGuire's name appeared. Turning back in the catalog, Leah found that Max had had a mastiff in Open Bitches, which I might add, is a conformation class that has nothing to do with Open Obedience—or, for that matter, with bitchiness, either, except in the strictly technical sense. Ginny's name appeared under the heading "Retrievers (Labrador) Open, Yellow Bitches" as the breeder, owner, and handler of Benchenfield

Prodigy CD, JH—Junior Hunter—the only owner-handled entry in the class. I wondered how they'd done. The judge had been Horace Lathrop, who's a friend of my father's and a fair judge, or so Buck says, anyway. Eric Grimaldi had had a long day. He'd started his breed judging with pointers at eight-thirty A.M., taken a lunch break between spaniels, English springer and field, and ended with Weimaraners; and then at six o'clock, he'd judged the Sporting Group and Brace.

I thanked Leah, asked her to keep looking through the catalog, and reminded her to check the dog magazines. She'd shown initiative in hunting up the catalog, and it had provided some information, but any show catalog is subject to what I guess you'd call false positives: dogs and people whose names were printed in the catalog, but who for one reason or another had never turned up. It happens all the time. Dogs go lame or blow coat. Exhibitors get the flu. Although the American Kennel Club is formally protesting the matter in the Highest Court of All, as of this date, even AKC judges are still subject to attacks of appendicitis and to the other sudden ills of ordinary mortals. And if a club is forced to use a substitute judge? If there's time, the club mails a notice to everyone who's entered, and the substitution is always posted at the show, but the original name still appears in the catalog, of course. Furthermore, although you can't enter a dog after the closing date for a show, there's nothing to prevent you from going there and wandering around with the hundreds or thousands of other spectators, none of whose names are recorded anywhere.

When I emerged from the stuffy heat of the phone booth, it was time for drill team, the prospect of which really put me off. For one thing, the day had become oppressively hot and humid. Mostly, though, the idea of heeling dogs around in would-be precision lines and pinwheel formation to the brassy, jolly strains of a marching band only a few hundred yards from where Eva had died felt uncomfortably like dancing on her grave. Perhaps my objection seems senseless. I don't really like the idea of tutued ballerinas pirouetting on the sod over my own remains, but I take comfort in advance from the vision of happy teams of handlers and dogs parading above while I'm down below—provided, of course, that the handlers insist on tight heeling and quick sits, and that the dogs invariably come when called. But remember! No forging, no lagging, no sloppy work at all, or the ground beneath your feet will rumble and shake, and you'll know that Holly Winter will keep rolling over until that dog shapes up.

But Rowdy and I went to drill team nonetheless. Janet, our instructor, conducted herself and the activity with admirable dignity. She omitted the music. What piece could we have used? The Dead March from *Saul?* With an air of brave determination to carry on, Phyllis Abbott took her position at the center of the line, moved briskly, and paid what must have been close attention to Janet's cues. I had the feeling that Mrs. Abbott was concentrating on setting a good example. The AKC would even have approved of her apparel, knitted coordinates that would have looked dowdy on a young woman, tailored pants and a matching twin set in a muted, demure shade of spruce, clothing too warm for what had become a July-hot day. As attentive as his handler, Nigel kept his bright dark eyes on her face. His task couldn't have been easy. Phyllis was a big, tall woman, so it was a long way up to her face from Pomeranian level, and the jut of her bosom must have blocked Nigel's view. From Rowdy's face to mine was no great distance, and my anatomy presented no natural obstacles to eye contact, but he remained as unfocused on me as I was on the pattern we were supposed to be following. Although we were practicing what we'd learned the day before, I kept forgetting the next move, turning in the wrong direction, and failing to keep tabs on the other handlers and dogs, thus throwing us as out of sync with everyone else as we were with each other. By the time drill team finally ended, I felt sorry I'd gone to it at all, not because we'd displayed any disrespect for Eva or for her memory—we hadn't—but because I'd literally misled Rowdy, who had deserved all my attention or none at all and had received a confusing mishmash of the two. To make amends, I stayed for flyball, which Rowdy had loved the day before and which, at his beginning level, required very little from me. Focused on the flyball box and on the tennis balls that sprang from it, Rowdy must have found the inanimate objects more responsive than I'd been during the previous hour. Except to cheer Rowdy on, I spoke little. Avoiding my friends, I exchanged a few aimless words with people I didn't really know: the couple with the beautiful English setters, Ms. Baskerville, the owners of the handsome basenjis, the woman named Jennifer with the obedience Doberman, Delilah.

Walking Rowdy back to our cabin, I had a sudden attack of homesickness. I missed Kimi so sharply that tears came to my eyes. With a leash in only one hand, a dog on only one side, I felt oddly unsafe. When we reached the cabin, I gave Rowdy a bowl of water. When he'd finished slurping it up, I presented him with a big dog biscuit. He didn't have to sit, give his paw, drop, watch me, or do anything else to earn the reward; it felt important to me to give him a simple gift. Furthermore, although I'd laughed at the presence of an air conditioner in a cabin in God's country, I turned the silly thing on and settled Rowdy under it. When he'd wrapped himself up in his classic heat-conserving sled dog position, tail curled to cover his nose and thus warm the frigid air, I sat at the desk and covered its surface with some of the material I'd used in drafting my article: copies of AKC rules, regulations, and guidelines; a couple of old issues of the *Gazette;* and pages of notes scribbled on yellow legal pad. Like everything else I write by hand, the notes were almost totally illegible, even to me. I was a prescient child, convinced that penmanship exercises were a waste of time. It's clear to me now that I foresaw the invention of the personal computer. I wished now that my clairvoyance had had a practical bent: A psychic pragmatist would also have divined the means to afford a laptop. With complete foreknowledge that unless I printed carefully, I'd soon be unable to decipher what I wrote, I took brief, careful notes about possible grounds for AKC suspension, reprimands, and fines. From the *Gazette* and from memory, I made notes of particulars, most of which were irrelevant to my purpose. If anyone at Waggin' Tail had committed any of the obvious AKC crimes, I'd certainly have heard by now. No one was guilty of any of the dramatic offenses for which people had been publicly shamed in the Secretary's Pages of the *Gazette:* No one had kicked a judge, shouted obscenities at a steward, or thrown a grooming table at another exhibitor. In search of subtle or private transgression, I studied the AKC rules pertaining to shows, the guidelines for conformation and obedience judges, and, for perhaps the millionth time in my life, the obedience regulations. From the beginning, it was clear that the person most likely to have risked reprimand or suspension was Eva Spitteler herself. Hers was the dog most likely to have caused a problem at a show, and it was easy to imagine Eva using abusive language to a fellow exhibitor, starting an altercation with an official, or arguing about a judge's decision. As I already knew, exhibitors were forbidden to threaten judges and to question their decisions. Judges were absolutely and repeatedly forbidden to solicit judging assignments. In all respects, the behavior of judges was supposed to be above reproach. Eric Grimaldi and Phyllis Abbott had judged at the Passaic show. Ginny, a tracking judge, had been an exhibitor.

As I was castigating myself for not having been there myself, a sharp rapping on the cabin door awakened Rowdy, who leaped up, wagged his tail, bounced around, and pointed his nose toward the source of the sound.

I opened the door to Phyllis Abbott. She stepped only a few feet inside, shook Rowdy's outstretched paw, and said, "I can't stay. I just stopped in to give you a message. You're supposed to call home. Maxine asked me to tell you."

My heart raced.

Kimi.

Five minutes later, I was in the stuffy phone booth frantically dialing my own number. Before Leah had finished saying hello, I demanded, "Is Kimi all right?"

"Would you relax?" my cousin said.

"I'll try."

"We were going to talk later. Remember? After I read the magazines? Well, it's later, okay?"

"Okay. So what'd you find?"

"About two million ads for dogs, a hundred boring articles about the search for a new AKC president when what's his name retires. It's supposed to be soon. All this stuff about qualifications, knowledge of dogs, business management skills versus dog stuff, lots of that kind of thing."

"Yes, but—"

"It's not 'yes, but.' That's why I called. Most of what I found is stuff we already knew—who was at Passaic, that kind of thing. But then two of the gossip columns had . . . Well, one of them said something about this Donald Abbott and John White—"

"John R.B.," I said.

"Yes. And so I sort of read between the lines, and then I called your father."

"You called Buck?"

"Yes. And he says he heard the same thing."

"What thing?"

"About this guy Donald Abbott."

"What about him?"

"That he's in line. Or really, he thinks he's in line. And that's why he's doing all this politicking. He's working on it."

"In line for . . . ?"

"He wants to be president of the AKC."

"That's ridiculous," I said.

"That's what Buck thinks, too."

"Well, Buck is right," I said.

But after I hung up, while I was charging down the steps of the lodge on my way to my cabin to change for dinner, I almost collided with Don Abbott, who said heartily, "Well, you're full of energy, aren't you? Good for you! Go get dressed, and come back up and enjoy yourself. I always say: You can't keep dog people down for long."

It was, of course, exactly what someone had done to Eva Spitteler.

Twenty-six

IF I'D BEEN THE POLICE, I'd have questioned everyone. I, for example, had a lot to say.

So what else is new?

Truly. If properly interrogated, I'd have told all. *(Nice dog you got there, lady. Be a shame to separate the two of you.)* But according to the rumors that spread from table to table at dinner that night, instead of making interesting and productive use of my loyalty by frightening me into revealing the secrets of the Order, the police had frittered away their time extracting dull facts about the A-frame from people who didn't even try to keep them secret. No one came right out and said that the police should've talked to me, of course; that's just my own conclusion. But according to gossip, the police had concentrated on Heather and Sara, who owned the A-frame; on Everett Dow, who'd built it; and on the proprietor of the hardware store where Everett had bought the hinges and chains. For information about Waggin' Tail, they'd turned to Maxine. Neglected, I was thus virtually forced to keep my knowledge of the grips, signs, and passwords all to myself. I don't blame the police. From the unenlightened perspective of their own fraternal order, they were following what must have seemed like the sensible course of posing questions about Eva's death to people who might have been expected to know the answers.

Having been seated among the elect on the previous evening, I was hoping to demote myself back to my own level, but Maxine McGuire snagged me, and I got stuck at her table again. Heather and Sara had escaped to a far corner of the dining room, but as on the previous night, Cam and Ginny were at Max's table, as were Don and Phyllis Abbott and Eric Grimaldi. Everyone but Phyllis was drinking pretty heavily, it seemed to me, and I'm not exactly a teetotaler. In the places previously occupied by the agility people were Craig and Joy, who were undergoing what I took to be the first steps in an initiation into the fancy.

"Craig's been bitten by the bug," Don Abbott informed me in a Scotch-thick voice smoothed by the burgundy he was pouring down. "He's been asking about where he can get a show dog."

Joy giggled. *Giggled.* "And what to do once we get it," she added in the tone of someone who deludes herself into believing she's uttered an exceptionally clever remark.

Craig, who apparently shared the delusion, gave her a protective hug. He squeezed her lightly, as if she were a fragile puppy unable to withstand a solid grown-up thump. What made me uncomfortable about the two of them, I realized, wasn't just Joy's stereotypical ultrafeminine, helpless, vulnerable, and infantile manner, or even the possibility that some misguided individual might misuse her as a basis for making assumptions about me or about other women. No, that was just the least of it. What really bothered me wasn't Joy alone, but the couple, Joy and Craig in combination, because taken together, Joy so little-girlish, Craig so unnaturally overmuscled, the two of them, despite the clean, wholesome appear-

ance of the individuals, somehow exuded an air of child mo-
lestation: victim and perpetrator, wife and husband. I
wondered whether Joy could possibly have remained a virgin
bride.

Don, Phyllis, and Eric gave no sign of entertaining such
speculations. Tactfully avoiding any reference to Lucky's deficiencies as a show dog, Eric offered numerous helpful recommendations about getting started in dogs. Go to a show, he
suggested. And read Don Abbott's terrific book! Stretching a
point, Don asked whether they were thinking of another
Cairn. Yes, they were. Well, Don would be happy to get the
names of reputable breeders in their area. Showing dogs was
really a lot of fun, Phyllis said. Among other things, you got to
meet wonderful people; you made friends for life.

Meanwhile, Maxine was expressing considerable annoyance
at Wayne Varney, who, she said, could have dealt with the
whole matter very competently himself. She'd never before
suspected Wayne of suffering from such low self-esteem. And
why on earth did they need an autopsy? When she lost a dog
for no known reason, she always had one performed, but this
was different. Plainly speaking, Eva had gotten conked on the
head. What more obvious cause of death could there be?

Paying no attention to the content of Maxine's complaints,
Ginny spoke almost exclusively about Bingo: good lines, sire
finished, dam pointed, eyes and hips clear on both sides,
lovely temperaments, and on and on in the eternal manner of
dog breeders. Cam listened patiently. What could she possibly
have replied?

Except to insert food, I kept my mouth shut. The clam
chowder was Cape Cod style, a white sauce with chopped
quahogs, not Maine clam chowder, which has a relatively thin
but strong-tasting broth and swims with whole steamers, bel-
lies, chewy necks, and all, delicious, but not to the squeamish,
I suppose. The main course, seafood lasagna, wasn't bad, and

I'd drenched my salad in Ranch. Dessert was bread pudding. A white meal.

After I'd eaten, I got a cup of coffee, and instead of downing it and excusing myself, I sat there as the passive observer of a ritual at which I'd often officiated. The liturgical phrases and sentences were ones I'd recited myself. Whole paragraphs had passed my own lips. Don's advice to Craig was my own, as were Eric's injunctions, and, most of all, Phyllis's enthusiasm. Time and again, in welcoming newcomers to the fancy, I'd offered the same grand incentives: the promise that shows were *such* fun and that dog people were *so* wonderful.

Our table dispersed when Don Abbott asked whether he could interest anyone in a cognac and no one but Eric accepted the suggestion. Craig, I felt sure, wanted to join the other men, but succumbed to the batting of Joy's tired, imploring eyes. He escorted her away with the genuinely reluctant but duty-first, no-choice, you-understand air of a parent forsaking a good party to get the baby-sitter home. As Ginny rose from her seat, the thought crossed my mind that for once, she looked her age. Then I realized that I had no idea what it actually was. Her skin was suddenly more wrinkled than weathered, and loose hairs were making their escape from what had always been the tight-security lockup of that narrow plait. Although Phyllis pleaded fatigue, her wide, glossy eyes and the tension in her jaw and hands predicted a choice between pills and insomnia. Maxine looked damp and overheated: Artificial-looking pink blotches burned on her cheeks, and the veins around her nose blazed red. In contrast to the rest of us, Cam looked neat, tidy, and precisely as sleepy as a healthy person should be at bedtime. In the lakeside humidity and the lingering warmth of the unseasonably hot day, everyone else's hair had broken out in everything from unexpected little crimps and waves to Orphan Annie mops to what looked like the kinds of bizarrely dual-purpose items advertised on late-night TV—voluminously pilose wigs that had only to be whisked off the head and lightly damped to serve as restaurant-size scouring pads guaranteed to remove even baked-on grease from commercial cookware. And I'm not just the president of the Hair Club for Pots! I'm also . . .

But Cam didn't believe in gimmicks. What she believed in was obedience. I imagined her standing in front of the bathroom mirror, where she'd command the full attention of her short, dark hair ("Ready! Watch me!") and go on to issue the same commands she gave to her dogs, and in some of the exact same words, too: Down! Stay! And stay down it did, in neat rows of controlled waves, until Cam released it. Or possibly she never did. For some people, no exercise is ever really finished.

So when I left the main lodge, Eric Grimaldi and Don Abbott were heading across the lobby to the little bar known as The Pub for what Eric had insisted was going to be one quick nightcap; and Joy and Craig were presumably in their cabin, where, I imagined, he was zipping her into or possibly out of a fuzzy pink bunny-sleeper. Since Cam, Ginny, Phyllis, and I were going in the same direction, we walked together. Phyllis, as I recall, did all the talking: Wasn't it exciting to encourage newcomers to get involved! Joy and Craig were people with a lot to contribute. Didn't we agree? Instead of waiting to hear whether we did, Phyllis switched to exclamations about the brightness of the stars and the beauty of the moon on the lake. I slapped at a mosquito and said nothing. When we reached Cam and Ginny's cabin, Phyllis said her good nights in exactly the same gracious tone she used in the ring, as if she were ordering them to prepare not their dogs, but themselves, for the long down. I'd always found Phyllis very pleasant in the ring—friendly, considerate, and fair. Judicial, too, of course. After all, she was a judge.

As Phyllis and I covered the short distance to our cabin, she remarked on what a trooper Ginny was. "You know, it's not every breeder who'd take full responsibility for that dog,"

Phyllis said. "Some people out there would decide they didn't like the impression people were getting of their lines, and they'd put him down. But not Ginny. I admire her spirit. I hope she's not setting herself up for disappointment."

I said I hoped so, too. Starting up my own stairs, I wished Phyllis good night. She told me to sleep well.

But every diligent dog owner is a sort of Robert Frost—dogs to walk before we sleep, dogs to walk before we sleep. Speaking of which, you know this book by Elizabeth Marshall Thomas? *The Hidden Life of Dogs*. That one. It's what I thought of as I walked Rowdy that night . . . or, pardon me, as I systematically applied my observational skills to his behavior in my trillionth effort to fathom how any sensate human being could ever have discerned anything even remotely discreet, reserved, or modest, never mind clandestine, disguised, covert, masked, obscured, kept under wraps, or otherwise *HIDDEN*, for heaven's sake, about the desire of a male dog to leave his mark as ostentatiously as possible on absolutely every object in the vicinity of which he could possibly cock a leg. In truth, it's a sad book, the pitiful story of a woman so terrified of a normal, protective human relationship with dogs that she fled the responsibility and mutuality that love entails.

But there's one phrase in the book that I adore: "pitiless domestication." You know what that means? The breeding of show dogs. Almost everyone else in the fancy loathed the book, you know. I'm unusual. Anyway, with my product of pitiless domestication oppressively reduced to an unnatural and abnormal condition, which is to say, with Rowdy safely hitched to his flex lead and thus, worse yet, linked to his devoted oppressor, I started out along the bank of the lake away from the main lodge. When we reached the thick woods, the path ended, and we reversed direction, strolled past the dock, the pebble beach, the upended canoes, the lodge itself, and the cabins on its far side. Circling around in back, we skirted the edge of the big field, passing the area where Eric

had held the breed handling class. Here and there in the field
and among the trees that formed its boundaries, dark shapes
loomed and stirred: other people, other dogs. Restless, I considered crossing the field to the blacktop drive and following
it through the high pines and thick undergrowth out to the
main highway. What kept me away from the dirt road to the
agility area was not, I conclude in retrospect, some supersti-
tious fear that Eva's avenging revenant lurked among the colorful obstacles, passed through them perhaps, invisibly
seesawed back and forth on the teeter-totter, whooshed
through the weave poles, cleared the jumps, or lingered on the
pause table gathering strength to spring off, brutally dismem-
ber the innocent pieces of equipment, and—brandishing
planks, poles, metal bases, thick wooden supports, and heavy
chains in its phantasmagoric hands—vent the rage of the
newly dead on any hapless intruder who had the ill luck to
stroll by. Not at all. I didn't fear the living, either: I was no
threat to anyone. Besides, despite Elizabeth Marshall
Thomas's fancy academic credentials—gee whiz, a Ph.D. in
anthropomorphism—the real expert on dogs was Carol Lea
Benjamin: Rowdy's heritage of pitiless domestication had, if
anything, brightened the big red S on his show-dog chest, and
I was his very own Lois Lane. So what stayed my steps? Not
the dead, not the living, but what I now identify as true panic:
the primitive, universal terror of the great god Pan. At the
time, though, all I felt was a muted, civilized disinclination to
approach the thick woods.

"Rowdy, this way!" I called softly. "Let's go!" I had to reel
in his lead. Pan was Greek, a god of trees and shepherds.
Rowdy's original people spoke Mahlemut. On the treeless
tundra, they kept no sheep. Survival itself was their only luxury. They could not indulge in pointless foreign gods.

"Rowdy, this way!"

Driven, as I now realize, away from the shadowy woods and
toward the expanse of the lake, I jogged past the lodge, slowed

my pace, and wandered by my cabin and down the slope to the water. A loon laughed. The bird's call is freakish, human and nonhuman, utterly animal yet disturbingly easy to mimic. It doesn't take much skill to ape loons well enough to call them in. I wanted to try, but I was no more eager to be overheard by the campers still awake than I was to awaken those who'd gone to bed. My loon imitation, although remarkably effective in achieving its goal, is not meant for human ears. I yodel even worse than I sing, and my singing exhibits the same leaden property that affects my efforts to float: negative buoyancy.

"And if I got the loon to come in," I told Rowdy, "you'd just scare it away."

In response to my voice, Rowdy wagged his tail. He doesn't even mind my singing. Dogs will forgive anything. Considering his tolerance and devotion, I should have stayed where I was, on good, reliable, and, above all else, blessedly dry land, albeit it at the edge of that nasty stuff that creeps through both layers of your coat, right to your skin, where it feels just horrible. But I stepped onto the dock and coaxed: "Come on, big boy! It won't hurt you! The dock is dry, and Kimi isn't here to push you in."

Kimi had done it once, at my father's place, whether accidentally or deliberately, I don't know. Rowdy hadn't blamed her. Instead, he'd thenceforth treated all wooden docks as members of a secret Rowdy-drenching society, fanatical conspirators devoted to the goal of getting him wet.

When he succumbed to my cajoling by placing all four paws on the planks, his resistance diminished, and I had no trouble in leading him to the end, where I stood and surveyed the lake. As I've mentioned, the day had been outright hot for Maine in late August. The evening, although warm for Maine, was cool by ordinary standards; before taking Rowdy out, I'd pulled on a sweater. Consequently, when I noticed the swimmer, my first thought was that it must be someone with a

thick layer of subcutaneous fat. All I could see was an uniden-
tifiable head and the slight wake left by arms and legs silently
stroking beneath the surface. If the lake had been a tidal river,
I'd have assumed that the head belonged to a seal. I remembered how hot Maxine had looked at dinner. Her face had
been damp, its veins prominent.

Goody-goody believer in the buddy system, I disappointed
Rowdy by settling down on the dock. Refusing to follow suit,
he turned to face the shore and whined softly. "Shh!" I whispered.

Far out on the lake, a boat putted. Although sound carries
and echoes over water, I heard nothing else until the lone
swimmer coughed, lightly at first, as if a few drops of water
had gone down the wrong way, then deeply and loudly, with
involuntary force. The head dipped, legs kicked, and arms
flailed. How far out? No farther than Elsa and I had swum
that morning, no distance at all to a lifeguard gifted with
buoyancy, as many yards as a powerful man can toss a rubber
toy. But the Red Cross course I'd flunked had cautioned even
the buoyant against impetuously plunging in. A flotation device should have been mounted somewhere on the dock.
None was. Dragging Rowdy after me, hollering, I dashed to
land, onto the little pebble beach, and to the first of the upended canoes—only to remember that the paddles were
stored in the main lodge. Even so, I reached in, fished around,
and found what I needed—a seat cushion, a flotation device.

Croaking out pleas for help and calling to the swimmer, I
stumbled back over the rough rocks and jumped onto the
dock, Rowdy bounding beside me. Only when I reached the
end, maddeningly close to the helpless, frantic swimmer, did
the problem hit me: What was I going to do with Rowdy?
The flat dock hadn't been designed for mooring boats; it offered not a single upright or cleat to which I could fasten a
leash. Furthermore, the flex lead, with its long cord and bulky
plastic handle, was meant exclusively for dog walking, not for

tying out. If I reached under the dock, I'd presumably find one of the wooden legs on which it sat. I could pull out a length of cord and, working underwater and in the dark, loop the cord around a support, knot the cord, and . . .

"Rowdy, down! *Gooooood* boy!" I removed his lead, yanked off my shoes, and showed Rowdy the palm of my hand. "Stay!" I'd done the best I could. If Rowdy broke, if he took off after a wild animal or another dog, or if he followed his nose to the kitchen of the main lodge or even into Rangeley in search of the golden with the come-hither scent, at least he wouldn't get fouled up by the flex lead. And if you're wondering why I didn't trust Rowdy, let's just say that if forced to choose between obeying me and zipping off after a raccoon or a porcupine, he'd act like a malamute every time.

With the seat cushion clutched in my hands, I jumped feet first off the end of the dock, bobbed up, kicked, and fought the weight of the sodden clothes that dragged me down. No wonder I'd flunked Red Cross. But the cushion was buoyant, the swimmer near. Too pumped to mind the cold, I frog-kicked hard.

How long was it, really, between the time the lone swimmer first sputtered and the moment that cold, strong hand grabbed the cushion from my grasp? As I've worked it out, approximately the length of the long sit in Novice obedience, what I'd heard kind judges, Phyllis Abbott among them, refer to as the "one-hour long sit," an exercise that lasts precisely sixty seconds. I'd dashed to the canoe, grabbed the cushion, run back, downed Rowdy, removed his lead and my shoes, hit the water, and kicked like hell. One minute? Certainly less time than the Novice long down. Objectively three minutes; subjectively, forever.

Minutes or hours, my relief in reaching the drowning swimmer was so great that when those powerful hands snatched at the cushion, I shoved it into them. Kicking to stay afloat, cold now, deeply chilled, weighted down by the sweater and the loose khaki pants I'd worn to dinner, eager only to head for shore, I missed the cues. The coughing and flailing had stopped. Choking, spitting out water, gasping for air, uselessly beating the lake's surface with frantic arms, my all-but-rescued victim had recovered all too soon, impossibly soon, had found breath never really lost, calmed feigned terror, and caught me unaware. Rigid fingers gripped my hair, dug into my scalp, and shoved me under. In some last-second reflex, I opened my mouth. Sucking for air, I breathed water that filled my nose and swelled in my throat. Stunned by the attack, bewildered by the underwater blackness, I kicked out blindly, fighting less for the surface than for some sense of where it was.

The hands gripped my head, but as I sank under a great weight, I finally fought back. My fists bounced off a heavy body. Sharp nails raked across my face. Bending my legs frog-fashion, I aimed, kicked, missed, and succeeded only in tightening the grip on my hair. Momentarily releasing it, freeing my scalp from that excruciating yank, the hands grabbed again and, this time, delivered a sharp snap that sent hot pain rushing down my neck. In that last moment, nothing passed before my eyes, not my own death, certainly not my life. I neither saw nor heard nor thought a single thing. To die by drowning means, I think, to leave this world as we enter it: wet and helpless, all feeling.

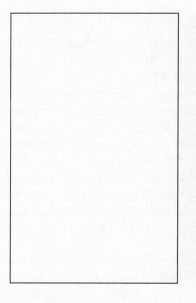

Twenty-seven

WITH THE STUPIDITY of panic, I kicked and strained. Finding my head inexplicably above water, I struggled to raise my entire torso, as if elevating my rib cage would somehow enable oxygen to enter my lungs through skin and bone, thus bypassing my impenetrable nasal passages and clogged trachea. Failing in my efforts to dodge nature's plan, I was saved by a single full-body blow, a powerful whole-torso Heimlich maneuver delivered from somewhere underwater, a massive WHAM! that knocked the wind out of me and, with it, the water.

The lake around me boiled and churned like the wake at the stern of some phantom powerboat, a ghostly Chris-Craft, the classic inboard, sleek and beautiful above, dangerous below, where the propellers slashed and drilled, slicing the water, grinding it up, disgorging it in twin waves of white-capped turbulence. My attacker thrashed and surged, bobbed, reappeared, lashed out, tried gliding under my rescuer, slipping around him, barging past him to regain that grip on me, shove my head beneath the water, and hold it there—this time—until I drowned.

He hated water, loathed it, always had—avoided even shallow puddles, balked at a walk in the rain, shrieked in the bathtub—but now, his big snowshoe paws transformed to whirling blades, his heavy-boned legs ripping through the water, the big guy blocked my attacker's every move.

"Help!" I screamed. "Help!"

Cries from shore answered mine. The beam of a big lantern flashlight played over the lake. From the dock, Cam's voice called, "What's going on there? Are you all right?"

Shaking and numb, I managed a feeble breaststroke toward shore. His combat finished, Rowdy chugged at my side until I reached the sharp rocks of the beach. Seconds later, I was on the dock, and Ginny was ripping off her warm, dry sweatshirt, pulling it over my head, chastising me, issuing orders: "What did you think you were doing? You could've drowned! You're shaking all over. What you need is . . ." And on and on, as if I were a naughty puppy.

Frantic to rid his coat of water, Rowdy was zooming around in elongated loops and figure eights, zipping past the cabins, vanishing into the night, reemerging, veering, dashing toward the lodge, whirling, passing through the lights outside the cabins and pausing only occasionally to convulse himself in audible efforts to decontaminate himself.

Her corpulence illuminated by the light mounted outside my cabin, my assailant stood on the slope above the dock. A towel in those strong hands, she rubbed vigorously. Although she addressed Cam, she spoke to me as well. Her tone was light, amused, and all-forgiving: "I inhaled a few drops of water, and while I was still coughing it up, Holly jumped to my rescue, and Rowdy leaped in after her." The note of surprise was utterly genuine. After a light, brittle laugh, she went on to elaborate: a total misunderstanding, a minor fiasco, a comedy of errors.

In emerging from the lake, two dissimilar creatures thus performed kindred rituals: In shaking off water, Rowdy was like an Orthodox Jew who'd been forced to consume *trayf*. Phyllis Abbott had also set about purifying herself. Phyllis, however, was concerned about her reputation; Rowdy, about his soul. Her superficial task was easier than Rowdy's, and of the two, she was the more successful. In Cam's position or in Ginny's, I'd have accepted her account as unquestioningly as they did. There was, after all, no reason to doubt Phyllis's word, especially in the presence of dripping proof that some fool had stupidly tried to play lifeguard.

I've wondered, of course, what would have happened if I'd spoken up. *Phyllis lured me in*, I could have proclaimed, *and then she tried to drown me!* Cam, I predict, would have raided her own or someone else's veterinary first-aid kit, administered a mastiff-size dose of acepromazine, packed me into an airline-approved Vari-Kennel, and assured me that I'd feel a lot better when the trip was over; and Ginny would've made sure I had a soft, clean crate pad and a bowl of fresh water.

I said nothing except a few words of thanks to Ginny, who had given me the sweatshirt off her back and, more importantly, caught the errant Rowdy by credibly baiting him with a fistful of imaginary liver.

Back in our cabin, even before I got into the shower, I treated him to the real thing. "Rowdy, *I* know what you did, big boy, and that's all that really matters." I stroked him gently, with the respect he deserved. The guard hair, his water-shedding outer coat, was almost dry, but his woolly undercoat remained damp. Since he was in no danger of contracting a serious chill, I let him enjoy the mal-deliciousness of being half frozen while I stood under the hottest shower my skin would tolerate and wished that I'd had the wisdom to stash a bottle of brandy among the extra leads, dumbbells, brushes, and other equipment I'd packed for Rowdy. My body turned a shade of red that reminded me of Phyllis Abbott's hair and Nigel's matching coat. In my rush to rescue her, I'd gone in fully dressed. My only visible wounds were the scratches she'd inflicted on my face, minor abrasions readily blamed on Rowdy. In a moment of petty nastiness, I hoped he'd raked Phyllis's exposed body with his thick claws. I even regretted having given his nails a recent trimming.

When I got out of the shower, I wrapped my head and body in the resort's thick red towels and stood under the red-bulbed heat lamp that was mounted in the ceiling. When I'd gently combed my hair, I plugged in my blow dryer, bent from the waist, trained warm air on my sore scalp, and hoped that I was simultaneously facilitating the flow of blood to my brain. Phyllis Abbott had had no reason to drown me. If she'd been trying to protect herself, the attack had been entirely misguided: Until it occurred, I'd seen Phyllis as only one of the people who could have murdered Eva Spitteler. Had Phyllis tried to kill me for the same reason she'd actually murdered Eva Spitteler? And why had she done that?

At least momentarily, we'd all had motives. If I read Craig correctly, he was a dog snob in the making; and in insulting Craig's dog, Lucky, Eva had hurt Joy, Craig's vulnerable child bride. She'd insulted Michael's Akita, Jacob, she'd ridiculed Rowdy, and she'd undoubtedly demeaned a lot of other dogs as well. If Everett Dow had really blamed the death of his wife on the death of the pet shop pup he'd bought for her, and if he really believed that Eva's business was a pet shop that sold dogs, he'd had a motive, too. Eric and Ginny, though, had had even stronger motives. Eva had slandered both of them. In spreading the malicious rumor that Judge Eric Grimaldi performed butchery to correct a common show fault, Eva had threatened Eric's ability to get what he wanted most—judging assignments—and in so doing, she'd constituted a threat to his identity as an AKC judge. Eva had also maligned Ginny, a tracking judge and a breeder with a reputation to protect, a reputable breeder who had tried everything to get Bingo away

from Eva—everything but murder. In trying to spoil camp by
seeding it with pet sympathy cards, material on pet funerals,
and scary clippings, Eva had annoyed the campers. In doing
our best to ignore her harassment and in avoiding direct con-
frontation and accusation, most of us, I thought, had had the
sense that in failing to give Eva the attention she evidently
sought, we were dealing with her as effectively as possible;
we'd followed the advice we'd have offered to anyone who
wanted to eradicate unwelcome behavior in an untrained dog.
In theory, Eva had constituted an economic threat to Heather
and Sara as well as to Maxine. She'd almost certainly have
done a better job of planning, organizing, and administering a
camp than Max had managed; and she'd have drawn campers
who wanted a more varied program than Heather and Sara
would offer. In doing her best to make Maxine, Sara, and
Heather look bad, and in recruiting campers at Waggin' Tail,
she'd tried to steal business from Maxine and, potentially at
least, from Heather and Sara. But I'd never been able to envision the agility people as Eva's killers. Among other things,
the personal animosity between Eva and Heather had cen-
tered on Heather's role as fecal inspector, and I couldn't really
believe that Eva had been murdered because of her failure to
clean up after her dog. Mainly, though, I was convinced that
tampering with the A-frame or with any other agility obstacle
was the last method that either Sara or Heather would have
chosen; on the contrary, either would almost have died herself
to protect the reputation of her sport.

But Eva's murder had obviously required knowledge of
agility—not expertise, not general information about it, but a
detailed understanding of the construction of Heather and
Sara's A-frame. Anyone could have heard Eva announce her
intention of going to the agility area at one A.M., but not
everyone could have planned the murder. Don Abbott, for
instance, would have had no idea that pins ran through the
hinges or that raising the obstacle would require going under

it to adjust the chains. The murder had had an obvious second requirement: the ability to predict Bingo's behavior. In a sense, when Myrna had joked about Bingo being the obvious murderer, she'd been right: Whoever had killed Eva had been able to predict that, left on a down-stay while Eva adjusted the A-frame, the Lab would break, head for the obstacle, miss the contact zone, land hard, and send it crashing down on Eva. Maxine hadn't attended agility: She was thus exonerated, as was Everett Dow. Cam met the requirements, and she also had the organizational skills to carry out the murder, a requirement that Maxine so demonstrably lacked. But if Cam had decided to murder anyone, she'd have used a neat, sure method. The uncertainty of this one bothered me, as I was sure it had bothered Phyllis Abbott. What if, for once in his life, Bingo had obeyed? What if he'd broken his stay before Eva reached the obstacle? What if . . . ? Phyllis Abbott was not a sloppy person. My hair dry, my body warm, I wondered what Phyllis's backup plan had been: for Eva Spitteler. For me, too.

Twenty-eight

IN DIMINISHING the momentous by magnifying trivia, death gives rise to vain, self-serving thoughts. I first noticed the phenomenon just after my mother died. Whenever I went to the bathroom sink to bathe my swollen eyes, I'd look in the mirror and admire the haircut I'd gotten the day before. Worse than this evidence of my coldhearted conceit was the jarring sense of self-congratulation that accompanied it, as if I'd anticipated the funeral and deserved credit for my cleverness and practicality. By chance, I wore new underwear that day. The panties had lace trim. The prettiness seemed important. I was young. At the time, these observations led me to conclude that I was a horrible human being. I have since learned to forgive myself for rejoicing in tokens of my own survival.

Tonight, I dressed with absurd care: new underwear, as on the day my mother died; navy socks with red toes and red stripes; a matching sweater, navy with a red sled dog team racing across my breasts; hiking boots tightly laced. It must have been midnight. The legendary loyalty of dogs extends beyond us to our daily routines. True to bedtime, Rowdy slept curled in his crate, its door open. As aware of Phyllis Abbott's presence on the other side of the cabin as if she'd been a corpse laid out there, I took a seat at the desk and pawed through the materials still strewn on its surface: a pen, legal pads, notes, magazines, lists of AKC transgressions, copies of rules, regulations, and guidelines, the Holy Writ applying to registration, dog shows, obedience trials, and AKC judges, the Word, the Commandments, all of it spread out where Judge Phyllis Abbott had seen it when she'd stopped in to say that Leah had called.

I ran my eyes over the written rules in search of one that Phyllis Abbott might have violated: attempting to obtain judging assignments, looking at a catalog before the judging was complete, smoking in the ring, dressing in clothes that offended the dictates of good tastes. *Phyllis Abbott?* I tried to picture her in a low-cut satin top, a brass-studded leather miniskirt, and fishnet stockings, one high-heeled foot fetchingly propped on a baby gate, a catalog in her hand, and a cigarette dangling from her mouth as she brazenly solicited assignments. I found it impossible to imagine her as anything but a model of judicial propriety and responsibility. Like every other obedience judge in the country, she probably got letters of complaint from OTCH people about such momentous matters as half-point deductions for sits that looked perfectly straight from one angle and ever so slightly crooked from another. I felt certain that she handled such routine griping with her usual courtesy and authority. Phyllis knew the regulations, followed the procedures, and met the requirements; and she did so with admirable fairness and impartiality. Neither on nor off show grounds would she ever have abused a dog, uttered obscenities, or done anything else I could think of to merit even a mild reprimand from the AKC. Phyllis's self-appointed priest, I examined her conscience and found it clean of sin—except, of course, that she'd murdered Eva Spitteler and then tried to drown me.

Neither crime, I realized, was specifically forbidden by any of the rules, regulations, or guidelines. In that respect, murder and attempted murder were not alone. A dignified body, the American Kennel Club refused to compromise itself, its judges, and the fancy as a whole by acknowledging the existence of the unspeakable. The need for judicial sobriety, for example, went without saying. A few judges—very few—occasionally broke the unwritten rule. The two or three I'd been warned to avoid were conformation judges. Somewhere, sometime, an obedience judge must at least have sipped a little wine before entering the ring. But Phyllis Abbott? Don Abbott was a heavy drinker. Phyllis wasn't. She didn't abstain, either. Nothing about her suggested a woman on the wagon. Secret drinking would have worked, especially tipsiness in the ring: It would certainly have been a violation of an unwritten rule. Eva could somehow have found out. Don Abbott had his eye on the presidency of the AKC. His hope didn't necessarily coincide with reality, of course. How many hopes do? He had the business background. And despite his obvious lack of interest in particular representatives of *canis familiaris*, Don was undoubtedly in dogs. He'd even written a book on getting started in the fancy. But married to a judge who entered the ring with alcohol on her breath? Damn! It would've done just fine. The American Kennel Club is possibly the single stuffiest, stodgiest, most conservative organization in the country. Especially on the grounds of an AKC show, its president's wife would have to be like Caesar's, above reproach.

What the hell could Phyllis have done?

Frustrated, I leafed through the guidelines for conformation judges and wished that Phyllis Abbott had become one. The guidelines were so tough! So specific, so clear, so rigid! And so rigidly enforced, too! Damn Phyllis! And damn the AKC for allowing obedience judges so much leeway, for leaving so much to their discretion and good taste. Without that freedom, as I well knew, the sport of obedience would lose its judges, almost all of whom worked for expenses, not fees, and who'd quit judging if judging meant abandoning all friendships in the world of dogs. Even so! The ban on travel: "Judges should not travel to or from shows or stay with anyone who is likely to be exhibiting or handling under them." *Conformation* judges. The warning about social functions: "Judges should not accept invitations to social functions immediately before a show where the host or guests are likely to be exhibiting under them." *Conformation* judges. But obedience judges? "A judge who has a shadow of doubt cast upon any of his decisions has caused his integrity, as well as the integrity of The American Kennel Club and of the Sport, to be compromised."

And I suddenly thought I knew, more or less, what Phyllis had done—almost nothing, really—and what Eva Spitteler had known. To firm up the guess, I needed a map of the area around the Passaic show site, a New Jersey map that would let me trace a route. The show site, Leah had told me, was in a place called Millington. I fished through my notes of our conversation. The Abbotts lived in a place called Chester, Cam and John R.B. White in Basking Ridge.

"Rowdy, wake up! Good boy. Go for a walk?"

I once had a dog named Rafe who loved to sleep. Day after day, year after year, Rafe slept through twenty-three out of every twenty-four hours. With only sixty noncomatose minutes a day in which to cram such life-sustaining activities as eating and drinking, Rafe was a challenge to train. After a while, I gave up. The only command I really needed, but needed frequently, was: "RAFE, WAKE UP!" Rafe was afraid of everything, especially consciousness. He obeyed reluctantly. I was very patient with Rafe. Therefore, Rowdy. Karma. With one hand locked on his leather lead and the other holding a flashlight, I made my way down the steps of the cabin. The Abbotts' lights were out. So were everyone else's.

Although no one but me was looking, Rowdy lifted his leg on every tree we passed and, in the parking lot, had to be reminded that tires were off limits. The parking lot at the Passaic show was the final scene in the narrative I was constructing. At Passaic, Eva Spitteler had entered Bingo in Novice A under Judge Phyllis Abbott. Eva had been there; she'd said so. Bingo hadn't qualified; if he'd earned a leg, Eva would definitely have bragged about it. Consequently, Eva, who'd always groused about everything, had been disgruntled. Later, Eva had watched Cam and Nicky in Phyllis's Open B ring; she'd said so. Eva had probably seen Phyllis hand Cam the blue first-place ribbon. At camp, Eva had intruded on the personal time of instructors. It would have been just like her to hang around the show until she found the opportunity to interrogate a judge about her dog's score. Dutiful obedience judge that she was, Phyllis would have been willing to discuss her scoring, but she'd have avoided participating in the kind of argument that Eva would have tried to start. To avoid creating even the appearance of a dispute, she'd have skillfully cut Eva off by denying her the opportunity to cause trouble. And if Phyllis had said she was busy, she'd have been telling the truth. She'd judged Novice A and Open B; and she'd undoubtedly had friends to see and social obligations to fulfill. Her husband had been there. Don had had politicking to do. He'd been seen with John R.B. White, a young Turk at the AKC, Cam's husband. And when Don was done with politics? He and Phyllis would have gone home together, of course. But that was the point: Don Abbott was never really done with politics. I didn't know how Phyllis Abbott had arrived at the show. But I was willing to bet that she'd gone home with her husband, Don, and that the two had traveled with John R.B. White. And with his wife, of course, with Cam, whose dog had just gone High in Trial out of Open B.

The U.S. atlas of road maps turned out to be wedged under the front passenger seat of my car. I pulled it out, opened to the map of New Jersey, and in the bright light of the flashlight beam, found Millington, site of the Passaic show. Basking Ridge, where Cam and John R.B. lived, was right nearby, a little north and west. Northwest of Basking Ridge was Chester, where the Abbotts lived. So who had ridden home with whom? I wasn't sure, but my best guess was that Don and Phyllis had gone with Cam and John R.B. White, mainly because of the four people, Cam had been the only one with a dog entered at Passaic. Cam and Nicky could have traveled with someone else, but I thought that she'd probably driven her big, beautifully organized van. To reach the Abbotts', Cam and John R.B. would've had to go out of their way, of course, past Basking Ridge to Chester, then back home. But the details didn't matter. The map answered my question: Leaving the Passaic site, the Whites and the Abbotts had to head in the same direction.

An obedience judge leaving a trial with an exhibitor to whom she'd just given a good score? Hey, no big deal. Among other things, conformation judges *give* opinions, but in obedience, scores are *earned*, not just handed out; and if an obedience judge *awards* an unearned point, the vigilant, outraged spectators write to *Front and Finish*, to the judge, and to the AKC; and the judge gets a call from On High asking what went on. Judges' decisions are final, and the AKC really supports judges. Even so, the judge in the obedience ring knows that she's under close scrutiny, and she scores accordingly. Consequently, riding home with someone who'd *earned* a good score in her ring was a situation that an obedience judge would prefer to avoid, certainly not a situation that an obedience judge would like to see bruited about, but in almost all circumstances, it was no big deal.

Almost all. There is at least one exception. Obedience fanatic, are you? If not, just take the following for what it was, a sentence spoken to me in a dream that night, a dream in which Rowdy and Kimi were dashing wildly around in a grassy field. But if you think you know your obedience, here's a *challenge*. That's the first hint. The second is what the voice said to me in the dream, a simple piece of advice, a broad hint. Here it is: "Tie your dogs so they don't run off."

I repeat. A challenge: "Tie your dogs so they don't run off." And therein lies the exception.

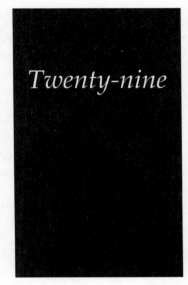

Twenty-nine

WHEN THE SUN ROSE on Wednesday morning, I knew almost everything and could prove absolutely nothing. Eva had followed Phyllis to the parking lot at the Passaic show and watched her drive off with Cam White. Eva had known why the ordinarily innocuous act of riding with Cam constituted a serious indiscretion, but she hadn't known just how serious. Phyllis's shaky marriage, her husband's ambitions, and her sense of who she was depended on her position as a respected AKC obedience judge. And Eva's ambitions for Bingo had been like Don Abbott's for himself: high and intense. Realistic? Realistically, were Rowdy and I ready to go up against Tundra and Anna Morelli at the national specialty? Realistically, was Rowdy prepared to limit his performance in the ring to the execution of the specified exercises and to delete from his repertoire such embellishments as the Drop on Back and Wiggle Feet, the Zoom out of Ring, the Slam into Handler, and that climactic crowd-pleaser, the infamous Kiss the Judge? Let's get it straight: We're talking dogs and hopes. Reality has nothing to do with it. At the forthcoming Long

Trail Kennel Club trial in Vermont, Eva Spitteler had been expecting Bingo to earn every point. In threatening Judge Phyllis Abbott, Eva had wanted only to make sure that Bingo got the score he deserved.

I'd slept restlessly. To protect the resort's plush, posh red velour blankets from Rowdy's fast-falling fur, I'd covered the bed with the sheet I'd brought from home. I wanted him next to me—and loose, too, not locked in a crate he'd have had to destroy if I needed protection. I got up three or four times during the night to go to the bathroom, to brush my teeth, to stare out at the lake. When the first light appeared, I gave up on sleep. I took a wake-up shower, got dressed, and fed Rowdy. A little later in the day, when I'd had some coffee, while I packed up the car, I'd be able to face Phyllis Abbott. I'd be able to lie to her, bluff, apologize for my silly misunderstanding. She wouldn't believe me; she wouldn't need to. Maybe she'd accept my groveling for what it would be: the assurance that I intended to do nothing. Maybe I'd drive the short distance to Bethel, Maine, to visit my grandmother. Maybe I'd go directly back to Cambridge. I'd make excuses to my editor and write whatever she wanted to see about Maxine McGuire's dog heaven. But it's hard to think creatively or to lie credibly before breakfast. I hesitated at the door and opened it only to prevent Rowdy from scarring it with impatient paws.

The lake was as flat as it had been the night before, but brilliant, a glass that reflected the clear sky, the morning light, and the pines along the shore. In the shallow water near the dock, fish jumped. Like droplets from a miniature cloudburst, tiny circles appeared on the surface. Straight out from the dock, a big fish jumped, a predator, maybe, in search of minnows. A door slammed shut. I leaped like one of the fish and jerked my head toward the Abbotts' side of the deck. Their door was closed, their blinds drawn.

A man whistled softly and called, "Elsa! Elsa!"

Rowdy caught sight of the Chesapeake before I did and, finding me slow to fly after her, hit the end of his leather lead and bounded down the stairs dragging me after him.

"Easy!" I told him. "Easy!" Serious obedience people don't believe in wasting all the work we've spent training our dogs on the inconsequential situations presented by real life. We reserve commands like "Heel," "Down," and "Come" for the context in which the dog's behavior actually matters: competition. But train your dog, anyway! When I'm bouncing down a flight of steps behind Rowdy, at least it's by choice. "Easy!"

Flashing his eyes in Elsa's direction in the futile hope that the sight of a macho male malamute anointing a tree would check her urge to hit the water, Rowdy paused at a pine and lifted his leg so high that he almost lost his balance.

"Dream on," I told him.

As Rowdy was lowering his leg, a bleary-eyed Eric appeared and greeted me. He wore tan swimming trunks and a souvenir sweatshirt from last year's Chesapeake Bay Retriever National Specialty, and carried Elsa's blue-and-white rubber toy. Pausing momentarily, Elsa turned her head, caught Eric's eye, and threw him a hopeful glance of defiance, as if all she needed to complete her joy was his disapproval. He laughed and said, "Elsa always likes to think she's getting away with something, even when she isn't." Beaming at Elsa, he held up the toy and clambered down the slope toward the dock. Rowdy and I followed. Another fish jumped, and without waiting for Eric to toss her toy, Elsa tore down the length of the dock, hit the lake, and vanished beneath the surface in apparent pursuit.

"Has she ever actually caught a fish?" I asked. I was eager to believe Elsa capable of almost everything. It's a view shared by all admirers of the Chesapeake, every sensible person who has ever known one.

Eric shook his head. "No, but she'll go under after rocks. If she's in a cooperative mood, she'll go after one for me, retrieve the one I throw."

As I was trying to imagine Elsa in a cooperative mood, her head bobbed up and disappeared. Rowdy stirred and made a high-pitched noise of impatience or, perhaps, of apprehension.

"How deep does she go?" I asked.

With a modest shrug, Eric said, "Well, not like a Portuguese Water Dog. I don't know, most of the time, not more than five or six feet. But a while ago, she . . . uh, I was visiting some people who had a pool, and I tried keeping her out, but she went down to the bottom of pool, at the deep end, and that must've been ten or twelve feet. They had her retrieving things from there. She knew she had a crowd, and she was showing off. Most of the time, it's not that deep. You can usually see the tip of her tail sticking out."

When I'd last seen Elsa's head, she'd been close to the area where Phyllis had attacked me, in what I guessed was seven or eight feet of water, certainly at a depth well over my head. "Not—" I started to say.

"What the . . . ?"

Elsa had surfaced with a shiny object in her mouth and was swimming toward the dock. What the morning sun had caught, what Elsa may even have seen as a sluggish perch or a languid trout, was a metal object that it took me a second to identify. At first, I wasn't sure, but as Elsa approached the dock, I moved out ahead of Rowdy, went striding down the wooden boards, came to a halt at the end, and got a good look. Clamped in Elsa's mouth was a piece of an agility obstacle, one of the smallest, heaviest parts of any obstacle: one of the iron legs of the pause table. Having glimpsed an interesting object underwater, Elsa had done what Chesapeakes do: She'd retrieved it. And what Elsa had retrieved was Phyllis Abbott's backup plan for me, the one she'd dropped when I'd fallen for the drowning-swimmer ruse.

Simply curious, Eric asked, "What's that you got there, Elsa?" He sounded pleased.

In response, Elsa—being Elsa—veered around and swam in the opposite direction, toward the middle of the lake.

"It's . . ." I stammered. "It's . . . Eric, it's important! I know what she has, and it's . . . Is there any way to get her to bring it in?"

Eric just laughed. I felt exasperated. Every once in a while, despite Rowdy and Kimi, I revert to my old rigid belief that, damn it all, dogs ought to do what they're told. I had no idea whether a night in the lake would have removed Phyllis's fingerprints from the table leg. A phrase came to me from a TV commercial for some kind of household cleaner: greasy finger marks. But what did it mean? That all finger marks were greasy, therefore hard to remove? Or that the product worked even on tough, hard-to-remove marks—greasy ones? And what did TV know about fingerprints, anyway? But I thought there was a chance that the leg of the pause table held a trace of evidence, and I damn well wanted Elsa to bring in that dab of proof.

Digging in my pockets for the bits of old dog treats they usually contain, I demanded, "Eric, will she work for food?"

Eric smiled. "You're welcome to try."

"Elsa, come!" I called cheerfully.

She ignored me, of course. No longer swimming toward the opposite side of lake, the Chesapeake had changed direction and was moving parallel to the shore, but away from us.

"Elsa!" I called in my best obedience voice, the one that expects to be obeyed.

Taking pity on my naïveté, Eric began a real effort to summon her. "Elsa! Elsa, come on! Come on, let's go!"

Suddenly inspired, I said, "Eric! Here, this'll work. Or it's worth a try."

"Elsa! Elsa, come!" he persisted.

I ran back down the dock to the shore. "Eric, come on! This really is worth a try. All you have to do is . . ."

Highly subject to contagious excitement and determined

not to be left out, Rowdy was adding his voice and producing long strings of the typiest syllable in the extensive malamute vocabulary: *"Woooooo! Woo-woo-woo!"*

My tone of expectation worked better on Eric than it had on Elsa. Looking puzzled, he joined me on the pebble beach. "Lie down!" I instructed him.

"You're joking," he said, or I think that's what he said. Rowdy was making a tremendous noise, and from the cabins and the woods, three or four dogs were answering his call.

"Rowdy, be quiet! Eric, really, *lie down!* Lie down and wave your arms or something. You have to do something she's not used to, something that'll get her attention and get her a little worried. It's worth a try."

Shaking his head and giving me a you-don't-know-Elsa smile, Eric ran his eyes over the sharp rocks, moved back to the dock, and spread himself out on it.

"Now call her!" I ordered. "Wave your arms around! Kick your feet!"

And once Eric caught Elsa's attention, the ploy did work. Awakened by the din we'd been making and curious to see what the fuss was about, campers began to appear, among them, Phyllis Abbott. Her soft-red hair looked freshly brushed and styled, but she wore nightclothes, a blue-and-white striped kimono over white pajamas with long legs, and a pair of fuzzy blue slippers.

Elsa was really close now, only three or four yards from where I stood on the pebble beach at the water's edge. "Good girl, Elsa!" I murmured. "Eric, can you get this from her?"

I should have done what Phyllis Abbott did, I suppose: I should have waded in. Without even removing her slippers, Phyllis beat me to it. Through the clear water, I could see that the wet pajama bottoms were clinging to her legs. When she was in up to her knees, she bent over and almost whispered, "What a good girl Elsa is! What's *that* you've got there, sweetie? Bring it to me! Good girl! Come on!" Phyllis stretched out a hand.

With rage, I realized that Phyllis didn't even need to get that metal leg out of Elsa's mouth to accomplish her purpose. To explain the presence of her fingerprints, all she needed to do was touch it.

" 'A judge,' " I quoted loudly, " 'a title that implies dignity and position.' "

Out of the corner of my eye, I saw Eric get up off the dock. He must have assumed that I was making fun of Phyllis.

I went on: " 'The manner in which judges exercise their authority has a direct impact on the sport.' "

"Holly," said Eric, no longer amused, "just what—?"

I spoke only to Phyllis. No, that's not quite right. I addressed only her conscience: " 'An individual's success as a judge rests on the basic attributes of good character and knowledge.' "

Attracted by the hubbub and probably by some sense of oddity in the air, Cam, Ginny, Maxine, Don Abbott, and six or eight other people had made their way down to the little pebble beach. Phyllis still faced away from us, toward Elsa and toward the lake.

"Mrs. Abbott," I continued, "I have always had the highest respect for you as an obedience judge. I have always found you to be one of the most knowledgeable, impartial, fair, responsible, and otherwise altogether estimable judges ever to enter an obedience ring. And, you know, when AKC says that judges represent the entire sport? I take that seriously. And I want to know something. Judges are allowed to discuss the regulations, right? It's part of your responsibility: to help people learn. So, is this mess really how you want to represent what we're about? Is this really it? Because if it is—"

Don Abbott's deep voice boomed over mine. "Phyllis," he told his wife, "turn around and get out of the water! You are contributing to a scene!"

"Mrs. Abbott can speak for herself," I said.

"She can't, you know." The voice was Cam's, as calm and controlled as ever.

"She certainly can," Don Abbott proclaimed, "and she can get out of that lake this minute. Phyllis, you are making a fool of yourself! Get out of there!"

"Leave her alone!" Cam told him. "The whole thing is your fault! Left to her own devices, Phyllis would never in this world have put me or herself or anyone else in anything even remotely resembling a compromising position! Phyllis didn't *ask* to judge that runoff! She was appointed! *You* were the one who had to go and make sure that you got John's ear and that once you had, you held it. *You* were the one who schemed and finagled and made damn well sure that John had no choice but to invite you home. I wish I'd never entered Passaic! You know, I *deserved* that trophy! I *earned* it! And now I wish that Sandy Battista had taken it home, after all."

Lost? I was, too. Turning to me, his face stubborn and ugly, Don said, "I don't remember you!"

"My name is Holly Winter. I'm in the other unit in your—"

Cam, who'd understood him, said, "Don, Holly wasn't even *at* Passaic." She paused. "Were you?"

"No," I said.

"Well," Cam said, "count your blessings. The rest of us should've stayed home, too. I don't know how you got involved in this, but the whole mess was Don's fault. We earned that one ninety-nine! How was Phyllis supposed to know that we'd end up tied for High in Trial? If she'd planned it, she'd have had a hard time pulling it off!"

"That's what the trophy was for," I said. "High in Trial." Cam looked surprised, as if I should already have known. I went on. "You had two legs. Did Sandy?"

"Yes. With her old dog. The one she's showing now is just getting started, Ogden. He's good. Obviously. Tied for High in Trial out of Novice B? One ninety-nine. Sandy was surprised."

"Easy judge?" I asked.

"Easier than Phyllis," Cam said. "Mr. McWhorter."

Let me remind you that Phyllis Abbott, clad in pajamas, a kimono, and bedroom slippers, was still standing in the lake. She had stopped calling to Elsa, who still hadn't come out of the water. At the time, however, I had no sense of the surrealism of the conversation, and I don't think that Cam did, either. Both of us spoke our lines as if we'd memorized them.

"And Phyllis judged the runoff," I said. "You won. You won for the third time, so you retired the trophy. And the runoff was very close. Nicky was good. Sandy's dog must've done really well, too."

Cam corrected me. "That sit was *crooked*. I don't know what anyone told you, but I was right there, and that sit was crooked. I saw it. If you'd been the judge, you'd've taken off a half-point, too."

"And then you and Phyllis left together. In your van?"

Cam nodded.

"All four of you. You and John R.B., Don and Phyllis. And Eva followed Phyllis. She pursued her. She followed her out to the parking lot. And she'd watched the runoff for High in Trial."

And that, of course, is what my dream meant. *Tie your dogs so they don't run off.* When two handlers are *tied* for High in Trial, the winner is determined in a *runoff* that consists of one exercise, off-lead heeling.

"Phyllis tried!" Cam insisted. "*I* tried! But John kept telling me that he couldn't just disinvite them! When they made this plan, when the men did, they didn't even know I was showing under Phyllis. Neither of them really knows anything about obedience. And John had gotten dragged into the politics. And both of them just said it didn't matter, and nobody'd know, anyway, and as long as there wasn't an obvious public breach of decorum . . . And it's not strictly illegal! It is for breed judges. But for obedience judges, the guidelines are ambiguous."

Phyllis swung around to confront Cam. "You're wrong," she said, very clearly. "The phrase you want is 'violative of the spirit of the guidelines.' It was not in the best interest of the Sport." You could hear the capital in her voice: the Sport. "Cam," she added, "I am really very grateful for your support. To compromise my own position was wrong; to compromise yours was inexcusable. I should have done what I threatened to do; I should have walked all the way home before I got in your van."

The American Kennel Club expects its judges to be treated with respect. Elsa had been slow to recognize authority, but she did not let the AKC down. Or maybe the metal table leg finally became burdensome. Maybe she just felt ignored. In any case, she dropped it in the shallow water at Judge Phyllis Abbott's feet. The American Kennel Club expects its judges to be ladies and gentlemen at all times. Like Elsa, Phyllis, too, did not let the AKC down. She was a perfect lady. Stooping to pick up the metal bar, frowning at it, turning it over in her hands, and wading out of the water, ridiculously costumed, she apologized to me. "I hope you understand," she added.

I accepted the apology. No one referred to the murder of Eva Spitteler.

Thirty

"YOUR MOTHER," said Rita. She spoke the words as only a therapist can. After a pause that apparently meant more to Rita than it did to me, she added, "and her representatives." Rita had used the phrase before. I liked it. *Your mother. (Pause) And her representatives,* as if my Marissa had thoughtfully anticipated her death by appointing a vast number of like-minded agents to administer and adjudicate her posthumous maternal affairs, emotional executors whose never-ending task it was to carry out the provisions of her iron will.

"Nonsense," I said. "My mother had golden retrievers. Phyllis Abbott has Pomeranians. There's no resemblance whatsoever." Rita thought I was joking. She is not a member of the fancy. The precepts of her own order are rather different from those of mine.

She raised an eyebrow. "So what's this Pan shtick, then? You grew up in the country. When did you suddenly develop some fear of the woods? You weren't afraid of Pan, for God's sake. What you were afraid of was betrayal—betraying your mother, betrayal by her." Rita paused. "And her representatives."

I ask you: What choice did I have? An objective examination of the facts will reveal that the decision was made not by me, but by a Chesapeake Bay retriever, and a particularly brilliant one at that. Besides, it would've been my word against the word of an AKC obedience judge, and Don would've alibied his wife, anyway. I did, by the way, learn something about him that shouldn't have surprised me at all. He's a Mason! And a Shriner, at that, a benefactor of the hospitals that provide free care to children with severe burns. So the next time you watch a parade, keep your eye on those minicars, because one of the guys in the fezzes just might be Don Abbott. And laugh all you want at fraternal organizations! But if you do, make sure the batteries in your smoke detectors are fresh, and keep your children and grandchildren away from the stove, or you just might have to take all this secret society business more seriously than you'd ever dreamed.

Curiously enough, as I found out from Cam, it was through Don's Masonic contacts that the Abbotts eventually traced Dog Beat's false report of Phyllis's death to Eva Spitteler and simultaneously cast light upon the mystery of the black ribbon for Bingo. Hanging around at shows, bad-mouthing the judges, the exhibitors, and the dogs, Eva Spitteler had, as I should have guessed, attracted the attention of Dog Beat's editor in chief, an individual about whom I prefer to say nothing except to report that this cancer on the fancy, recognizing Eva's natural potential, recruited her as a so-called contributor to his vile publication, thus enabling her easily to feed the report of Phyllis's death to Dog Beat's office, a single room in Manhattan staffed by a struggling young would-be romance novelist named Clarissa B. Good, who happened to be a number of things—and whether good numbered among them, I won't presume to judge. I continue: Clarissa B. Good happened to be the daughter of a member of Don Abbott's lodge and a former Rainbow Girl, who, while waiting until her recently submitted manuscript raised itself above the ordinary Brunos and bodices of Harlequin's slush pile, was forced to work a loathsome day job as *Dog Beat*'s trash compactor, in which capacity she answered the phone and keyboarded the copy. Clarissa did, however, get to take her dog to work, a really quite decent-looking Norwich terrier, Cam says, a dog that certainly didn't merit the insults that Eva Spitteler had spewed forth the time that she'd burst into *Dog Beat*'s office to demand immediate cash reimbursement for a paycheck that had just bounced. Eva was, of course, so memorable that when she called *Dog Beat* to report the death of Judge Phyllis Abbott, Clarissa not only recognized Eva's voice, but questioned her veracity and her motives even more than had become routine for her since she'd started the job. Checking up on Eva, Clarissa's editor in chief called the Abbotts' number, asked to speak to Phyllis, and, when told that he was already doing so, hung up and published the report anyway. As Clarissa's story reached me, it was he who decided to teach Eva a lesson about using *Dog Beat* for her own ends. It's possible, however, that Clarissa herself was responsible for the false black ribbon.

Whether you read *Dog Beat* or any of the reputable dog publications, you know by now that Don Abbott did not become the president of the American Kennel Club. I believe that he overdid the politicking and that his efforts backfired. Or perhaps John R.B. White used his considerable influence. Speaking of John R.B. White, *Front and Finish* included him in the photo of Cam and Nicky that appeared with the article about the Wilhelmina E. Pruett Memorial Challenge Trophy. Also present in the picture were Phyllis Abbott, who'd judged the runoff, and Adelaide J. Barnaby, who offered the trophy, which was the kind of big silver fruit bowl you never see anymore, and sterling, too, not plate. When I read the details, I was sorry I'd missed Passaic. Cam and Nicky, with a 199 out of Open B, had been tied for HIT with Sandra Battista and her young golden, Shoretowyn's Candy's Dandy, out of Novice B. Like most important trophies, this one was for permanent possession by the owner who won it three times, not necessarily with the same dog, and what made the runoff really exciting was that Cam and Sandy had each won it twice before. Whether Sandy and Ogden really deserved to lose the half-point that Judge Abbott deducted for a slightly crooked sit, I don't know. I wasn't there. I am convinced, however, that in Judge Phyllis Abbott's eyes, the sit was not perfectly straight. I have never doubted Phyllis's impartiality and fairness in the ring. One of these days, I may show under her again. After all, my mother is dead. Her representatives are all I have left. Who am I to oppose my mother's wishes?

In her own way, Eva Spitteler, too, left me a legacy. I used to go around telling myself and everyone else that scores don't count. I've learned better. These days, Rowdy and I are training harder than we used to, and not just because Rowdy is going up against Tundra, either. No, the real reason is that a half-point deduction for a crooked sit was ultimately what cost Eva Spitteler her life. If Rowdy and I ever end up in a runoff, I'll know that the outcome may be highly consequential. I intend to be ready. I intend to win. Victory is, after all, what my mother would have wanted. My mother. And her representatives.